RESTRUCTURING CARING LABOUR

DISCOURSE, STATE PRACTICE, AND EVERYDAY LIFE

RESTRUCTURING
CARING
LABOUR

DISCOURSE,
STATE PRACTICE,
AND EVERYDAY LIFE

EDITED BY
SHEILA M. NEYSMITH

OXFORD
UNIVERSITY PRESS

OXFORD
UNIVERSITY PRESS

70 Wynford Drive, Don Mills, Ontario M3C 1J9
www.oupcan.com

Oxford University Press is a department of the University of Oxford.
It furthers the University's objective of excellence in research, scholarship,
and education by publishing worldwide in

Oxford New York

Athens Auckland Bangkok Bogotá Buenos Aires Calcutta
Cape Town Chennai Dar es Salaam Delhi Florence Hong Kong Istanbul
Karachi Kuala Lumpur Madrid Melbourne Mexico City Mumbai
Nairobi Paris São Paulo Singapore Taipei Tokyo Toronto Warsaw

and associated companies in Berlin Ibadan

Oxford is a trade mark of Oxford University Press
in the UK and certain other countries

Published in Canada
by Oxford University Press

Copyright © Oxford University Press Canada 2000

The moral rights of the author have been asserted

Database right Oxford University Press (maker)

First published 2000

Canadian Cataloguing in Publication Data

Main entry under title:

Restructuring caring labour : discourse, state practice, and everyday life

Includes bibliographical references and index.
ISBN 0-19-541480-2

1. Women – Employment – Canada – Social aspects.   2. Women – Canada – Family
relationships.   3. Caring.   4. Women – Canada – Economic conditions.   5. Women –
Canada – Social conditions.   6. Canada – Economic policy – 1991–   .   7. Canada –
Social policy.   8. Feminist theory.   I. Neysmith, Sheila.

HV541.R47 1999   362'.042   C99-932400-4

Cover image: © David McGlynn/FPG International LLC
Cover design: Brett Miller
Text design: Tearney McMurtry

1 2 3 4 — 03 02 01 00
This book is printed on permanent (acid-free) paper ∞
Printed in Canada

Contents

Contributors

Jane Aronson teaches in the School of Social Work at McMaster University. Her research addresses women's work in both giving and receiving long-term care. Her current research and writing focus on health care reorganization and privatization's impacts on women who rely on home-care services because of disability, chronic illness, or frailty.

Carol Baines is a professor in the School of Social Work at Ryerson Polytechnic University. Her research interests and publications focus on the history of women in the professions, social work history, and child welfare.

Michael Birmingham has a Ph.D. from the Faculty of Social Work at the University of Toronto. He is presently the executive director of Carlington Community and Health Services, a community health centre in Ottawa. His recent research interests have focused on the nature of work and unpaid labour.

Marie Campbell is a professor in the Faculty of Human and Social Development at the University of Victoria, where she teaches in the Multidisciplinary Master's Program. Her area of scholarship focuses on organizational analysis; women's work in the human services; and the social organization of knowledge. She is co-editor of *Knowledge, Experience and Ruling Relations: Studies in the Social Organization of Knowledge* (1995).

Patricia M. Evans is an associate professor in the School of Social Work at York University. Her research is in the area of women and the welfare state with a particular focus on work, welfare, and single mothers. She is a co-editor of *Women and the Canadian Welfare State* (1997) and *Women's Caring: Feminist Perspectives on Social Welfare* (1998).

Evelyn Ferguson is an associate professor in the Faculty of Social Work at the University of Manitoba. Her research and writing interests include feminist approaches to Canadian social policy, with a focus on child daycare, particularly gender and parental involvement.

Belinda Leach is an associate professor in the Department of Sociology and Anthropology at the University of Guelph. Her research and writing focuses on economic restructuring; formal, informal, and domestic work; and gender, development, and industrial homework.

Janet Mosher is an associate professor at the University of Toronto and is cross-appointed between the Faculty of Law and the Faculty of Social Work. She is director of the combined LLB/MSW program. Her research and teaching interests include women and violence, women and poverty, legal ethics, legal process, and the law of evidence.

Sheila Neysmith is a professor in the Faculty of Social Work at the University of Toronto. Her research and writing has focused on the effects of social policy on women as they age. She is co-editor of *Women's Caring: Feminist Perspectives on Social Welfare*, 2nd edn (1998) and editor of *Critical Issues for Future Social Work Practice with Aging Persons* (1999). Her current research is a longitudinal study of the effects of policy changes on Ontario households.

Roxana Ng is a professor at the Ontario Institute for Studies in Education at the University of Toronto. She developed immigrant women as a field of feminist scholarship based on her work as a community researcher in Vancouver in the mid-1970s. In addition to her theoretical work on feminism and antiracism, she is involved in two research projects aimed at understanding how globalization is altering the lives of marginalized communities in Canada and how they develop strategies for resistance.

Susan Prentice is a member of the Department of Sociology at the University of Manitoba, and former Margaret Laurence Chair in Women's Studies. Her research focuses on the intersections of family, social policy, and social movements. She is currently working with Evelyn Ferguson on a SSHRC-funded study of parental involvement in daycare centres. From 1997–9 she was a board member of the Canadian Child Care Advocacy Association, and has been involved with child care advocacy since the early 1980s.

Marge Reitsma-Street is an associate professor in the multidisciplinary Master's program in Policy and Practice in the Faculty of Human and Social Development at the University of Victoria. Trained as a social worker with a Ph.D. in policy from the University of Toronto, Marge is an activist researcher focusing on poverty and people's contributions to community life. She is co-editor of *Changing Lives: Women in Northern Ontario* (1996).

Karen J. Swift is an associate professor in the School of Social Work at York University. She does research on women's issues, particularly as they intersect with child welfare policy and practices. She is the author of *Manufacturing Bad Mothers* (1995).

Acknowledgements

I am writing these acknowledgements as editor of this particular volume and as coordinator of 'The Caring Network', the nickname by which the authors of this book came to be known to ourselves and others. For over three years we met formally and informally to discuss the work that appears in the following pages, as well as other research and writing endeavours we were pursuing. This book reflects only a fraction of the exchange that actually took place during those years. Thus, we owe a debt of gratitude to the Women and Change Strategic Grants Division of the Social Sciences Research Council of Canada. This debt is as much for the specific grant, which allowed us to come together from across this large country, as it is for the council's foresight in setting up such a vehicle as the network grant stream in the first place.

For all of us, fashioning the content and process of our analysis and evolving with it was an exciting and challenging process. There was enormous excitement in seeing ideas ferment and sharpen in focus through our successive discussions and exchanges. There were also challenges as we tried to delineate where we agreed, where we differed, and what was important to think through and change. Working through these processes of debate and contestation could be complex. In the spirit of truly engaged knowledge-building, we brought heads, hearts, and personalities to the process and, inevitably, encountered some conflicts and tensions. I thank you for not walking away from these encounters but rather struggling through them. I trust you all got as much out of the overall project as I did.

The network—all thirteen of us—were not alone in our endeavours and thanks are due to our various supports and companions. I particularly want to thank Donna Baines, a former doctoral student of mine, who is now assistant professor of Labour Studies and Social Work at McMaster University. She assiduously recorded the ongoing debate. Although she dubbed herself as the network 'scribe', she knew the area well and frequently helped me interpret some of the more obscure mutterings from network members. Several babies were party to our debates while still *in utero*. All seem to be thriving in spite of the experience! On behalf of all network members, I thank family, friends, and relatives for taking over when we were away and/or welcoming us as we landed on you during visits to Toronto. Formal meetings were held in the School of Social Work at Ryerson Polytechnic University. Thank you for so generously providing a sunny, cheery room for our meetings, and thanks to Carol Baines, who organized the necessities and indulgences of coffee, meals, and a place to meet.

Finally, many thanks to Laura Macleod of Oxford University Press, who agreed to look at the manuscript in the first place and then sent it out for review. Two anonymous reviewers raised some important questions, which led us to examine several aspects of the analysis. Thank you for generously giving of your expertise. Valerie Ahwee edited our frequently less-than-elegant prose into a smooth delivery. We owe you all a debt of gratitude. The contributions have been many and rich, but ultimately we, as a group and as individuals, are responsible for the final project.

Publisher's Acknowledgement

Excerpt from *The Diaries of Jane Somers* by Doris Lessing (London: Michael Joseph; New York: Alfred A. Knopf, 1983). Copyright © 1983 Doris Lessing. Reprinted by kind permission of Jonathan Clowes Ltd, London, on behalf of Doris Lessing, and Alfred A. Knopf, a Division of Random House, Inc.

Chapter 1

Networking Across Difference: Connecting Restructuring and Caring Labour

Sheila M. Neysmith

More Than an Edited Volume

A perusal of the contents suggests that this book is made up of independent studies that examine the changing social conditions that shape the paid and unpaid work that women do. Indeed, each chapter is an original contribution to a field of enquiry, whether it is child-welfare policy or the changing work patterns of women who live in rural communities. However, adding to specific substantive literatures is a secondary aim of this book. The primary goal is to document how economic and social restructuring affect the responsibilities that women carry in caring for others. This analytical framework is the outcome of four years of debate among the authors who shared and risked works in progress, works that eventually became the chapters that follow.

A discourse on restructuring has ballooned over the last decade. The concept describes the magnitude of economic, political, and social changes that are occurring in numerous countries. Restructuring is frequently discussed as a necessary and inevitable response to globalization—the international flow of capital and its associated corporate influence across national boundaries. The sufficiency of this causal connection as the explanator of national policies may be debatable. However, the consequences of restructuring for women are very real. In the pursuit of free trade, countries have lowered tariffs and enacted massive social and economic changes. Not only has this perpetuated national and international inequities but, we argue, many costs that never appear in policy debates accrue to women. Specifically, there is very little recognition of how restructuring increases and changes the caring labour that women do and how these get played out in gendered, classed, and racialized ways. Women share a common responsibility to care for society's members who are defined as dependent; women differ in their social locations—and therefore the resources available to them—to carry out these socially assigned responsibilities.

In this chapter I discuss various dimensions of the relationship between restructuring and the caring labour that women do that emerged from discussions among the contributors to this volume. It is important to note that the following themes, and the provisional framework that finally emerged, were anything but apparent when we started our interchange. Until very recently, the literatures on caring and restructuring have been quite separate, which at first impeded our making what turned out to be a key analytical connection. In the following section I take up these separate literatures, outlining some of their debates. There follows a discussion of the methodology that informed the focus of our individual research endeavours and the themes/concepts upon which our debates as a group centred. Issues of power and agency arose time and again in our work—and in our professional and personal lives. The discussion links the concepts of power and agency, which are important to theories of social change, to caring and restructuring. The next section considers the differing social locations of women, which we see as critically important in the experience of the restructuring-caring labour nexus. Changing ideas of citizenship are explored and evaluated for their potential to provide pathways for various groups of women to participate in some of the decision-making processes that affect their communities, themselves, and their families. The foregoing themes are taken up separately in writing this introduction so that I can highlight specific features that informed our discussions. However, as revealed in the case-studies that make up the following chapters, they are enmeshed in the daily lives of women. I start, however, with a brief discussion of the network that was the structural vehicle for facilitating the discussions that resulted in this book.

I frequently refer to the contributors in this book as members of a network. This term is used by the Social Sciences and Humanities Research Council of Canada to describe an interdisciplinary group of scholars who apply for a research grant to come together to work over a period of time in a thematic area. Normally research funding agencies are relegated to footnotes and do not distract from the substance or the author of the text. I am naming the Council here because public funding was part of our strategy to ensure that this work had visibility. The network grant accorded legitimacy and some material support for bringing us together across disciplinary and geographic boundaries, and made space for work that is often squeezed out and marginalized in academia.

The original focus of the network was to develop an analysis that would help change the conditions that shape caring labour. The examination of social conditions was the focus of most of our discussions. Slowly we took apart our individual work and wove together the strands that reflected our common concerns about caring labour and the changing welfare state. Changing ideas of power and citizenship were the conceptual woof and warp of the analytical fabric, but towards the end a consensus began to emerge that what we were struggling to understand were the effects of restructuring on the paid and unpaid caring labour done primarily by women. The process and change that we all underwent was instructive in underlining the importance of debate to developing an analysis. Analysis does not occur in isolation.

Two processes facilitated our work on the deconstruction of restructuring costs. First, our interdisciplinary focus illuminated the extent to which the caring labour of women was being affected and how the private/public spheres dichotomy contributed to the disappearance of this work. It became increasingly apparent that women, not business, government, and service agencies that are the focus of much policy and popular literature, were bearing the brunt of restructuring. In fact, public bureaucracies, such as hospitals, have considerable control over how and when they implement changes; not so the participants in our studies.

My participation in the other network is now finished. . . . I seem to spend most of my time catching up with students; it's a workload issue; I'm appointed to two departments. My mother has been through a lot of chemo these past months, so I try to visit her as often as possible. . . . I think the hormones from the second pregnancy are interfering with my finishing this chapter!!

—Network member

Costs that were ejected from the public world frequently landed in the private world of households where women picked them up with little control over the terms and conditions under which the resulting additional work would be done. The process effectively reproduced the social conditions that make restructuring so profitable for some and so costly for others. Secondly, it emerged that these cost shifts were surfacing not only in our research findings but in the lives of network members. As specific issues such as child care or contract work were discussed, data were explicated and clarified by reference to other studies and by examples drawn from our experiences as professionals, mothers, daughters, members of different community groups, employees, and so on; our daily lives were being affected in parallel (if not identical) ways. We have no doubt that this constant blending of the personal and political helped us to articulate the connections between restructuring and caring labour that are documented in the following chapters. The vignettes in this chapter give insight to some of the lived realities of network members that surfaced during the 'check-in' sessions with which we routinely started our biannual meetings. We hope that by revealing some of the issues facing a relatively privileged group of women, the connections between globalization and restructuring that have resulted in increased demands on women for their caring labour will become apparent to readers.

Why Restructuring? Why Caring Labour?

We focus on restructuring because it seems to offer analytical possibilities for explaining the vast amount of unpaid work that women across countries continue to do. The 'hollowing out' of welfare states since the 1970s (Jessop 1993) and their adoption of various renditions of a mixed market approach to social policy have been such that priority must now be given to understanding the impacts of these processes on different groups. In the late 1990s it is states' retreat from social commitments across countries rather than differences among them that is of overriding concern. Our analysis of this downloading builds on insights from several streams of research: analyses of gender, histories, and restructuring of welfare states, of caring and of citizenship, and philosophical perspectives on care and justice.

We owe a particular debt to those feminist scholars who have sought to infuse gender into the traditional dimensions used for comparing welfare states (Fraser 1998; O'Connor, Orloff, and Shaver 1999; Orloff 1993; Sainsbury 1994; Williams 1995). Their work exposed welfare regimes as gendered. For instance, one classic dimension for evaluating a welfare state was how much it 'decommodified' the life of its citizens; that is, what types of programs were in place that allowed people to enjoy benefits that did not depend on their attachment to the labour force and/or their ability to pay. However, this is a dubious criterion for women who never enjoyed the 'benefits' of being in the market and were thus dependent on either a male breadwinner or state provisions. Furthermore, for women in many countries, comparisons based on state-market distinctions break down because the state is a large employer of women (Daly 1994).

The introduction of a critical literature on care allows state welfare models to be retheorized, changing the traditional focus on insurance schemes and income provisions (Ungerson 1997) in which men get positioned as claimants with rights whereas women are primarily recipients of targeted programs that define them as dependants (Fraser 1989). In Chapter 4 Patricia Evans and Karen Swift show how these definitions are taken up by the media, a powerful definer of culture. They discuss how these images are part of a process that disentitles women. In Chapter 2 Janet Mosher lays out the specific welfare legislative processes that result in disentitlement. Thus, a restructuring discourse that eulogizes the traditional family may be less about the particulars of family form than it is about ensuring that dependency remains defined as a private responsibility. Part of the disentitlement process is the narrowing of grounds (e.g., targeting) for making claims to public provisions. Thus, the push for a national child-care scheme is redefined and narrowed to early intervention, residual, 'Head Start' types of programs. Academics, as experts, play a role in developing, giving legitimacy to, and reproducing social categories. One of the outcomes of our debates as a network was an enhanced consciousness that we need to take a critical look at what we spend our time on as researchers and activists.

Our analysis does not question the importance of international comparisons so much as it argues that restructuring, only some of which can be linked to globalization, is experienced by citizens in the form of national, regional, and local programs. These changes have a particular salience for women, who will be differentially affected depending on their social location. This book documents this process and theorizes the results in terms of Canadian policies and programs, but the international literature on the gendering of welfare states suggests that similar effects are occurring in other countries.

I am trying to stop feeling guilty for saying no to students. . . . Janet and I didn't get our international grant after all that coordination with community partners. Feedback was [that] I didn't have enough Chinese experience. This year I have been to Hong Kong and twice to China. Mandarin [is] coming back, but physically, being in China is difficult. Restructuring is occurring everywhere, but many women's issues in the West are not so in China. . . . I really see a trajectory now between what I am working on and the globalization of the economy.

—Network member

On the one hand, the shape of things to come seems ominous when one examines what is happening as old bureaucratic welfare states change into what is now called welfare pluralism. These changes have serious implications for the caring labour and unpaid work done by women. On the other hand, this observation does not stem from nostalgia for the post-Second World War welfare regimes that actually existed in most Western countries; few were 'women friendly' (Neysmith 1997). Indeed, one might even voice some cautious optimism that a critical literature that connects restructuring processes to caring labour outcomes offers possibilities for rethinking the meaning and benefits related to citizenship. The analysis points to policy directions that might expand options for various groups of women, possibilities that do not exist under current models.

The separate literatures associated with social policy, philosophy, social psychology, law, and political science, to name but those that influence the chapters in this book, emphasize different aspects of the above debates. Disagreements abound and attempts to draw on several traditions (as we did during our discussions as a formal network) come with their own dangers. One tends to tread lightly when borrowing concepts from disciplines other than one's own. However, this is a risk that is inherent to cross-disciplinary work. What really frustrated network members was not just how insular disciplinary debates can be, but how the concept of care is being appropriated in policy and commercial rhetoric. At best, the concept is used in statements of policy goals rather than operationalized in terms of a process for actually implementing them. This may be discouraging, but is fairly predictable. One of the strengths of neoliberalism is its capacity to absorb critiques and transform them in ways that reproduce the very conditions that launched the critique in the first place. Thus, the work of critical analysis is never done. That said, the cutting edge of the caring critique is its challenge to the elements of what is considered ethical decision making, ideas of choice and justice criteria. These understandings delineate the responsibilities as well as the rights of citizenship and its privileges. It gives us an alternative lens for assessing the process and effects of restructuring.

In 1987 Mary Dietz argued for the importance of articulating a feminist version of citizenship that avoided both maternalist thinking and the blindness to power imbalances that underlies many versions of pluralism (Dietz 1998). Ten years later Ruth Lister (1997:13) elaborates on this articulation: besides questioning the allocation of responsibility for the care and welfare of dependants to women, she highlights and challenges the fairness of citizenship entitlements that rest on a model of labour market involvement that is only possible if women do most of the caring labour. In the interim, several theoretical perspectives on caring and citizenship developed that offer ways of responding to this challenge.

The multifaceted literature on caring (see Baines, Evans, and Neysmith 1998) has remarkably different orientations. There are the feminist studies from the early 1980s that document the burden borne by female kin who were providing the lion's share of daily care for elderly parents (see, for example, Finch and Groves 1983; Lewis and Meredith 1988). The class, race, and heterosexist biases in that literature are now apparent, but these pioneering efforts made visible the extent of the work and its costs to the physical, mental, emotional, and economic well-being of women. There is also a vast health care literature with considerable professional/management analysis of the organization and funding of services (Abel and Nelson 1990; Armstrong and Armstrong 1996). Here, the driving force continues to be a fear that health care costs will sky-rocket as the population ages. The strength of this assumed association, aptly coined 'apocalyptic demography', has stimulated a critical political economy of aging (Barer, Evans, and Hertzman 1995; Estes, Swan, and Associates 1993; Robertson 1991, 1997). For instance, many so-called intergenerational conflicts on social spending priorities were revealed to conceal disparities rooted in gender, class, and racial inequities. Unfortunately, this critique is still only on the fringes of many health care policy debates. Policy makers in Canada, like those in other Western countries, are restructuring our health care systems. This entails far more than the implementation of a new health care model that substitutes care in the home for institutionally based programs. The process is redistributing current and future costs. Sometimes the outcome is transferring a service from one column in the health ledger to another; in other cases services are moved out of the public sector and into the market sector; frequently, however, programs are just cut, leaving individuals and families to cope with whatever means are at their disposal. Each move affects the paid and unpaid caring labour done by women.

These shifts in the distribution of caring work—which is unfolding in the everyday lives of those giving and receiving care and taken up in applied literatures on social policy and health care—have occurred quite separately from a theoretical debate in philosophy, which juxtaposes an ethic of care with an ethic of justice (Card 1990; Clement 1996; Noddings 1984; Tronto 1993). In their extreme forms these arguments pit an understanding of ethics, which sees individuals engaged in ongoing relationships that influence how moral decisions are made, against one that presupposes an autonomous individual who makes decisions about what is right or just in terms of a set of moral rules or codes. The former—the caring ethic, and the research and theory in that tradition—has been accused of being local, even parochial. Its critics charge that it focuses on personal relationships, is in constant danger of essentializing women, and, at least in its current renditions, is unable to specify principles for ethical decision making among the different voices that are making justice claims (see, for example, Koehn 1998).

This concern seems to assume that if an ethic of care is translated into principles for guiding the development of policy, history will repeat itself and we will get a twenty-first century version of late nineteenth-century maternalism, which romanticized domesticity. Recognizing this as a danger in an ethic of care is different, however, from rejecting such an ethic completely. The alternative would be some rendition of a personal rights argument grounded in an individualism that ignores relationship claims, and in the power differentials inherent in prevailing theories of justice. Authors such as Gordon (1996) outline the complex debates of those studying relatedness today. In this literature, the emphasis is on recognizing the conditions that lead to responsibility towards others rather than on specifying those conditions that ensure that individuals can exercise freedom of choice. Feminist advocates of the ethic of care point out that Kantian and utilitarian thinking results in an approach to justice that relies on abstract reasoning and on ideas of autonomy that are individualistic. In this frame, the social relationships of people are not considered relevant in evaluating either their behaviour or what is just. Thus, the analytical dilemma is how to think about the two perspectives without subjecting an analysis of care to the conceptual assumptions about choice, equality, rights, and individualism that permeate dominant models of justice (see, for example, Slote 1998).

Throughout much of the 1980s the justice and care debates seemed to be travelling on separate and incompatible paths. It seemed that debates about questions of justice and questions of caring occurred in isolation without bridges or links. There were more nuanced accounts of both caring and justice arguments during the 1990s. Clement (1996) and Tronto (1993), for instance, are careful to outline care and justice as modes of moral reasoning rather than modes of practice and both make the point that there are better and worse versions of the focus on the ethic of care. The relational turn in their developing ideas is what is of interest and proved so useful to network members as we examined the changing conditions under which women negotiated their caring commitments.

Scholars are also revisiting conceptualizations of autonomy and agency, which are central to theories of justice and, we would add, to those of caring. This work, picked up in the next section, has the potential for dealing with one of the major shortcomings of the early writings on women's caring labour. In pursuing policy goals people are engaged in making normative judgements. There is no avoiding the articulation of moral obligations. On the one hand, it seems to us that an ethic of justice and the related dominant discourse on rights and choice, anchored in concepts of autonomy that assume a disembodied individual acting according to a set of rational rules of moral judgement, is simply not adequate for addressing the contradictory claims and obligations that social relationships make on people. These claims are particularly evident in women's lives, yet prevailing ideas of justice and citizenship exclude them. On the other hand, an ethic of care, although it distinguishes between difference and relatedness as noted earlier, is not par-ticularly strong in either articulating obligations for non-personal relation-ships or delineating criteria for deciding among competing just claims. Such criteria and decision rules based on them are inherent to the social policy process. Without them, an ethic of care is a poor compass for pursuing gender justice, let alone dealing with inequities that arise from different social locations, some of which are discussed in the following chapters.

Feminist scholars have raised the concern that theorizing about care tends to ignore the fact that the relationships in which care is given are frequently not forged in ways and under terms or conditions of women's choosing. Scaltsas (1992:23), for example, underlines the importance of distinguishing between making moral choices and having a responsibility imposed upon one. It is the difference between an agent herself recognizing a responsibility and deciding to act on it and the arbitrary assignment of the responsibility to care for others. The effects of restructuring documented in the following chapters suggest that women are increasingly being given assignments rather than operationalizing social justice through a process wherein such responsibilities are negotiated and shared among different groups of citizens. In their analyses of justice feminist scholars like Young (1990) emphasize how differences in American society matter. For instance, Young postulates five faces of oppression connected to social structures that affect choice but cannot be accounted for by resorting to an individual differences explanation: exploitation, marginalization, powerlessness, cultural imperialism, and violence. Policies that emphasize redistribution of resources to individuals without regard for these major definers of social location can be criticized on several grounds—they reproduce structural inequalities by focusing on individual solutions; they reproduce a model of the passive consumer citizen who, with adequate resources, can exercise choice; and perhaps of most concern for many women, such policies ignore the fact that while resources are important, so too is their source and the social location of their presumed beneficiaries. For example, the limited redistributed resources that women receive from the state when the policy model sees men as workers and women as carers has been particularly detrimental for women with dependent care responsibilities who live in violent relationships. In Chapter 2 Janet Mosher provides an in-depth analysis of this issue.

Critiquing restructuring through an examination of how it changes caring labour allowed us to document how restructuring actually gets played out in the lives of women who move in different sectors of Canadian society. Our research and discussions led us to conclude that there is a gap between what is happening and official accounts of what is happening. Not only are these accounts silent on restructuring costs that fall outside the responsibilities of public institutions, but even the limited data presented in this volume reveal that women bear a disproportionate share of the costs of restructuring while the benefits accrue to others. Let me hasten to add that not all women bear these costs equally—social location is a key determining factor, and its effects on women's varying citizenship claims are taken up in the next section. What became increasingly clear to us over the period of our discussions, however, was that the media and professional commentary on globalization and restructuring (the two terms are always linked) dwelt so single-mindedly on funding and organizational issues that there was little opportunity to consider how other sectors are affected, particularly households in which women do unpaid work. As a group, we found that the tendency in popular literature to link globalization and restructuring effectively obfuscates dimensions of restructuring that have little to do with the globalization of markets but much to do with federal, provincial, and local politics of containment of those groups (such as the unemployed and single mothers) seen as 'abusing the system'. In this construction of the problem, organizations (such as firms that downsize or move their plants to other countries—see Leach, Chapter 10, this volume) are said to be responding to globalization pressures and the state disappears as a visible actor. Of course it does not, but we did find that the exercise of power, in terms of the discourse and ruling relations that make up the state, had to be once again 'unpacked' and examined. On the other hand, the rhetoric of scarcity that accompanies restructuring efforts, which are presumably necessary because of globalized finances, results in a politics of containment; that is, the expectations of Canadian who are poor or who are marginalized in some way are lowered as the threat of disentitlement becomes very real. In theoretical terms, power in the restructuring discourse is exercised by limiting the relevant restructuring issues discussed in public policy.

The context of globalization is important because it affects the economics of individual nations. Nation-states, such as Canada, are persuaded to decrease social provisions and reorganize the funding and delivery of services under the banner of increasing efficiency and improving competitiveness. Efficiency tends to be equated with using market sector budgeting and delivery mechanisms and the imposition of more stringent criteria for determining who should receive services based on assessments of need, which are referred to as targeting programs (Bakker 1996; Brodie 1995).

I feel that my efforts around workfare and social justice have been largely unsuccessful as well as exhausting, although we learned a lot about dirty tactics and policy changes. . . . My 'ups' include the publication of a book; the community project I'm writing about now has full funding. It is no longer a demonstration project. . . . I accepted a position on the west coast and will be moving the household! . . . I have here some great photos from our last network meeting.

—Network member

While global capital and national responses to it need to be controlled if developed nations are to have some say in the quality of life of their citizens, as Stryker (1998) points out, globalization is often invoked by nation-states as an excuse for both systematic and programmatic retrenchment. Furthermore, these are different phenomena that need to be examined both separately and together, but they should not be conflated. Systematic retrenchment is most apparent in a neoliberal discourse, which equates globalized finances with the complete impotence of national level policy making. The argument is that since national policy making cannot change the occurrence or consequences of transnational markets, governments can and should do nothing except reduce tariffs and increase competitiveness by reducing the size and cost of their social programs. This rhetoric contributes to changing the political environment, which in turn facilitates reductions in program expenditures and changes in social programs.

Economic and social policies are never static. It is the job of governments to introduce new legislation, and to change funding and program priorities as the political environment changes. Restructuring is a given in that sense. The restructuring that we and others (O'Connor, Orloff, and Shaver 1999; Stryker 1998) are criticizing is part of a discursive practice in which changes in social programs are rationalized in terms that relate the specific measures taken to the imperatives of international markets. For example, policy priorities for eliminating the deficit are presented as necessary responses to the pressures of globalization rather than as one response, the results of which will not fall equally on all segments of the population. Debate is effectively foreclosed rather than stimulated.

The chapters in this book expose some of the mechanisms through which restructuring operates and affects women's lives. For instance, Chapter 10 by Belinda Leach and Chapter 11 by Roxana Ng illustrate how this happens in rural and urban job markets. One of our goals is to include in the restructuring debate an analysis of its effects on the caring labour that women do. Recognizing the costs to women and addressing their conse- quences for various groups of women cannot be put on hold until global- ization issues are resolved. Women are experiencing restructuring in very particular ways. If women are central in the analysis, the list of policy priorities and how to address them will change. For instance, Marie Camp- bell's research in Chapter 9 shows how the reorganizing of nursing relies on nurses' unrecognized knowledge and labour to make the restructured system work. It may not seem like news that the system mediation work done by nurses is not specified as a nursing task and thus is lost in the reor- ganizing, but this has serious implications for patient-centred care—the title of the restructuring scheme. If nursing continues to be conceptualized and resourced as a set of tasks (as is the case with the restructuring strategy described by Campbell), when the current generation of nurses who hold things together with their unrecognized labour retire, dangerous gaps will appear in patient-centred care. This model does not operate in practice as it appears to in managerial designs that leave out nurses and family members as active agents. The design is assessed in terms of an efficiency standard that values fewer days in hospital. All players recognize that many patients will need more care, and assume that it will be delivered at home by the family. In this private sphere, who will do the work, under what conditions, and with what quality control is not the concern of a public institution. In addition, while the restructuring literature may be sensitive to tracking job loss, retraining, and movement of labour, it does not track how industry changes differentially affect options available to women and men to prepare for restructured jobs. As Belinda Leach shows, the caring responsibilities of rural women are directly linked to their job decisions, which in turn open up options for male household members. Women are twice disadvantaged, once by losing their jobs and again by finding it impossible to take up new jobs that conflict with their family responsibilities.

Focusing on Daily Issues to Understand Restructuring

The research we present documents the everyday nature of restructuring effects. In specifying how they unfold and influence daily life, we hope, first, to show that women are not just victims of restructuring. Women have agency, but this agency's limits and possibilities are constructed within social conditions that vary over time and location. Furthermore, women live the contradiction of being actors in, and thus reproducing, aspects of the restructuring process. Second, the research agenda is to create opportunities for resistance and transformation. Third, we wish to contribute to an analysis that will redefine what forms of labour are socially valuable and change the paid/unpaid work dichotomy that undergirds existing citizenship entitlements and responsibilities. I start, however, with a discussion of methodology because it is central to the questions asked and our interpretation of study findings.

Throughout the life of the network, members had individual programs of research, usually grouped into categories with labels such as child welfare, sole-support mothers, poverty, community development, professionalization, violence, etc. Each area has its own theoretical and policy questions. Consequently, network discussions meant negotiating different disciplinary terrains. The process required a continuous struggle with language and concepts. In addition, these professional and disciplinary literatures have not, for the most part, systematically addressed issues of restructuring and globalization. That is, there has been minimal interrogation of the process beyond organizational change. The connections we present in these pages were the outcome of a persistence in pursuing, and finally naming, connections. At first individual network members discussed their work and others would remark at the similarities to what was happening in their own disciplines/professions. It took considerable probing, however, before we concluded that we were witnessing the downloading of social care costs onto and into the lives of women.

I spent a lot of time over the summer putting two research proposals together so that I can compare women with disabilities and old women. The money and teaching buy-out will allow me to do the interviewing myself—an RA doesn't help in this type of analysis. . . . My mother died recently. I have been doing a lot of stuff locally and got myself onto a community care appeals board.

—Network member

Much of the data presented in the ensuing chapters were collected using research designs and data collection tools that are commonly referred to as qualitative methods. The term is used to describe studies in which the information is not converted into variables that are assigned a numerical value. The term can actually be misleading because it often refers only to design or data collection methods and does not address the more substantive question of a researcher's epistemology, the framework or theoretical perspective used by a writer for specifying the content and generation of knowledge about our social world. Qualitative data collection tools are, in fact, used in all research traditions. They are frequently chosen by feminist scholars, however, because within the social sciences at this particular historical moment they seem to offer more conceptual space than do quantitative research approaches for alternative voices to be heard. Tools, however, are not the distinguishing characteristic of feminist methodology even though they might be the most obvious (Cook and Fonow 1990; Maynard and Purvis 1994; Neysmith 1995). Methodology is important because it connects what we know with how we know it. Feminist methodology shares with the critical school of social research the aim to 'develop a theory of society that sustains and promotes the possibility of practical action in the service of constructing a fair and just society' (Schwandt 1997:124). In other words, each chapter is concerned with feminist praxis. The term 'praxis' is used because it signifies that knowledge building is directed towards an end beyond the intellectual. Its aim is not only to produce knowledge but to realize some goal. Furthermore, the ends of praxis are not immutable or fixed but are constantly revised as goals are pursued (Schwandt 1997:124). In this case, the goal is not only to make visible the restructuring costs borne by women but to do so in a way that will promote change in the social conditions that disenfranchise those who take on caring responsibilities. The project of social transformation or changing social conditions introduced the need in our analysis to conceptualize those social relations in our lives wherein we are empowered and/or oppressed.

There has been an intensive discussion over the last decade within the feminist/critical literature of the concepts of power and agency: how discursive practices promote or hinder aspects of both, and how women's choices and actions are part of a process of social transformation. Network members are participants in this debate, so they do not all speak with the same voice. Consequently, as they take up various aspects of these issues in the chapters that follow, differences among the authors will be apparent. Sometimes this is merely a question of emphasis; at other times it reflects the stress taken by a particular discipline; on occasion it signals a different understanding of social phenomena. However, as a network we shared the common goal of developing social theory that does not immobilize purposive social action, as do some renditions of structuralism, but also does not preclude it, as some versions of postmodernism seem to do (Fraser 1998). Documenting how restructuring affects different areas of caring labour became for us a site to test out debates on several concepts and think through strategies for social change.

Power is one concept that received a lot of attention in our discussions. We took seriously the challenge of explicating through our research how it operates, not just recognizing it as a part of the context. We place ourselves with those analysts who do not associate power with a person or an institution but see it as a social enactment, often the product of discursively organized relations. Power, as enacted and relational, is not centralized in a state or other ruling apparatus and thus is not an entity that can simply be overthrown. Consequently, women are in the contradictory position of exercising power as well as experiencing its effects, albeit in varying degrees depending on their social location.

If we conceive of power as being exercised rather than possessed, then we can understand how it works by examining the effects of action on others. As noted earlier, one of the important effects of power is structuring the field of choices, decisions, and practices. Power shapes, creates, and transforms social relations, practices, and institutional processes. One of its depersonalized forms is knowledge and disciplinary power. In Chapter 8 Carol Baines analyses the particular form it took in the development of child protection services during the post-Second World War era. The needs of children were seen through the lens of expert knowledge and class-based perceptions of proper child-rearing practices. Similar types of competing claims are evident today as documented in the chapters by Jane Aronson and Marie Campbell. Power operates so effectively because it is purveyed in various ways (Cooper 1994). Thus, the mothers in Susan Prentice's and Evelyn Ferguson's studies (Chapter 6) discipline themselves as surely as they are disciplined by the regulations about parental involvement on daycare boards. They are partners in shared ideas (ideology) about good parenting. Individual women may see dominant definitions of good parenting as heterosexist, class based, or ethnocentric, but they internalize them nevertheless. Thus, the involvement of parents (primarily mothers) can be more regulated than participatory: their presence on decision-making bodies such as boards controls the power of child care professionals, but board obligations are work for these mothers, work that is piled on top of their other unpaid and paid labour. Thus, as the data show, participation can be both an advantage and a disadvantage. These statements are made with no intention of denying the agency that board membership can promote for women. The point is that agency is bounded by the costs of such involvement to women. Other boundaries include the limited discourses that are available to women to draw upon. In Chapter 7 Marge Reitsma-Street and I specify some of the elements that promote engagement with community programs, but we also document the problems with a volunteering discourse, which was the only linguistic currency in circulation to describe the contributions made by women living in poor neighbourhoods.

The word 'discourse' is now an established part of the academic lexicon. The meaning of this concept, and how it is used by professionals and policy makers, was commented upon frequently by network members. We were constantly pulling this concept back to earth, finding that it was somewhat ethereal in many policy discussions. Hopefully, in the chapters that follow we have succeeded in making clear that it is discursive practices that we are exploring. Discourse is not a thing or talk; it is performed or practised. When the term is used in this book, it refers to particular ways of talking and writing about, but also doing or performing, one's practice. The practices we examine frequently take place in particular social settings such as hospitals, agencies, and universities, in which certain discourses dominate. Discursive practices, and the languages of practice, function as signs of social identity and difference for their practitioners. What we frequently refer to as professional discourse is more than the technical language that many professions develop. It encompasses ethical and political understandings of society (Schwandt 1997:31–2). Different discourses help (make?) us think differently. Consider, for instance, the language of managerialism and how it creeps into the everyday life of the old women in Jane Aronson's chapter. This expert discourse structures old women's views of themselves. 'Being managed' is the price these women pay if for any reason they cannot define themselves into the privileged category of managing, with its image of competence, and independence, and not making demands on public resources. Similarly, in the focus groups discussed by Karen Swift and Michael Birmingham (Chapter 5), participants used managerial discourse to describe what they do. It was the only language available to them even as they defended their caring work.

One might conclude that public policy assumes that all the women in this book ought to be managing, regardless of whether they are old women, kin caregivers, young women on welfare looking after children, mothers in the labour force with child care issues, or network members! They *ought* to be managing, but should they fall short, the opposites of independence and autonomy are standing there in the shadows, ready to be invoked at a moment's notice.

Got pregnant. . . . My department head reminds me to publish more. . . . Was part of my daycare board that got a big grant, but had difficulty coping with it within an advocacy agency. I tried hard to persuade them to get rid of the grant. It took a lot of hours. It's interesting to argue for giving money back. . . . Broke my leg when I was six months pregnant and became a bad dependent person. . . . My daughter is sick and will shortly go in for surgery; I'm preoccupied with her health. Got a chapter done for a book.

—Network member

Dichotomies and their consequences characterize Western thought (Mahoney 1994) and are difficult to override. In the caring literature, the concept of interdependence is often presented as if it were the synthesis that resolved the dependence/independence split. Such a resolution, however, hides the power differentials between actors in these situations. Similarly, the concept of autonomy has been proposed as a possible way of avoiding the victim/agent dualism. It might, however, as Janet Mosher shows in her chapter on violence against women, either/or conceptual thinking quickly fills in opposites; it seldom transcends them.

Dominant discourses can (but do not necessarily) cast women in ways that preclude agency. Agency comes up directly and indirectly in all chapters. As noted earlier, network members rooted their analyses by reflecting on their own multidimensional lives—one dimension being their feminist activism. Thus, analyses that facilitated social change were important. Praxis assumes the presence of agency. Unfortunately, particularly in its professional rendition as 'empowerment', agency is another term that may not accurately describe what actually happens. Examining various aspects of the concept may enable us to see some of the interplay between the reproductive and transformative dimensions of social action. As graphically depicted by Emirbayer and Mische (1998:1001), we perform in dramas in which we know our parts, but we can and do improvise continuously. These authors examine some dimensions of the concept's implication for social action. They emphasize a point that proved central to our discussions:

> . . . human agency [is] a temporally embedded process of social engagement, informed by the past (in its habitual aspect), but also oriented toward the future (as a capacity to imagine alternative possibilities) and toward the present (as a capacity to contextualize past habits and future projects within the contingencies of the moment) . . . the structural contexts of action are themselves temporal as well as relational fields—multiple, overlapping ways of ordering time toward which social actors can assume different simultaneous agentic orientations. Social actors are imbedded in these and thus are oriented to past, present and future (Emirbayer and Mische 1998:963).

This captures several dimensions of the restructuring/caring labour relationship while avoiding the structural determinism/individual liberty types of dichotomies that can be so immobilizing. First, it emphasizes that judgement is situationally based and relationships are part of the situation. Thus, it includes social relations (and their potential to be empowering or oppressing), but avoids personalizing such relationships. Second, the primary locus of agency lies in the contextualization of social experience. This may be done in debate with others and sometimes reflexively with oneself, but it cannot be done in isolation. This means that over time, actors can gain in their capacity to make considered decisions that may challenge their usual patterns of action. Daycare boards, older women's networks, community projects, labour force readjustment committees, to name but those discussed in this book, can promote social change in so far as they are arenas for participants to examine jointly how power is exercised and provide an experiential basis for articulating alternatives.

I have been on leave for six months so am in a better space than last time. . . . The three agency, three funding sources community project is going well. There is an issue over control of the project, and writing [about] it is an ethical problem. . . . On leave I went to Australia. I feel totally renewed and really recommend getting away. It gives you time to reflect on those things that are making all of us deeply unhappy. Alliances with progressive people may be what saves us; it gives you new ways of thinking. . . . I fell in love with an organic farm on the beach. I realize I could move. It's probably a dream, but . . . (smile and a sigh).

—Network member

Earlier I mentioned how the restructuring/caring labour framework only emerged over time as network members tried to deal with the various fragments of women's lives, fragments that rang bells of recognition for quite some time before they led to an analysis. Framing is critical because it is both diagnostic and prognostic. In proposing new social ends as well as different means for arriving at them, actors draw upon and sometimes extend, rearrange, and transform the master frames extant in the broader political culture. Thus, the sole-support mother can be cast as an innocent or demon, depending upon whether she is seen as a victim of restructuring or as the welfare cheat who epitomizes what is wrong with our society. As several chapters highlight, she has been increasingly positioned as a suspected abuser of the system, misusing hard-earned taxpayers' dollars by staying at home rather than seeking employment. We might well ask why she is the scapegoat. Even more important is asking ourselves who and what escapes our attention if the spotlight is on the sole-support mother. Portraying the sole-support mother as a social problem also delegitimizes, in passing, the work she does in meeting the daily needs of her children. The situation is not only contradictory, but an ethos of consumerism increases the demands put on these women. As Karen Swift and Michael Birmingham show in Chapter 5, these women must meet, on an extremely limited budget, their families' basic needs for food and shelter *and* their children's socially constructed but nonetheless pressing demands for trendy clothing and activities. Ironically, even a sole-support mother's contribution as a consumer is invalidated. In a culture where service users are defined as customers, where exercising choice is often limited to being a consumer, the sole-support mother's budget is expected to include only basic necessities.

The language of need permeates social policy. The language is very powerful yet vague as service providers and analysts consecutively invoke the images of client, consumer, and even customer to describe service users. The concept of need has its own contested definitional history in the policy and management literatures, but a differentiation between basic needs and other needs that might easily be called 'wants' misses the point of the strength and persistence in people's lives of so-called manufactured needs. In addition, expert discourses about people's needs become the currency for defining everyday situations (see Fraser 1989 for an in-depth discussion of the interpretation of need). We contrast the power of this discourse to the data in our studies, which describe the amount of shadow work women are doing—volunteering, providing the infrastructure, 'making do'. This effect of restructuring is not part of public dialogue. Its reality was caught in a comment by a network member who told of a women among the decimated support staff in her university department who wears a t-shirt emblazoned with 'I AM infrastructure!'.

Thanks for your concern around the time of the floods. . . . The RAs on my project finished collecting child daycare legislation from across Canada this summer. . . . I don't need to run behind my children any more so had a quality summer vacation! . . . I'm offering a new course this year. . . . My daycare board keeps me connected, but is work. I'm becoming aware of how I get sucked into voluntary work. . . . Decided to take on care of my mother-in-law. Jane's paper was very powerful in helping me understand what is happening to her. . . . It's nice coming here and not being responsible for everyone for a few days.

—Network member

The downloading of work has become normalized, a fact of life in this day and age of restructuring, not something that a good team player constantly complains about. Naming this shadow work—only some of which we could articulate—was a challenge for the participants in our various studies and, I might add, for network members. Centring the concepts of power, agency, discourse, and need in our discussions of how caring labour is restructured helped in disrupting the private/public split in women's lives and allowed some of the unseen work to emerge and be problematized. Doing so is pivotal if women's citizenship claims are to be realized.

The Importance of Social Location

An analysis of social location is integral to understanding how restructuring is changing the caring labour done by different groups of women and identifying policies and pathways to more equitable outcomes for women who experience restructuring in their daily lives. We are using the term 'social location' to highlight how the experiences of women are not uniform but are shaped by the privilege and oppression that permeate Canadian society. Looking at feminist theory and politics over the last dozen years reveals the growing diversity of what was once a White, middle-class social movement. Although countercurrents always existed, 'certain apparently innocent concepts and methodology strategies in much feminist enquiry lead quietly but inexorably to putting the lives of white middle class women at the logical centre of such enquiry' (Spelman 1988:x). Increasing analytical sensitivity to the presence of voice, diversity, and marginalization has forced a rethinking of how women experience gender and how this experience changes depending upon where women are located in society in terms of these powerful definers of identity. Not surprisingly, such an analysis comes with its own difficulties. How these are resolved will influence pathways to social change. First, a discussion of intersectionality or analyses that factor in social location is readily understood if one is discussing an individual or trying to explain individual variation. It works less well when the concept is used to describe a group because members of any group will inevitably include individuals who will differ in meaningful ways from each other. For instance, in this book some women are old, others are mothers of young children, some are poor, while still others are lesbian or visibly ethnoracial. In what way would such women self-define into a group or be included in a policy category designed to remedy harms arising from these differing aspects of their social location?

Second, in the process of recognizing multiple vectors along which oppression can exist, it is very easy to slip into either a hierarchy of oppression or the equating of all differences as equally important. At any moment in history some differences will be far more consequential for the quality of a person's life than others. In addition, each of these dimensions has its particular theoretical tradition; each can have assumptions that clash with those of others. For example, in many studies of social class differences the individual is not so much the unit of analysis as is the household. This makes it almost impossible to see the operation of intrahousehold disparities arising from gender, age, sexual orientation, or ability differences among members.

At any historical moment, and depending upon the particular context, groups will comprise individuals who vary along multiple dimensions. As Ng argues in Chapter 11 and Swift and Birmingham document in Chapter 5, categories such as gender, race, and class are too broad for understanding the effects of policies on various groups of women. Even where stable categories might work for theoretical purposes, they can too easily play into rather than challenge a politics of restructuring where resources can be used to divide groups by emphasizing their competing claims and thus are not useful for building a politics of democratic alternatives to the reigning one of neoliberalism. I am arguing that these analytical categories are too broad and static as a basis for articulating praxis. However, I am not arguing that they be abandoned. Class, for instance, describes a relationship among social groups unequal in power. This relationship aspect moves the focus from a structurally static one of people described, for example, as being 'poor' or 'in the upper fifth income percentile' to one where the individuals in these groups start to develop a consciousness of each other *and* recognize that their relationships with other groups reflect the dynamics of power; they are not interest groups competing on an equal basis (Collins 1998: 217). The debate on agency is important because it might provide a bridge between the micro level (where intersectionality is experienced by individuals and can be documented) and the macro level of policy (where categories are used as part of the politics of containment). Categories that are used to foster competition can also be deconstructed to reveal how power operates. The idea of agency makes it possible to move from analysis to engagement as citizens.

The citizenship debate is an excellent arena for examining how power relations reproduce class and race, as well as gender inequities. Although feminist debates about how to conceptualize as well as promote citizenship have consistently highlighted the deleterious effects of the private/public split, in the 1990s the issue took on a certain edge as neoliberalism, in its restructuring form, began to equate citizenship rights with ideas of choice, particularly choice in the market-place (for a synopsis of some of the arguments, see Lister 1997). The new citizen became the consumer of goods and services in one domain and the taxpayer in another. Such a rendition permeates professional as well as market and government programs. Totally absent from this discourse is an awareness of some women's exclusion because one needs time and money to be both consumer and taxpayer. At the same time, the politics of diversity had deepened as well as broadened. The citizen/consumer was exposed as a White, heterosexual, middle-class male. Excluded were women, children, poor people, racialized groups, people with disabilities, lesbians, and gay men (Boyd 1997; Dean 1997; *Feminist Review* 1997; *Hypatia* 1997; *Theory and Society* 1997). Some feminists joined communitarians and social democrats in mounting a critique of the passive citizenship neoliberal model in which participation in deliberation and social action were no longer fundamental to citizenship (Abrahams 1996; Bussemaker and Voet 1998; Demaine and Entwistle 1996; Kulynych 1997; Narayan 1997). There are numerous fractures among these groups, but they have opened up conceptual spaces for considering alternatives for legitimate engagement as a citizen. I will limit my comments to a few areas that are particularly relevant to the chapters in this book.

Commitments to inclusiveness in policy development are often limited to participating in deliberations as to the nature, extent, and possible public action to be taken on a problem. By omission, there is the assumption that once this process has been engaged in, the powers that be are the only legitimate vehicle for carrying out the public will. This is certainly the consultation model that has been used around long-term care and child welfare policy, both of which have changed very little during the post-Second World War era. Community activists contend that the rules are stacked against them in the consultation process so that the message is suppressed before it gets into the wider public domain. A competing approach is to visualize many modes for legitimate engagement in the public domain, including strikes and public demonstrations. The history of protest in social movements supports these counterstrategies as effective means of getting the message out, particularly because the media responds to such images (see Chapter 4). Sparks (1997) theorizes this in terms of dissident citizenship. For the purposes of this book, her analysis is important for its focus on broadening the locale from which political participation takes place. Examining traditional sites of political activity is unlikely to reveal alternative modes of participation. Countersites include women's local helping networks that have traditionally been viewed as private and apolitical (Sparks 1997:22). Chapter 7 in this volume documents such in terms of the community work done by poor women.

This broadening of locale makes the private/public formulation that underlies theories of the state more problematic than ever. This split has meant that women's contribution had to be defined in public sphere terms in order to count as political activity. Under existing public sphere rules, it is easy to discount many contributions. When women's political action is noticed, their contributions (for example, organizing the local community or campaigning against drunk drivers) get renamed or diminished. The history of women's professions shows how this happens. Sarvasy (1997) and Carol Baines (in Chapter 8) revisit this history, showing how women argued that the kinds of work they did at home could be transferred to the community. This is not how historians using a private/public sphere model of political contributions have interpreted women's community work. The losers have been women whose work was not seen as valuable and thus potentially the basis for citizenship entitlements. Part of the problem, of course, is that most discussions of citizenship start with Marshall's model in which a citizen is assumed to be an independent worker participating in civil society (Stewart 1995; for a collection of several key pieces, see Beiner 1995). This male model ignores the unpaid work that women do. The caring literature is caught in this conundrum of exclusion. Writers like O'Connor et al. (1999), Pateman (1992), and Young (1990) widen the theoretical space by introducing family into the traditional model of the welfare state. The family is key in most areas of social policy, but not being part of the welfare state model means that policy effects on it are not questioned and caring costs are not considered. A cautionary word is in order, however. Too much stress on state/market/family relationships could erode existing safeguards on the autonomy of individuals in any of these three domains (Yuval-Davis 1997). Secondly, in countries such as those in

Eastern Europe or parts of the Middle East whose histories differ from those of the traditional Western welfare states, the state has striven to incorporate under its control all facets of the familial and the civil, which has resulted in restricting rather than promoting the welfare of women (Heinen 1997; Sainsbury 1994). These effects of globalization can no longer be ignored as we in traditional welfare states rethink a politics of engagement that will redefine citizenship.

Reaching Conclusions That Point to Possibilities

As activists as well as scholars, we are keenly aware of how the historical moment within which ideas and action occur shape the analysis. In each chapter the authors have tried to document how restructuring as it is experienced and reproduced at the local level connects to a discourse on globalization, which was changing even as we wrote.

I have finished facilitating the faculty task force on funding ethics. It was a lightning rod for every tension in the place! This funding issue isn't going to go away but my blood pressure said to cool my involvement for the moment. . . . The longitudinal study of policy impacts on provincial households is going really well, but time consuming as well as exciting. . . . Got a lot of doctoral students defending this year—then I go on sabbatical! . . . Feel like I'm always whining about lack of time.

—Network member

Feminists' road to social change holds many reminders of hard-fought battles for change that were taken up in ways that blunted their transformative potential. The most frequently documented have been in the area of violence against women. Shelters and changed police protocols, which are important but limited responses, have not addressed the ongoing problem of violence in our society. At other times professionals and state agencies have responded to women's experiences by putting in place or recommending a structure or procedure that ignores the context. Thus, specific practices that seem like a good thing at the time, including those suggested in the various chapters in this volume, will not necessarily remain so. As contexts change, so must our analysis and action. Indeed, parts of the critical work done today will be incorporated into regulations and mechanisms for exercising power tomorrow. The contradictory discourse that has surrounded caring debates is a prime example of this. In these pages we have tried, not always successfully, to avoid giving the idea that once an area is deconstructed and a more progressive interpretation offered, the struggle, at least on that particular aspect of the issue, is resolved. The desire to get the work done once and for all and move on is understandable, but probably stems more from fatigue than a belief that it is possible. Continuing analysis, like the examination of caring labour documented in the following chapters, is an essential ongoing activity that promotes a healthy polity. On the up side, each critical foray can open up sites for resistance.

Ideas of resistance have been given prominence in recent years as scholars and activists have struggled with envisioning new models of citizenship. However, even analyses rooted in a relational understanding of how power operates embody contradiction. Namely, if we accept that our actions constitute relations of power, how do we simultaneously enact and resist power? To what extent does the form of power exercised determine the form that resistance will take? In other words, possibilities of resistance seem to mirror how power is exercised. In that sense the idea of resistance presents individuals or members of groups as responding to existent conditions rather than building alternatives. This emphasis is apparent in the current use of the word 'oppositional' rather than 'feminist' or 'socialist' in some of the resistance literature (Cooper 1994:443). This sometimes happens in the analyses presented in these chapters. We would nonetheless argue that there is a safeguard if a steady gaze is kept on the context within which resistance is occurring. Resistance can be a catalyst for transformation, just as surely as it can be a dead end. At this point, it is helpful to return to the individual/ group issue discussed earlier under social location. Just as intersectionality serves as a heuristic tool for understanding the experiences of individual women but does not seem applicable to delineating the basis for group affiliations, so resistance seems to offer a way for individuals to counter the exercise of power. Although it is limited as a basis for group action, resistance can define a place, a starting-point for articulating alternatives. In fact, the history of feminist analyses supports such a position. Many readers will be familiar with the research priorities of the 1960s and 1970s. The challenge then was to fill in the gaps that male stream scholarship never explored. This was followed by the 'add sex and stir' thinking that nonetheless exposed how the model changes when gender was added, for example, to the string of variables used to predict labour force participation. As gender was no longer thought of as a variable but became increasingly seen as a dimension in the construction of knowledge, the possibilities for new understandings and actions blossomed. I have listed things chronologically, but, of course, events are never quite so neat. The point is that these analyses may seem today to be rather modest efforts. However, they did open up possibilities. How we theorize concepts like power is important because it 'highlights certain social issues and marginalizes others. If it is theorized in a way that dampens struggle then it may be of less value to those seeking change than a framework that allows for resistance and transformation and sees future social relations as whilst contingent, without theoretical closure' (Cooper 1994:453).

The analysis presented in the following chapters inevitably reflects the historical moment in which it was done and the social conditions that shaped the lives of network members. By the time the network formally concluded, all members were tenured university professors. However, the relative privilege of this status did not produce the promised peace and contemplative space of the proverbial ivory tower. Instead, we found ourselves balancing an array of teaching, research, and administrative tasks; child and parent care responsibilities to our families; and community commitments, constantly pushing the boundaries of time and energy. One of the themes that surfaced repeatedly in our discussions was that precious resource called time: time to think; time to communicate, laugh, and love; time to take action. From day one it was a scarce asset. The network freed up some time and space to theorize differently and thus made the following chapters possible. For that we are grateful. This particular space is no longer available to us, but our individual and joint analyses have been changed so the influence of the network lives on as we form new collaborations and start down new paths. In that way the network fulfilled the important function of providing a protective space for developing a group-based analysis that was more than the sum of our individual inputs. Thus, although the following chapters have named authors, the other network members are 'shadow' authors who have read, debated, and influenced the analysis.

References

Abel, Emily K., and Margaret K. Nelson, eds. 1990. *Circles of Care: Work and Identity in Women's Lives*. Albany: State University of New York Press.

Abrahams, Naomi. 1996. 'Negotiating Power, Identity, Family and Community: Women's Community Participation'. *Gender and Society* 10, no. 6:768–96.

Armstrong, Pat, and Hugh Armstrong. 1996. *Wasting Away: The Undermining of Canadian Health Care*. Toronto: Oxford University Press.

Aronson, J., and S. Neysmith. 1996. '"You're Not Just in There to Do the Work": Depersonalizing Policies and the Exploitation of Home Care Workers' Labor'. *Gender and Society* 10, no. 1:59–77.

Baines, Carol, Patricia Evans, and Sheila Neysmith. 1998. 'Women's Caring: Work Expanding, State Contracting'. In *Women's Caring: Feminist Perspectives on Social Welfare*, 2nd edn, edited by C. Baines, P. Evans, and S. Neysmith, 3–22. Toronto: Oxford University Press.

Bakker, Isabella, ed. 1996. *Rethinking Restructuring: Gender and Change in Canada*. Toronto: University of Toronto Press.

Barer, Morris L., Robert G. Evans, and Clyde Hertzman. 1995. 'Avalanche or Glacier: Health Care and the Demographic Rhetoric'. *Canadian Journal on Aging/La revue canadienne du vieillissement* 14, no. 2:193–224.

Beiner, R. 1995. *Theorizing Citizenship*. Albany: State University of New York Press.

Bickford, Susan. 1997. 'Anti-identity Politics: Feminism, Democracy, and the Complexities of Citizenship'. *Hypatia* 12, no. 4:111–21.

Boyd, Susan, ed. 1997. *Challenging the Public/Private Divide: Feminism, Law, and Public Policy*. Toronto: University of Toronto Press.

Brodie, Janine. 1995. *Politics at the Margins: Restructuring and the Canadian Women's Movement*. Halifax: Fernwood Publishing.

Bussemaker, Jet. 1998. 'Vocabularies of Citizenship and Gender: The Netherlands'. *Critical Social Policy* 18, no. 3:333–54.

———, and Rian Voet. 1998. 'Citizenship and Gender: Theoretical Approaches and Historical Legacies'. *Critical Social Policy* 18, no. 3:277–307.

Card, C. 1990. 'Caring and Evil'. *Hypatia* 5, no. 1:101–8.

Clement, G. 1996. *Care, Autonomy and Justice*. Oxford: Clarendon Press.

Collins, Patricia Hill. 1998. *Fighting Words: Black Women and the Search for Justice*. Minneapolis: Minnesota Press.

Cook, J., and M. Fonow. 1990. 'Knowledge and Women's Interests: Issues of Epistemology and Methodology in Feminist Sociological Research'. In *Feminist Research Methods*, edited by J. McCarl Nielson, 69–93. Boulder: Westview Press.

Cooper, Davina. 1994. 'Productive, Relational and Everywhere? Conceptualizing Power and Resistance within Foucauldian Feminism'. *Sociology* 18, no. 2:435–54.

Daly, Mary. 1994. 'Comparing Welfare States: Toward a Gender-Friendly Approach'. In *Gendering Welfare States*, edited by Diane Sainsbury, 101–17. London: Sage Publications.

Dean, Jodi, ed. 1997. *Feminism and the New Democracy: Re-siting the Political*. London: Sage Publications.

Demaine, Jack, and Harold Entwistle. 1996. *Beyond Communitarianism: Citizenship, Politics and Education*. Hampshire and London: MacMillan Press.

Dietz, Mary G. 1998. 'Context Is All: Feminism and Theories of Citizenship'. In *Feminism & Politics*, edited by Anne Phillips, 378–400. Oxford and New York: Oxford University Press.

Emirbayer, Mustafa, and Ann Mische. 1998. 'What Is Agency?' *American Journal of Sociology* 103, no. 4:962–1023.

Estes, Carroll, James H. Swan and Associates. 1993. *The Long Term Care Crisis: Elders Trapped in the No-Care Zone*. Newbury Park: Sage Publications.

Feminist Review. 1997. Special Issue. *Citizenship: Pushing the Boundaries* 57.

Finch, Janet, and Dulcie Groves, eds. 1983. *A Labour of Love: Women, Work and Caring*. London: Routledge & Kegan Paul.

Fraser, N. 1989. *Unruly Practices: Power, Discourse and Gender in Contemporary Social Theory*. Minneapolis: University of Minnesota Press.

Fraser, Nancy. 1998. 'From Redistribution to Recognition? Dilemmas of Justice in a Post-Socialist Age'. In *Feminism & Politics*, edited by Anne Phillips, 430-60. Oxford and New York: Oxford University Press.

Gibson, D. 1996. 'Broken Down by Age and Gender: The "Problem of Old Women" Redefined'. *Gender and Society* 10, no. 4:433–48.

Gilligan, C. 1982. *In a Different Voice*. Cambridge: Harvard University Press.

Gordon, L. 1994. *Pitied But Not Entitled: Single Mothers and the History of Welfare*. New York: Free Press.

Gordon, S. 1996. 'Feminism and Caring'. In *Caregiving: Readings in Knowledge, Practice, Ethics, and Politics*, edited by S. Gordon, P. Benner, and N. Noddings, 256–77. Philadelphia: University of Philadelphia Press.

Graham, Hilary. 1993. 'Social Divisions in Caring'. *Women's Studies International Forum* 16, no. 5:461–70.

Heinen, Jacqueline. 1997. 'Public/Private: Gender—Social and Political Citizenship in Eastern Europe'. *Theory and Society* 26:577–97.

Houston, B. 1990. 'Caring and Exploitation'. *Hypatia* 5, no. 1 (Spring 1990):115–19.

Hypatia. 1997. Special Issue. *Citizenship in Feminism: Identity, Victim and Locale* 12, no. 4.

Jenson, J. 1997. 'Who Cares? Gender and Welfare Regimes'. *Social Politics* 4, no. 2 (Summer):182–7.

Jessop, R. 1993. 'Toward a Schumpeterian Workfare State? Preliminary Remarks on Post-Fordist Political Economy'. *Studies in Political Economy* 40 (Spring):7–39.

Knijn, Trudie, and Monique Kremer. 1997. 'Gender and the Caring Dimension of Welfare States: Toward Inclusive Citizenship'. *Social Politics* 4, no. 3:328–61.

Koehn, Daryl. 1998. *Rethinking Feminist Ethics: Care, Trust and Empathy*. London and New York: Routledge.

Kulynych, Jessica. 1997. 'Performing Politics: Foucault, Habermas, and Postmodern Participation'. *Polity* 30, no. 2:315–46.

Leira, A. 1993. 'The "Woman-Friendly" Welfare State? The Case of Norway and Sweden'. In *Women and Social Policies in Europe: Work, Family and the State*, edited by J. Lewis, 49–71. Aldershot: Edward Elgar.

Lewis, Jane. 1997. 'Gender and Welfare Regimes: Further Thoughts'. *Social Politics* 4, no. 2:160-77.

_____, and Barbara Meredith. 1988. *Daughter Who Care: Daughters Caring for Mothers at Home*. London and New York: Routledge.

Lister, Ruth. 1997. 'Dialectics of Citizenship'. *Hypatia* 12, no. 4:6–27.

Mahoney, M. 1994. 'Victimization or Oppression? Women's Lives, Violence and Agency'. In *The Public Nature of Private Violence*, edited by M. Fineman and R. Mykitiuk, 59–92. New York: Routledge.

Maynard, Mary, and June Purvis, eds. 1994. *Researching Women's Lives from a Feminist Perspective*. London: Taylor & Francis.

Narayan, Uma. 1997. 'Towards a Feminist Vision of Citizenship: Rethinking the Implications of Dignity, Political Participation, and Nationality'. In *Reconstructing Political Theory: Feminist Perspectives*, edited by M.L. Shanley and U. Narayan, 48–67. Cambridge: Polity Press.

Neysmith, S. 1995. 'Feminist Methodologies: A Consideration of Principles and Practice for Research in Gerontology'. *Canadian Journal on Aging/La revue canadienne vieillissement* 14, no. 1:100–18.

_____. 1997. 'Toward a Woman Friendly Long-Term Care Policy'. In *Women and the Canadian Welfare State: Challenges and Change*, edited by P. Evans and G. Wekerle, 222–45. Toronto: University of Toronto Press.

_____, and J. Aronson. 1996. 'Home Care Workers Discuss Their Work: The Skills Required to "Use Your Common Sense"'. *Journal of Aging Studies* 10, no. 1:1–14.

Noddings, Nel. 1984. *Caring: A Feminine Approach to Ethics and Moral Education*. Berkeley: University of California Press.

O'Connor, Julia, Ann Shola Orloff, and Sheila Shaver. 1999. *States, Markets, Families: Gender, Liberalism and Social Policy in Australia, Canada, Great Britain and the United States*. Cambridge: Cambridge University Press.

Orloff, A. 1993. 'Gender and the Social Rights of Citizenship: The Comparative Analysis of Gender Relations and Welfare States'. *American Sociological Review* 58, no. 30:303–28.

Pateman, C. 1992. 'The Patriarchal Welfare State'. In *Defining Women: Social Institutions and Gender Divisions*, edited by L. McDowell and R. Pringle, 223–45. Cambridge: Polity Press.

Phillips, Anne. 1993. *Democracy and Difference*. University Park: Pennsylvania Press.

_____. 1998. 'Introduction'. In *Feminism and Politics*, edited by Anne Phillips, 1–20. Oxford and New York: Oxford University Press.

Robertson, Anne. 1991. 'The Politics of Alzheimer's Disease: A Case Study in Apocalyptic Demography'. In *Critical Perspectives on Aging*, edited by M. Minkler and C. Estes, 135–50. Amityville: Baywood.

_____. 1997. 'Beyond Apocalyptic Demography: Toward a Moral Economy of Independence'. *Ageing and Society* 17, no. 4:425–46.

Sainsbury, Diane, ed. 1994. *Gendering Welfare States*. London, Thousand Oaks, and New Delhi: Sage Publications.

Sarvasy, Wendy. 1997. 'Social Citizenship from a Feminist Perspective'. *Hypatia* 12, no. 4:54–74.

Scaltsas, P. 1992. 'Do Feminist Ethics Counter Feminist Aims?' In *Explorations in Feminist Ethics: Theory and Practice*, edited by E. Cole and S. Coultrap-McQuin, 15–26. Bloomington: University of Indiana Press.

Schwandt, Thomas. 1997. *Qualitative Inquiry: A Dictionary of Terms*. Thousand Oaks: Sage Publications.

Slote, Michael. 1998. 'The Justice of Caring'. *Social Philosophy & Policy* 15, no. 1:171–95.

Smith, D. 1990. *The Conceptual Practices of Power: A Feminist Sociology of Power*. Toronto: University of Toronto Press.

Smith, J.K. 1993. *After the Demise of Empiricism: The Problem of Judging Social and Educational Inquiry*. Norwood: Ablex Publishing Corporation.

Sparks, Holloway. 1997. 'Dissident Citizenship: Democratic Theory, Political Courage, and Activist Women'. *Hypatia* 12, no. 4:74–111.

Spelman, E. 1988. *Inessential Woman: Problems of Exclusion in Feminist Thought*. Boston: Beacon Press.

Stewart, A. 1995. 'Two Concepts of Citizenship'. *The British Journal of Sociology* 46, no. 1:63–78.

Stryker, Robin. 1998. 'Globalization and the Welfare State'. *International Journal of Sociology and Social Policy* 18, no. 2/3/4:1–49.

Theory and Society. 1997. Special Issue. *Recasting Citizenship* 26.

Tronto, J. 1993. *Moral Boundaries: A Political Argument for an Ethic of Care*. New York: Routledge.

Ungerson, Clare. 1997. 'Social Politics and the Commodification of Care'. *Social Politics* 4, no. 3:362–81.

Walby, Sylvia. 1994. 'Is Citizenship Gendered?' *Sociology* 28, no. 2:379–95.

Williams, Fiona. 1995. 'Race/Ethnicity, Gender and Class in Welfare States: A Framework for Comparative Analysis'. *Social Politics* 2, no. 2:127–59.

Yeatman, Anna. 1998. 'Trends and Opportunities in the Public Sector: A Critical Assessment'. *Australian Journal of Public Administration* 57, no. 4:138–47.

Young, Iris. 1990. *Justice and the Politics of Difference*. Princeton: Princeton University Press.

_____. 1997. *Intersecting Voices: Dilemmas of Gender, Political Philosophy, and Policy*. Princeton: Princeton University Press.

Yuval-Davis, Nira. 1997. 'Women, Citizenship and Difference'. *Feminist Review* 57:4–27.

Part 1

The Powerful Presence of a Retreating State in Daily Life

Chapter 2

Managing the Disentitlement of Women: Glorified Markets, the Idealized Family, and the Undeserving Other[1]

Janet E. Mosher

A dramatic shift in the Canadian welfare state is now well underway as federal and provincial governments continue their retreat from social programs. Valorization of the market (in particular a global market) and a corresponding practice of privatization are eroding the already imperfect twin notions of state responsibility to meet the needs of its citizens and of citizen entitlement to state support. This is not to suggest that faith in the market's ability to provide for all is a new idea, but rather that it has gained a new position of pre-eminence in the Canadian polity (Day and Brodsky 1998; Little 1998). Assent to this shift has been garnered largely through the construction of a fiscal crisis for which social welfare programs were (are) to blame (Cohen 1997). As Cohen maintains, the notion that 'we cannot afford these programs' has become part of our cultural mindset (Cohen 1997). Constructed in this manner, the solution to the crisis appears obvious—withdrawal from social programs. This 'solution', however, creates the unsettling problem of how those needs formerly met by the state will now be addressed. Here, visions of an idealized and hegemonic family and of glorified international markets come into play; both are valorized as not only able to address our needs, but to do so in ways preferable to the state interventions of the past.

In this schema of things, it is important to observe that government retreat and market ascension are understood to be not only desirable but indeed inevitable. This inevitability is linked to the understanding that Canada's debt has launched the country into crisis (so something dramatic must be done) and to the understanding of 'globalization' as an unstoppable force beyond human control. As such, the state's retreat is portrayed as an apolitical imperative, not a choice with winners and losers.

Using a case-study of the reform of social assistance ('welfare') in Ontario, I debunk several of the claims central to this schema. As reviewed more fully later, the state's retreat from its responsibilities, as manifested in recent welfare reforms, has 'disentitled' women. Drastic reductions in benefit levels and changing conditions of eligibility (including a new definition of spouse and new workfare requirements) have significantly curtailed women's entitlement to state benefits. This retraction has, I show, profoundly negative implications for women's equality and women's safety. As such, it becomes clear that the state's retreat entails a normative judgement with consequent winners and losers; it is not an apolitical imperative. I also explore how this disentitlement has been 'managed'; that is, how the state has made the retraction of entitlements seem not only acceptable but indeed desirable.[2] I argue that three principal strategies have been (and continue to be) employed to this end. Two of these—the invocation of an idealized, hegemonic family and the glorification of the market—are not specific to welfare reform and have been, as I suggested earlier and as reviewed elsewhere in this volume (see chapters 3, 4, 5, 7, 9, 10, and 11), integral to the state's retreat and the market's ascension. These strategies, however, manifest themselves in particular ways and with particular consequences for women in the context of welfare benefits. Rather than meeting the needs of women, as the crafters of the state's retreat would have us believe, the market and family—particularly as idealized within present discourse—do much to increase women's responsibilities for meeting the needs of others, including within relationships not of their choosing. The third strategy, while not unique to welfare reform, is absolutely central to the management of women's disentitlement to welfare. This strategy entails the active construction of a deeply negative stereotype of welfare recipients in general and of single mothers in receipt of welfare in particular. Central to this strategy has been the state's 'anti-fraud' campaign, but the idealization of the nuclear family and the glorification of the market (and of paid work) fuel the stereotype as well. This stereotype, which resonates with the media accounts of single mothers that Swift and Evans review in Chapter 4, casts single mothers as undeserving of public support and, as such, justifies their disentitlement.

Rather than promoting women's equality, as the state's many domestic and international undertakings would seem to commit it to do, or enhancing women's safety, as many recent criminal justice strategies are ostensibly designed to do, these reforms and the strategies employed to garner assent to them (that is, the strategies to manage disentitlement) actively compromise women's equality and safety, often exposing them to harms, including the multiple harms of wife abuse. By creating conditions that make it more difficult for women to leave abusive relationships and more difficult to protect and otherwise care for themselves and their children, the state is implicated as an active participant in sustaining violence against women.

I begin by reviewing several key features of social assistance regimes of the past. I then review recent reforms and how they have disentitled women. I then examine the three strategies identified earlier and document the harms wrought not only by the disentitlement of women but by the strategies themselves. While the reforms I examine are those that have occurred in Ontario, it would be wrong to credit Ontario with originality in undertaking these reforms; reforms of this general nature are occurring throughout North America. Thus, while I focus upon a particular case-study, the analysis is relevant to many other jurisdictions.

Welfare Then and Now

Social assistance ('welfare') in Ontario has, since its inception, been a residual program based upon demonstrated need for assistance. As such it has always been a means-tested program, unlike many other programs characteristic of modern welfare states that are tied to labour market participation, such as unemployment insurance (Little 1998). The receipt of welfare has also been associated with a deeply negative and harmful stereotype. While variations of this stereotype exist, its dominant features are those of idleness or laziness, sloth, ignorance, and, increasingly, dishonesty. To this stereotype is added that of promiscuity and immorality for single mothers in receipt of welfare (Little 1998). The existence of this stereotype means that the receipt of social assistance is accompanied by stigma, prejudice, and discrimination.

The receipt of social assistance is deeply gendered and, as such, welfare reforms affect men and women in differential ways. Women are more likely than men to be recipients of social assistance and to remain on social assistance for longer periods. Aboriginal women, women with disabilities, immigrant women, and racial minority women are more vulnerable to poverty than other women (Day and Brodsky 1998). Single mothers experience the highest rate of poverty (57.3 per cent, but as high as 82.8 per cent when their children are under seven) and the greatest depth of poverty in the country (National Council of Welfare 1997). In Ontario two-thirds of all single mothers receive social assistance (*Falkiner et al. v. Director of Income Maintenance Branch*, Appellants' Submissions 1997). Moreover, the reasons why women and men turn to social assistance are gendered: women because childcare responsibilities make paid employment difficult; men because of unemployment (Bakker and Brodie 1995). As many analyses have shown, women's poverty is strongly linked to their care-giving responsibilities (Bakker and Brodie 1995; Day and Brodsky 1998; Evans 1998).

So too the structure of social assistance has been and remains gendered in multiple ways. For example, social assistance regimes in Ontario have long been premised upon a particular form of family constituted by clearly demarcated gender roles of a male breadwinner and female dependant (Little 1998). Also, various categories of deservedness have existed over time within social assistance regimes, with able-bodied, employable men treated less favourably than single mothers, at least those women who were demonstrably celibate. And the evolution of the treatment of single mothers over time, as discussed more fully later, reveals social assistance policy as being grounded in, and thus perpetuating, a particular view of how women were (are) to behave.

Social assistance rates have never been generous. Even before Ontario's welfare reforms in the latter half of the 1990s—which included a 21.6 per cent reduction in benefit levels—rates were below all common measures of poverty. One reason for maintaining low benefit levels has always been to motivate people to get off welfare and into paid employment, and to discourage people from leaving employment for welfare (Little 1998). Even in what is perhaps the most progressive of welfare reform reports in Ontario, *Transitions*, it was recommended that benefit levels be below those of the lowest paying employment for these very reasons (Social Assistance Review Committee 1988). Employment—no matter what kind—has always been more highly valued than the unpaid care that single mothers provide day in, day out.

Notwithstanding these (and other) deficiencies and inequities, social assistance did, however, reflect something of society's commitment to provide for its neediest. A person in need no longer had to depend upon the largesse of the more fortunate; rather, she or he had a right—an entitlement—to assistance from the state. The legal basis of the right was embedded in the Canada Assistance Plan Act (CAP), an act that provided the framework for cost-sharing agreements between the federal government and the provincial and territorial jurisdictions. Pursuant to CAP, the transfer of federal funds required that the provincial and territorial jurisdictions meet certain conditions: that welfare be provided to those in need; that the amount of benefits provided take into account basic requirements/needs; and that no conditions—such as workfare—be attached to the receipt of benefits.

Moreover, notwithstanding its inadequacies, social assistance did, at least for some women, provide the necessary financial support that enabled them to leave abusive relationships (*Falkiner et al. v. Her Majesty the Queen*, Affidavit of Usha Gici George 1996; OAITH 1996, 1997; Pollack 1996). While the precise number of women in receipt of social assistance in Ontario who have been abused is not known, we do know that women experience violence and abuse at the hands of their intimate partners in staggering numbers. The Violence Against Women Survey, undertaken by Statistics Canada in the early 1990s, found that one in three women had suffered acts of violence, as defined by the Criminal Code, at the hands of their marital or common-law partners (Rodgers 1994). Women married or living in a common-law relationship at the time of the survey, and with annual family incomes of less than $15,000, reported double the rate of assault in the twelve-month period preceding the survey than those with greater incomes (6 per cent as compared to 3 per cent). Given these statistics, Little's estimate (*Falkiner et al. v. Her Majesty the Queen*, cross-examination of Margaret Hillyard Little 1996) that 50 per cent of women in receipt of assistance have experienced abuse seems reasonable, if not conservative. One Toronto study of young mothers, most of whom were in receipt of social assistance, found that 50 per cent had lived for some time with a partner who had physically assaulted them or had abused drugs or alcohol (*Falkiner et al. v. Her Majesty the Queen*, Affidavit of Robert Fulton 1995). Various studies undertaken in the United States have found rates of abuse at the hands of a current or former partner among recipients of Aid to Families of Dependent Children to be in the range of 50–80 per cent (Allard et al. 1997; Cooley et al. 1997; Ehrenreich 1995; Pollack 1996; Raphael and Tolman 1997).

Shortly after its election to office in 1995, the Conservative government of Ontario introduced various measures that together with the federal government's revocation of the CAP, have fundamentally altered social assistance. The federal government's revocation of the CAP left it open for provinces to provide welfare other than on the basis of need, and to attach conditions to its receipt. Ontario moved quickly to do precisely this. The first two reforms introduced in Ontario changed existing regulations: a 21.6 per cent reduction in benefit levels (Regs 384 and 385/95), and a new definition of 'spouse' (Regs 409 and 410/95). Then came Bill 142, the Social Assistance Reform Act (SARA, SO 1997, c. 25), the first major welfare reform in thirty years, which was proclaimed in force in the spring of 1998 (portions were proclaimed on 1 May, the remainder on 1 June). The SARA enacted two separate acts: the Ontario Works Act, 1997 (OWA); and the Ontario Disability Support Program Act, 1997. The OWA (which is the focus of the discussion that follows) is in many respects simply a shell because it gives the government of the day sweeping regulatory powers. There are virtually no rights set out in the OWA that cannot be taken away by regulation; indeed, by regulation the responsible minister may even make regulations 'prescribing classes of persons who are not eligible for assistance' (subsection 74 [1] 11). As such, the act is profoundly antidemocratic, permitting further changes to welfare policy without even the benefit of legislative debate (Steering Committee on Social Assistance 1997). Pursuant to these broad regulatory powers, several other welfare reforms were introduced in the spring of 1998, including several that operationalized the new 'workfare' requirements of the act.

As will become clearer below, consistent with the general direction of social policy in a number of areas, the effect of these reforms is to shift much of the state's responsibility for meeting needs to the market and 'the family'. Below I review several of the reforms and how they disentitle women in significant ways. I consider these reforms through the lens of the three strategies, which I identified at the outset as being central to current restructuring: glorified markets, the idealized family, and undeserving others.

Glorified Markets

Section 1 of the Ontario Works Act provides that the purpose of the act is to establish a program that: (a) recognizes individual responsibility and promotes self-reliance through employment; (b) provides temporary financial assistance to those most in need while they satisfy obligations to become and stay employed; (c) effectively serves people needing assistance; and (d) is accountable to the taxpayers of Ontario.

By its very terms the OWA represents a clear departure from the principles underlying the CAP. The OWA, reflective of the more general shift towards faith in the market and market values, is premised upon an understanding of poverty as rooted in individual failing rather than as an inevitable consequence of a market economy. While past welfare regimes never fully embraced an understanding of poverty as systemic and structural in nature, the OWA moves us much further away from such an understanding. Because individuals are understood to be at the root of poverty, its remediation is also seen to rest in their hands. Within this frame of reference, individuals need to be reformed—to develop a stronger work ethic, to learn not to be dependent upon welfare—hence the OWA requires people to participate in various work or job readiness activities ('workfare'). More specifically, the act provides that 'a recipient and any prescribed dependants may be required as a condition of eligibility' to 'satisfy community participation requirements; participate in employment measures; accept and undertake basic education and job specific skills training; and accept and maintain employment' (OWA subsection 7 [4]). While this provision is framed permissively ('may be required'), the regulations make it clear that all recipients and adult dependants, except those falling within a few defined categories (reviewed below) are required to do so (Reg. 134/98, Section 27). As such, the act draws upon, and hence sustains, the negative stereotype of welfare recipients reviewed earlier: lazy, unmotivated, slothful individuals who require discipline. Indeed, there is much state discourse that explicitly portrays this stereotype and actively constructs welfare recipients as undesirable 'others', people who are clearly not deserving of state benefits. The state promises, for example, to get 'these people' off the welfare rolls, to get them working, to put an end to rampant fraud, to make the system accountable to the 'taxpayers of Ontario' (assuming wrongly, of course, that welfare recipients are not taxpayers). This rhetoric, and the reforms that it shoulders, require one to ignore the effects of restructuring: the job displacement, the high levels of unemployment, the changing nature of the employment market, etc.

In many respects, the OWA reflects a fundamental redrawing of the social contract, moving from an idea that people within a market economy would become unemployed and potentially impoverished through no fault of their own and hence that society had an obligation to provide for them by establishing a social safety net (Moon 1988), to one wherein individuals who receive financial support from the state incur a debt or obligation that must be repaid through participation in 'workfare'.

While, as noted earlier, prior welfare regimes attached greater value to paid employment than to the unpaid caring labour provided by women, the

OWA exacerbates these value differentials. Reproductive labour does not, in the main, entitle one to benefits from the state. Single mothers (fathers too, but there are not many of them) are exempted from the workfare requirements of the act unless there is publicly funded education for their children, which means that at present they will be exempted until their children turn four years of age (Reg. 134/98, subsection 27 [2]1.).[3] While this, construed in its most favourable light, may reflect an acknowledgement that single mothers with young children are making a contribution—albeit less valuable than paid employment—the caring/giving labour otherwise performed by women is completely ignored. It is productive labour, not reproductive labour, that is valued (see also Chapter 5).

Once required to participate in workfare, neither the act nor the regulations oblige the state to address the constraints that care-giving responsibilities (be they children or adult dependants) place upon women's participation in paid employment or in job readiness activities. The act ignores the reality that the labour market is structured against the backdrop of an assumed gendered, nuclear family with its resident wife/mother caring for the children and performing virtually all of the domestic labour so that her husband can report to work fed, clothed, and rested (Mosher 1991). Women, including single mothers, are expected to perform this reproductive labour and participate in a market economy that assumes someone else—not its employees—are performing it.

Moreover, neither the act nor regulations create any exceptions for women abused in their intimate relationships, nor do they create any supports for their participation in paid employment or job readiness activities.[4] This is especially troublesome for a number of reasons. To appreciate this, it is first necessary to sketch out the role that economic domination plays as one of the many strands in the web of constraints that limits women's options while they are in an abusive relationship and often after they leave such a relationship (Mosher 1998). Abusive men will often go to great lengths to ensure that their partners are economically dependent upon them, for economic dependence gives them tremendous power and control. To ensure this dependence, an abusive man may engage in any number of tactics: he may prevent his intimate partner (present or past) from participating in paid employment; he may not permit her to attend employment readiness or skills-training programs; he may prevent her from acquiring the language skills she needs to become gainfully employed; and if she is employed, he may control her pay. Studies document the enormous amount of time that women are absent from work due to the debilitating consequences of wife abuse and the incredible extent of harassment that abusive men perpetuate at women's places of work, often causing them to lose their jobs (Cooley et al. 1997; OAITH 1997).

These forms of abuse do not necessarily end once a woman has 'left' an abusive relationship. For many women, violence and other forms of abuse increase after separation (Rodgers 1994). And the act of separation is often an extremely dangerous one for women; indeed, it is at this point that women are at the greatest risk of lethal violence (Crawford and Gartner 1992; Crawford, Gartner, and Dawson 1997).

Thus, a woman who has been abused in her intimate relationship may have few marketable skills; she may have little or no marketable job experience; she may be unable to meet job or workfare requirements because of ongoing harassment and abuse by her (ex)partner; she may have sustained psychological scars that have undermined her self-esteem and confidence; she and her children may be vulnerable to further attacks (particularly in the workplace); and/or she may need to be with her children to help them and herself recover from the trauma of the abuse (OAITH 1997; Raphael and Tolman 1997).

Two important implications for welfare reform result from these observations. First, without financial support that is not dependent upon labour market participation (because she may not be able to secure a job, or may not be safe while employed) or upon unsupported labour market participation (because she may only be able to find and retain work with supports in place), many women are virtually trapped in abusive relationships (OAITH 1996, 1997). Cuts to social assistance benefit levels, and the attachment of conditions to eligibility that mandate employment, trap women in or force them to return to abusive relationships, thus exposing them to the ongoing harms of wife abuse. In August 1996 the Ontario Association of Interval Houses (OAITH) conducted a survey of its member organizations (sixty shelters across Ontario) to assess the impact upon abused women of the cuts to social assistance, as well as a range of other cutbacks. One hundred per cent of the shelters that responded said that cuts to social assistance had a severe impact on survivors of abuse. Over two-thirds of the shelters reported that women were remaining with or returning to abusive men as a direct result of the decrease in financial support they could receive. The survey also documented the emotional costs of the cutbacks: depression, despair, hopelessness, and stress. As OAITH's report concludes, 'With little support or assistance to return to a life free from violence, women are locked in with abusers who endanger the lives of themselves and their children. When they try to get away, they discover they cannot financially support themselves and their children. . . . Women who are trapped with or forced to return to an abuser will certainly be subjected to further abuse. Already, far too many women die because they lack options and support for escape' (OAITH 1996:35).

A second important implication is that any 'employment readiness' or community participation programs must be designed with these realities in mind. Recent studies conducted in the United States suggest that the most significant impediment to women's successful participation in employment readiness programs is the abusive conduct of past or current male partners (Raphael 1995; Raphael and Tolman 1997). The studies document men hiding or destroying women's work clothes, physically preventing them from attending programs, and interfering with their sleep or study to undermine their abilities to perform (Raphael 1995). As Raphael (1995) puts it, men sabotage women's efforts to become gainfully employed. Nothing in the design of 'Ontario Works' (owa) or in its regulations attends to these realities.[5] Instead, women who 'fail' to participate as required will be penalized. Their benefits will be cut for a period of time: three months for the first 'failure', six for the second (Reg. 134/98, Section 33) and women and their children will suffer grievous harm as a consequence, either the harms of abject poverty or the harms inflicted by the abusive partners that they are forced to return to.[6]

In sum, the reforms reviewed earlier presuppose that the market has a place for all and will adequately meet our material needs. The reforms valorize participation in the market as the only meaningful contribution, and not only devalue but demean those who are not engaged in paid employment.

The Idealized Family

Welfare, like other areas of social policy, has long been premised upon an image of a hegemonic and idealized nuclear family, with clearly demarcated roles for men and women. Within 'the family', men were assumed to be breadwinners who provide adequately for their wives and children. It was the responsibility of men, not the state, to provide for women and children. It was assumed that 'the family' provided for material needs, as well as our needs for comfort, security, nurturance, and belonging.

Single mothers exist outside the boundaries of 'the family' and as such represent a challenge to it. Historically, in the context of welfare, whether single mothers were seen to be deserving and thus entitled to benefits depended on the reasons for their status as single mothers. At the inception of Mothers' Allowance (a precursor to welfare regimes), only those who were widowed and 'fit and proper' persons were eligible; those who bore children out of wedlock or whose husbands had deserted them were not (Little 1998). Of course, widows posed no challenge to 'the family', while unwed mothers did. Over time, other single mothers became entitled to Mothers' Allowance as mores about the family began to change slowly (Little 1998). Eventually, the eligibility of a single mother came to depend on whether she was 'living as a single person'; put differently, she was eligible provided there was no 'man in the house'. If there was a man in the house, it was assumed to be his responsibility—not the state's—to provide for the woman and children in the house ('the family' was assumed). It did not matter whether he was in fact providing for them. Because women's initial and continuing eligibility for benefits depended on the absence of 'men in the house', women's lives became subject to intrusive investigations and often to the arbitrary or capricious termination of benefits (*Falkiner et al. v. Her Majesty the Queen*, Affidavit of Margaret Hillyard Little 1996; Leighton 1987; Little 1998). In the period immediately preceding 1987, determinations of whether a woman was living as a single person depended mostly on whether welfare investigators concluded that there was a sexual relationship. Often benefits were terminated based upon a mere suspicion of sex, suspicions arising from, for example, the presence of men's clothing or toiletries. As such, women were subjected to an indirect moral test; if they wished their benefits to continue, they had to avoid heterosexual sex (as 'good' single women did) or avoid any kind of a relationship with a man (Little 1998). This policy drew upon and sustained the idealized nuclear family. Sex outside of marriage—outside of family—rendered one undeserving of state support; sex outside of marriage challenged the institution of marriage itself and could not be condoned by the state through the provision of welfare benefits. Rather, the assumption underpinning welfare policy was that men provided (or should provide) economic support for the women with whom they had sex, for to engage in sex was to participate in a 'spouse-like' relationship, and spousal relationships carry with them this responsibility. As such, welfare policy was embedded in the ideology of the nuclear family with its breadwinner husband and economically dependent wife, who provided, among other things, sex (Leighton 1987).

In 1987 a constitutional challenge to the definition of spouse resulted in amendments to the regulations as part of the settlement of the litigation (Rosenberg, J. in *Falkiner et al. v. Her Majesty the Queen* 1996).[7] The new definition largely mirrored the definition of spouse within Ontario's Family Law Act (FLA) and included people who were subject to a support obligation under the FLA and people of the opposite sex who had resided together continuously for a period of three years (at which point support obligations would arise under the FLA). This meant that benefits would only be terminated where there was a coexisting legal obligation to provide support under the FLA, whereas in the past benefits could be terminated on the basis of a 'spousal' relationship, even though there was no legal obligation to provide support. It also meant that people could cohabit for three years before they would be treated as spouses for welfare purposes. As such, the 1987 amendments represented an important move forward for women. In addition to changing the definition of spouse, the amendments contained an express prohibition on the investigation or use of sexual factors to establish a spousal relationship. The intent of the provision was to eliminate intrusive investigations into women's intimate lives and thus to provide at least a modicum of privacy.

This period of liberalization was short-lived. A new definition of spouse, introduced in the fall of 1995, provides that two people of the opposite sex who reside in the same dwelling place are assumed to be spouses for welfare purposes (Regs 409 and 410/95, now Reg. 134/98, Section 1). The onus is on the person who has applied for, or is in receipt of, benefits to prove that she is not a 'spouse' within the meaning of the act. In fact, it turns out to be difficult to prove that one is not a 'spouse', for if a man with whom a woman is residing provides financial support, or if she provides financial support to him, or if they have 'a mutual agreement or arrangement regarding their financial affairs' (an ambiguous phrase at best that has been applied to even an agreement to share household appliances), and if the 'social and familial aspects of the relationship between the person and the applicant or recipient amount to cohabitation' (again, a wildly ambiguous phrase), they are spouses for the purposes of welfare (Reg.134/98). Moreover, 'sexual factors shall not be investigated or considered in determining whether or not a person is a spouse'. As a direct consequence of the new definition, 10,013 recipients were cut off welfare; 89 per cent of these were women and 76 per cent were single mothers. Of those terminated, 6,947 have not returned to welfare (as, for example, applicants as a 'family') and of these, 97 per cent are women (Rosenberg, J. in *Falkiner et al. v. Her Majesty the Queen* 1996). While this and other declines in the welfare rolls have delighted the present Conservative government, it is a cause for concern for others because inevitably many of these women are now destitute or have been compelled to return to abusive relationships.

The new definition has been the subject of a recent and successful constitutional challenge before the Social Assistance Review Board (SARB), (*Falkiner et al. v. Director of Income Maintenance Branch* 1998).[8] I do not propose here to review the Charter arguments at length, but rather to consider more fully the facts of the case that led the board to the conclusion that Section 15 (the equality guarantee) and Section 7 (the guarantee of life, liberty, and security of the person) had been violated. These facts assist in revealing the consequences of the new definition to women.

Each of the applicants (Sandra Falkiner, Cynthia Pauline Johnston, Deborah Ann Sears, and Claude Marie Cadieux) had one or more dependent children, and each had been residing for less than one year with a person of the opposite sex who was not the father of the child or children. Each was receiving benefits as a sole-support parent with dependent children, and each had these benefits terminated when the new definition of spouse was enacted. Each of these women had suffered serious abuse; three by a former partner, and one by her father. In their affidavits, they attested to their reluctance to make a commitment to a new relationship in light of their past experiences, and of the importance of maintaining their economic independence until they were prepared to make a more permanent commitment. They also attested to the importance of living together before making that commitment, with the pressures and demands that entails. The effect of the new definition was to deny them this—each was presumed to be living with her 'spouse' and not entitled to benefits in her own right. Women in this situation have, as the SARB found, three choices: (1) to end the relationship (a relationship that may be—and was to these women—

beneficial in a host of ways); (2) to seek the financial support of their partners (but partners have no corresponding legal obligation to provide
support to either the women or their children); or (3) to make a joint application for welfare with their deemed spouses (but again, men have no obligation to do so and even if they do and are found to qualify, the welfare
cheque is likely to go to the man as the 'head of the household'). The board
observed in its decision that this approach to the definition of spouse 'seems
to be throwing the sole support parent into the water and waiting to see if
she will sink, or if the co-resident will throw out a financial lifeline'
(*Falkiner et al. v. Director of Income Maintenance Branch* 1998:59). But
even this dire analogy fails to capture the full impact of the definition. The
analogy of 'wait and see' erroneously implies that should her coresident fail
to throw a financial lifeline, the state will respond (it won't). Also, both of
the latter options are problematic because they render women economically
dependent upon men, creating a situation that abusive men will exploit.

As a result of the new definition, sole-support parents (women) in receipt
of welfare are denied the opportunity to live with a man on a trial basis to
determine, among other things, whether he is non-abusive. Forming a
heterosexual relationship at all puts a woman at risk because, given the
very ambiguous definition of spouse, she does not know in advance how
many visits to her home by a male will be 'permitted' before he is deemed
to be living with her and thus presumed to be a spouse. Sharing accommodation with a man, either to help make ends meet or to provide some
measure of protection for herself and her children, exposes her to intrusive
investigations and puts the onus upon her to prove that he is not her
'spouse'. If she does not, in the opinion of her welfare worker, prove that
she has been receiving benefits as a single person, her benefits will be cut
and she may be charged with fraud and assessed with an overpayment of
welfare benefits. And the onus is difficult to discharge for she cannot rely
upon sexual factors as the 1987 amendment prohibiting the investigation
and use of sexual factors to establish a spousal relationship continues (thus,
a provision intended to protect women's privacy and enhance their access
to benefits now helps to disentitle women) and mutual arrangements
regarding financial affairs can be and have been found in virtually any case
where people share accommodation (*Falkiner et al. v. Her Majesty the
Queen*, Cross-examination of Kevin Costantes 1996).

As the board held in coming to its conclusion that sole-support parents
were deprived of personal autonomy (a dimension of 'security of the
person' within Section 7 of the Charter), 'a constant sense of not knowing
whether sharing a meal with the co-resident or meeting his family will be
the act that tips the balance and put one's means of subsistence into jeop-
ardy is psychologically stressful and would affect the immediate relationships as well as the possibility of entering new relationships in the future'
(*Falkiner et al. v. Director of Income Maintenance Branch* 1998:44).

In light of these multiple harms to women, it is interesting to consider the reasons offered by the government for its adoption of this definition of 'spouse'. In a document released by the Ministry of Community and Social Services (the responsible ministry), a series of questions are posed and answers provided (Ministry of Community and Social Services 1995). With respect to the definition of spouse, there is the question, 'Why are you making this change?' The answer provided: 'Social assistance recipients, (principally sole support parents and single persons) who live with unrelated adults often receive an economic benefit from these relationships. It is important to take into account the economic benefit that occurs in a common law relationship for social assistance purposes because of the need to ensure taxpayers' dollars are used for the most needy.' But this answer is clearly unsatisfactory. Prior to the new definition, benefits were, in accordance with the regulations, reduced in these situations to reflect the fact that a coresident was contributing to household expenses; hence the economic benefit was already being taken into account. Moreover, even if it were not, the logic of the answer provided surely could not be limited to 'common law' relationships (by which they mean whenever a man and woman live in the same dwelling) since in a whole variety of relationships (friends sharing accommodation, for example) there is an economic benefit. Later in the same document there is a question of whether the new rules apply to same-sex couples. The answer: 'The new regulation will apply to opposite sex couples only. This is in keeping with the current understanding of the family unit in the Ontario *Family Law Act*.' While it is true that the FLA defines spouses to include only opposite-sex couples, as noted, the very definition of spouse introduced by these regulations departs fundamentally from the FLA definition. As such, being in step with the FLA definition seems merely a subterfuge for the real purpose of the new definition. That purpose would seem to be to rekindle the ideology of the heterosexual nuclear family based upon a gendered division of labour, a purpose perfectly in keeping with the state's withdrawal and its replacement with private provision through the market and family. Its effect, if not its purpose, is to cut the welfare rolls; more specifically, to cut off women from welfare in order to save money and to force them into, or to return to, relationships—whether abusive or not—with men.

In the *Falkiner* case, the board flatly rejected the government's claim (made in the context of its argument that any infringements of the equality interests of sole-support parents—and it argued that there were none—were demonstrably justified within the meaning of Section 1 of the Charter) that the purpose of the new definition was to treat common-law spouses like married spouses. As I have noted earlier, and as the board points out, such a claim flies in the face of reality. The secondary purpose claimed by the government was to save money, and grounding welfare policy upon an idealized family wherein men provide materially for women and children, a situation that is presumed to exist upon sharing a dwelling, allows it to do so. The board found this to be the primary purpose and went on to find that it was not a 'clear and pressing' interest (part of the Section 1 test) that could outweigh the equality interests of sole-support parents (who are over-whelmingly women). Significantly, the board's analysis does not compart-mentalize economic policy and the interests of women. Rather, unlike the government, it clearly identifies the harms to sole-support parents of the particular reform (a reform driven by economic policy) and makes a normative judgement that prioritizes women's equality interests.

Undeserving Others

Soon after coming to power in 1995, the Ontario Conservative government undertook in earnest the task of eradicating welfare fraud. It introduced a 1–800 'hotline' (snitch line) and encouraged people, under a cloak of anonymity, to report suspected fraud. It created a new 'central fraud prevention team' and promised 'taxpayers' savings in the order of $100 million in the first year (Ministry of Community and Social Services 1995). The OWA permits the director of Ontario Works and each delivery agent (designated by the minister to administer the act and provide assistance in each geographic area) to establish a social assistance fraud control unit to investigate the eligibility of present and past applicants and recipients (Section 57). 'Eligibility review officers' (those who undertake the investiga-tions, e.g., welfare cops) are given many powers, including the right to enter any place other than the home to obtain information pertaining to eligibil-ity and to do so without a warrant (the home may be searched with a warrant), and to require any person therein to cooperate with the investiga-tion by answering questions under threat of penalty (Reg. 134/98, Section 65). Moreover, the OWA allows municipalities to set up a system for the biometric identification (fingerprinting, for example) of welfare recipients (Section 75). These and other measures have been accompanied and supported by a discourse about rampant fraud in the welfare system. But the empirical data—including the government's own—and the anecdotal evidence paint a very different picture. A 1994 Ministry of Community and Social Services report concluded that there was no reason to believe that fraud is more widespread in social assistance than in any other public insti-tution and suggested that the rate was between 1–5 per cent (Little 1998; Rosenberg, J. in *Falkiner et al. v. Her Majesty the Queen* 1996). An investi-gation of 40,000 supposedly high-risk cases in 1993–4 led the government to claim that there was either error or fraud in approximately 20 per cent of these cases. However, only 1,029 of these cases were suspected fraud and reported to the police, representing .15 per cent of the entire caseload (Little 1998; Ontario Social Safety NetWork 1994). Yet this was picked up by the media and the Conservative Party (which was then in Opposition) as proving fraud in 20 per cent of the entire welfare caseload (Little 1998).

While this antifraud campaign has profoundly negative consequences for all welfare recipients, it also works hand-in-hand with the new man-in-the-house regime to create particularly troublesome outcomes for women, especially those abused in their intimate relationships. As noted, if it is concluded that a welfare recipient has been collecting benefits as a single person or single parent (and it will almost inevitably be a woman in this context) while living with her 'spouse', she may be charged and prosecuted for welfare fraud, as well as assessed for an overpayment of benefits that she will be obliged to repay. The stepped-up campaign to eradicate welfare fraud means that the state is actively seeking to locate men in the houses of single women on welfare. Women are watched, interrogated, and required to answer questions about the most intimate details of their lives and subject to home visits. Their landlords, neighbours, their children's teachers, and a multitude of others who may have 'evidence' relating to intimate aspects of their lives are questioned. Their privacy is virtually ignored. They are unable to shield themselves and their children from the harmful negative stereotyping of welfare recipients by keeping their welfare status private. Many women are threatened with fraud charges if they do not admit to living with a spouse (*Falkiner et al. v. Director of Income Maintenance Branch*, Appellants' Submissions 1997:paras. 58, 211). Having 'admitted' to living with a spouse to avoid a fraud charge, a woman is then ineligible for benefits as a sole-support parent. Her alleged 'spouse' may provide some financial support; he may jointly apply with her for welfare benefits, but, as noted earlier, he may have no legal obligation to do either. If he chooses not to do either of these, she may be left destitute and desperate.

For abused women, the combined effects of the campaign against fraud and the new man-in-the-house legislation are even more pernicious. As noted earlier, abusive men seek to establish and maintain their power and control. They are often obsessively jealous and possessive. Imagine the power that the threat of a call, or an actual call, to the welfare snitch line gives him. He threatens to report—anonymously and falsely—that the woman who has left him and is trying to make it on her own is living with a man. Imagine the terror this would cause women. While there is no empirical evidence as to the extent of snitching by abusive former partners, there is sufficient anecdotal evidence to suggest that it is not uncommon (*Falkiner et al. v. Her Majesty the Queen*, Affidavit and Cross-examination of Margaret Hillyard Little 1996; *Falkiner et al. v. Director of Income Maintenance Branch*, Appellants' Submissions 1997:para 95; Thompson 1997). The compounding difficulty is that, not surprisingly, most abusive men do not graciously and silently accept their partners' decision to leave. On the contrary, many step up their efforts to establish their power and control. Calling a snitch line is completely consistent with this behaviour; so too are following, stalking, harassing, and appearing regularly at a woman's home and workplace. In other words, abusive men often refuse to exit women's lives, and the greater the presence he can assert in her life (the more he stalks, harasses, refuses to leave, etc.), the more likely it is that he will be found to be a 'spouse' for welfare purposes. The case of *R. v. Lalonde* amply demonstrates several of these concerns.

Lise Lalonde was charged with and prosecuted for welfare fraud. She was the mother of five children. Peter Van Deyl was the father of four of these children, who were born between 1983–9. Over a ten-year period, Lise Lalonde received family benefits as a single mother with dependent children. She represented to welfare authorities that she was not living with Van Deyl. The trial judge held, based upon the evidence, that Van Deyl and Lalonde lived in the same residence, within the meaning of the legislation (this case preceded the 1995 amendments), for approximately half of the ten-year period. The trial judge describes the relationship as follows;

> Throughout their relationship Peter Van Deyl rarely worked and when he did, he spent most of his earnings on alcohol. He is an alcoholic. Additionally, he was both physically and emotionally abusive towards this accused from the beginning of the relationship to the end. . . . He assaulted this accused on a number of occasions. He constantly referred to her as stupid. When things went wrong in the household she was blamed for them. He was domineering and controlling throughout. . . . He stalked the accused. He had her underclothes checked for semen. He was possessive and jealous. On a number of occasions the accused moved in an attempt to get rid of him. On one occasion he came to visit on the pretext of seeing his children and ended up unlawfully confining Lise Lalonde, dragging her by the hair across a courtyard, assaulting her and telling her that he would kill her. Throughout the relationship Peter Van Deyl told the accused that if she left he would take the children and she would never see them. Lise Lalonde describes her love for her children. She testified for me that they were her whole life and Peter Van Deyl knew it and knew how vulnerable she was.

After her final separation from Van Deyl, Lise Lalonde went to a women's shelter. While there, Van Deyl secured an order from the courts on an *ex parte* basis (without notice to Lalonde) for interim custody of four of the children. Thus he managed, with the assistance of another court, to make good on his threat. The trial judge observed that had Lalonde and Van Deyl applied as a couple, the welfare cheque would have been made out to Van Deyl as the head of the household. 'She was concerned and rightly so that she and the children would be at serious risk that he would drink the money from welfare and they would be without food or shelter or both. It was suggested in cross-examination by the Crown, that she could apply to have the cheque made payable to her. . . . [That] fails to take into account Peter Van Deyl's reaction. I can fairly infer from the evidence that it would be violent.'

The trial judge acquitted Lise Lalonde, finding that she was afraid to act while in the relationship, that she suffered from battered woman syndrome, that her intention had not been to defraud the state but to feed her children, that the state had not been deprived since Lalonde and Van Deyl could have obtained benefits as a couple, and that the ministry had turned a blind eye to a situation that they must have known existed. Again, I do not propose here to go into the merits of the legal analysis employed by the trial judge to arrive at his decision. Rather, I use it to bring more vividly to life the realities of the lives of abused women and the harmful consequences of particular welfare policies. It demonstrates the difficulties many women have in getting abusive partners out of their lives. Women whose abusive partners assert (often violently) their physical presence, despite women's attempts to get rid of them, are caught in a no-win situation. They are desperately trying to end an abusive relationship, to protect and care for themselves and their children; instead their abusive partners are deemed to be spouses and their welfare benefits are terminated. Many women, with nowhere else to turn, resign themselves to the abusive relationship they had struggled so hard to end. And as if this were not bad enough, they may be charged and prosecuted for welfare fraud, criminalized for trying to sustain themselves and their children. But the picture gets even worse; some women will lose their children to child welfare authorities because they 'failed' to protect them from the harms of witnessing wife abuse.

> One of the greatest tragedies of the rate cuts to social assistance is that many more women remain in abusive relationships. Here economic security means food in your child's belly and a fist in yours. Those who do leave are often pursued with a vengeance. Where abusive ex-spouses are aware that the parent now relies on income assistance, they frequently make spiteful allegations of fraud. It is then the fraud investigators [start] hounding their neighbours and friends for information; stalking is contracted out with tax payers' dollars and made 'legal' (Thompson 1997).

The discourse on welfare fraud also dovetails with that surrounding market participation and the family. In each case the idea that those claiming benefits are not genuinely in need and are thus not deserving of benefits is invoked: those making fraudulent claims; those who are able to work but are too lazy and unmotivated to do so; and those who receive or ought to receive financial support from the men with whom they 'dwell'. As described, government rhetoric and policy actively construct welfare recipients as lazy, unmotivated, unskilled, sexually immoral, and deceptive (if not fraudulent). Premier Harris, for example, when asked why the pregnancy benefit (additional funds payable when pregnant) was being terminated, invoked a negative stereotype of mothers on welfare by his response: 'what we're making sure is that those dollars don't go to beer; don't go to something else' (Girard and Orwen 1998). By deepening the negative stereotype of the 'welfare recipient' (presented as a homogeneous category), the 'welfare recipient' is distanced from the 'taxpayer'. This distance is also created by the common government trope when implementing and justifying these reforms that the welfare system is being made accountable to 'taxpayers' and benefits are paid only to the 'truly needy'. This creates the impression that welfare recipients are taking advantage of taxpayers (because they are not genuinely in need, or are otherwise not deserving of benefits) and that welfare recipients are not themselves taxpayers. Welfare recipients and taxpayers are constructed as adversaries. The distancing of the taxpayer from the welfare recipient (including, of course, economically secure women from poor women) is important since the less they have in common, the greater the support for cutbacks. In perpetuating this discourse to support its welfare reforms, the state, rather than working to promote equality, plays a significant role in perpetuating the negative stereotype that is at the core of discrimination against welfare recipients generally and poor women in particular.

This stereotype obscures the actual recipients of welfare benefits and the realities of their lives. It hides the fact that many welfare recipients are single women, frequently mothers, seeking refuge from an abusive relationship. All too often the effect of these welfare reform policies is to deny them that refuge and in doing so to enhance rather than disarm the power of abusive men. In this way, the state is implicated as an active player in sustaining violence against women. Barbara Ehrenreich sums up the situation well:

> But only a fool, or a smug male legislator, could think of crafting welfare policy as if domestic violence doesn't exist. The closer you look at the real narratives of women's lives, the more you realize that there is a war going on, a hidden war of men against women—fought with fists and blunt objects, over such issues as why the baby makes so much noise or dinner wasn't ready on time. In this war the wounded don't get much help; they are often stigmatized and reviled for seeking it.
>
> Enter, stage right, the welfare reformers, full of helpful advice for downtrodden women. Get a job, they say, not noticing that some batterers will do anything to prevent that, including stalking their victims at job sites. Get married, they say, not noticing that the potential bridegroom may be a practicing sadist. . . . The fact is that domestic violence, ugly as we pretend to find it, seems to be becoming part of our national policy. Despite our pious concerns for the battered, the message from the welfare reformers is clear and cold: stand by your man, they're saying, even when he's knocked you to the floor (Ehrenreich 1995:36).

Conclusion

The cumulative harm of these recent welfare reforms is staggering. The freedom of women in receipt of welfare to form heterosexual relationships is significantly curtailed, for if they form such relationships, they put their economic survival and that of their children at risk. They are subject to intrusive investigations. They are denied personal autonomy. They are required to participate in unsupported and, in some instances, dangerous job readiness and employment programs. Many are trapped in abusive relationships. Cutbacks have forced others into greater reliance upon food banks, and some must give up their children to children's aid societies. The idealized family and glorified markets are not meeting the needs of many women; on the contrary, not only are fewer of women's needs met now than prior to the reforms but greater expectations have been placed upon women to meet the needs of others. Social assistance has never been generous, it has never adequately met women's needs, and those who receive it have always been subject to negative stereotyping, but women's circumstances have become decidedly worse; women are being disentitled.

Welfare reform is being pursued at the expense of women's safety and equality. It is not an apolitical imperative but a clear choice with winners and losers. The case-study reveals what Day and Brodsky (1998) have described as the 'disturbing disconnection between the economic and social policy decisions that are affecting women's lives and the commitments that have been made over the last five decades, both domestically and internationally, to the equality of all women'. One might hope that this is simply a case of omission; that the state, through some oversight, failed to consider the implications for women when crafting these reforms. I am inclined to think that the situation is far graver. The state actively defended its new definition of 'spouse' in the *Falkiner* case, arguing that neither equality nor security of the person rights were infringed. More tellingly, it argued that if such rights were infringed, such infringements were justified—*in order to save money*. In other words, the state is prepared to carry out its economic reforms on the backs of women who are already multiply oppressed. This speaks volumes as to the depth of the state's commitment to women's equality and safety.

Notes

1 I have drawn extensively upon the evidentiary record and submissions filed by the applicants in the case of *Falkiner et al. v. Her Majesty the Queen in Right of Ontario*. As such, I am deeply indebted to the many people who worked so hard to make that litigation a success.

2 The idea of 'managing disentitlement' comes from network member Marie Campbell.

3   It is also important to note that because this exemption is contained in the regulations, it can be altered at any time by the government of the day.
4   This can be contrasted against the present situation in the United States. New federal legislation that mandates workfare and limits the total receipt of benefits to a five-year period over one's lifetime permits states to exempt women who have experienced domestic violence. There is currently much activism at the state level by women's advocates to secure these exemptions (Pollack and Davis 1997).
5   An exemption from participation in employment activities may be granted in 'exceptional circumstances, approved by the Director, that apply to the participant' (Reg. 134/98, subsection 27 [2] 5). The Ministry of Community and Social Services has issued a directive to guide the exercise of discretion granted by this subsection, which provides for a three-month deferral (with possible further extensions where approved by the administrator) where 'the applicant or participant has declared himself or herself to be a victim of family violence'. This directive is completely inadequate: it depends upon a voluntary disclosure of abuse (which is unlikely to occur); the three-month period is arbitrary and disconnected from the realities of women's lives; it operates in a vacuum without a general policy on family violence, nor training with respect to family violence; and its status as a directive means that it is virtually unenforceable and can be altered at any time.
6   In the event that the benefit unit includes a dependant(s), benefits will be reduced by the budgetary requirements of the person who failed to comply. While this is, of course, preferable to the complete revocation of benefits, all members of the benefit unit, including children, will nevertheless be harmed by the reduction in total income available.
7   Minor changes to the definition of spouse were also introduced in 1986.
8   The challenge was originally brought before the Ontario Divisional Court. Two of the three judges hearing the case ruled that the Charter challenge was premature; the matter first had to be brought before the Social Assistance Review Board, the tribunal then having statutory jurisdiction with respect to welfare matters. The third judge, Mr Justice Rosenberg, disagreed on this point and after engaging with the substantive issues, found that the new definition of 'spouse' violated Section 15 of the Charter.

References

Allard, M.A., et al. 1997. *In Harm's Way? Domestic Violence, AFDC Receipt, and Welfare Reform in Massachusetts.* Boston: University of Massachusetts.

Bakker, I., and J. Brodie. 1995. *The New Canada Health and Social Transfer (CHST): The Implications for Women.* A report for and funded by Status of Women Canada.

Canada Assistance Plan Act, R.S.C. 1985, c. C-1.

Cooley, T., et al., for the Maine Coalition for Family Crisis Services. 1997. 'Safety and Self-Support: The Challenge of Welfare Reform for Victims of Domestic Abuse'. Bangor: Maine Coalition for Family Crisis Services.

Cohen, M.G. 1997. 'From the Welfare State to Vampire Capitalism'. In *Women and the Canadian Welfare State*, edited by P. Evans et al., 28–67. Toronto: University of Toronto Press.

Crawford, M., R. Gartner. 1992. *Woman Killing: Intimate Femicide in Ontario 1974–1990*. Toronto: Women We Honour Action Committee.

_____, R. Gartner, and M. Dawson. 1997. *Woman Killing: Intimate Femicide in Ontario 1991–1994*. Toronto: Women We Honour Action Committee.

Day, S., and G. Brodsky. 1998. *Women and the Equality Deficit: The Impact of Restructuring Canada's Social Programs*. Ottawa: Status of Women Canada.

Ehrenreich, B. 1995. 'Battered Welfare Syndrome'. TIME 145 (3 April):14–36.

Evans, P. 1998. 'Gender, Poverty and Women's Caring'. In *Women's Caring: Feminist Perspectives on Social Welfare*, edited by S. Neysmith et al., 47–68. Toronto: Oxford University Press.

Falkiner et al. v. Her Majesty the Queen in Right of Ontario as Represented by the Ministry of Community and Social Services, 29 October 1997, Court File No. 810/95 (Ontario Court [General Division] Divisional Court). The judgement and the record in general, but in particular: Affidavit of Robert Fulton, 25 October 1995 and exhibit A, Young Mothers in Metro Toronto; Affidavit of Usha Gici George, 29 January 1996; Affidavit of Margaret Hillyard Little, 28 January 1996; Cross-examination of Margaret Hillyard Little, 16 May 1996; Cross-examination of Kevin Costante, 15 May 1996.

Falkiner et al. v. Director of Income Maintenance Branch, Ministry of Community and Social Services and Attorney-General of Ontario, 1997, Appellants' Submissions on the Charter.

Falkiner et al. v. Director of Income Maintenance Branch, Ministry of Community and Social Services and Attorney-General of Ontario (Board File: P1031–22; P1026–05; P1221–25; Q0828–43), August 1998, unreported decision of the Social Assistance Review Board.

Girard, D., and P. Orwen. 1998. 'Harris Sorry for "Beer" Crack'. *Toronto Star* (17 April):A1, A32.

Leighton, M. 1987. 'Handmaid's Tales: Family Benefits Assistance and the Single-Mother-Led Family'. *University of Toronto Faculty of Law Review* 45:324–54.

Little, M. 1998. *'No Car, No Radio, No Liquor Permit': The Moral Regulation of Single Mothers in Ontario, 1920–1997*. Toronto: Oxford University Press.

Ministry of Community and Social Services, Communications and Marketing Branch. 1995. 'Government Fights Fraud and Tightens Welfare Rules', 23 August.

Moon, D. 1988. 'The Moral Basis of the Welfare State'. In *Democracy and the Welfare State*, edited by A. Gutmann, 27–52. Princeton: Princeton University Press.

Mosher, J. 1991. 'The Harms of Dichotomy: Access to Welfare Benefits as a Case in Point'. *Canadian Journal of Family Law* 9, no. 2:97–156.

———. 1998. 'Caught in Tangled Webs of Care: Women Abused in Intimate Relationships'. In *Women's Caring: Feminist Perspectives on Social Welfare*, edited by S. Neysmith et al., 139–59. Toronto: Oxford University Press.

National Council of Welfare. 1997. *Poverty Profile 1995*. Ottawa: National Council of Welfare.

OAITH (Ontario Association of Interval and Transition Houses). 1996. *Locked In Left Out*. Toronto: OAITH.

———. 1997. 'Some Impacts of the Ontario Works Act on Survivors of Violence Against Women'. A brief to the Standing Committee on Social Development. Toronto: OAITH.

Ontario Social Safety NetWork. 1994. 'Enhanced Verification Report Released'. 'Newsletter of the Ontario Social Safety NetWork', Issue 7.

Pollack, W. 1996. 'Twice Victimized—Domestic Violence and Welfare "Reform"'. *Clearinghouse Review*, Special Issue, 329–41.

———, and M.F. Davis. 1997. 'The Family Violence Option of the Personal Responsibility and Work Opportunity Reconciliation Act of 1996: Interpretation and Implementation'. *Clearinghouse Review* (March-April):1079–98.

Raphael, J. 1995. 'Domestic Violence and Welfare Receipt: The Unexplored Barrier to Employment'. *Georgetown Journal of Fighting Poverty* 3:29.

———, and R.M. Tolman. 1997. *Trapped by Poverty, Trapped by Abuse*. A research compilation from the Project for Research on Welfare, Work, and Domestic Violence, a collaborative project of the Taylor Institute and the University of Michigan Research Development Center on Poverty, Risk and Mental Health.

Regina v. Lalonde (1995), 22 O.R. (3d) 275.

Rodgers, K. 1994. 'Wife Assault: The Findings of National Survey'. *Juristat* 14, no. 9:1–22.

Steering Committee on Social Assistance. 1997. *Brief on Bill 142*.

Social Assistance Reform Act, S.O. 1997 c. 25.

Social Assistance Review Committee. 1988. *Report of the Social Assistance Review Committee*. Toronto: Queen's Printer.

Thompson, J. 1997. 'Ontario Works Legislation—Bill 142 Legislated Poverty for Women'. *LifeSpin* (Fall).

Chapter 3

Restructuring Older Women's Needs: Care Receiving as a Site of Struggle and Resistance

Jane Aronson

Government retreat from the public provision of health and social welfare programs is accomplishing the 'downloading of social care costs onto and into the lives of women' (Neysmith, Chapter 1, this volume). This chapter explores aspects of this downloading process in the lives of elderly women in need of care and assistance. It focuses particularly on how older women's identities and interpretations of their needs are narrowed by changing state practices and their discursive manifestations in long-term care.

The dominant discourse on long-term care and community care emphasizes the cost-effective use and rational organization of the scarce resources to which elderly people are likely to turn when frail, disabled, or ill; elderly people are rendered passive bearers of needs to be efficiently managed and serviced. This managerial and minimalist construction of societal responses to older people's needs has not, of course, gone unchallenged, for example: feminist critiques have highlighted the oppressive consequences of devaluing women's paid and unpaid caring work and, by implication, devaluing the people for whom they care (Graham 1993; Rose and Bruce 1995); critics of federal and provincial governments' efforts to offload responsibility for care and to model public services after private markets underscore their negative effects (Aronson and Neysmith 1997; Shapiro 1997); and senior citizens' organizations protest the reduction and poor quality of public health and social services (e.g., Canadian Pensioners Concerned, Ontario Division 1998; National Advisory Council on Aging 1995). However, these various critiques do not directly explore the reductive images of elderly people embedded in the dominant policy discourse, and they seldom focus centrally on what it might mean to need or receive care or on the work involved in influencing its form and delivery. This absence of attention may be attributable, in part, to the ageist cultural surround. As well, the imperatives of opposing the dominant discourse (e.g., fighting cuts, resisting privatization) consume so much critical energy that attention is diverted from developing or envisioning alternatives to it and debate can remain locked into the discursive terms of the status quo (Graham 1993). Nonetheless, it is ironic that in contemporary debates about elderly people and health and social services, we hear little from elderly people themselves.

This chapter seeks to redress this pattern of inattention by looking at the imagery of elderly women in the dominant discourse on long-term care and by elaborating some alternative interpretations and images of elderly women's positioning. I focus particularly on elderly women: women make up the majority of the elderly who depend on assistance and care and, in later life, women's lifelong experiences of inequality combine with the cultural devaluation of women, age, and bodily frailty to generate the conditions for highly gendered forms of subordination and invisibility (Arber and Ginn 1995). My interest lies in particular in exploring and amplifying interpretations of older women receiving care that are relatively muted but that provide vocabularies and images of older women as active, political participants in meeting their own needs and shaping their own journeys through illness, disability, and care in later life. Given the tendency of current policy debates to stifle anything but narrow interpretations of needs and services and, by implication, limited understandings of older women's positions, articulating these possibilities and making them visible is important and timely.

In her analysis of the politics of needs interpretation, Nancy Fraser reminds us that:

> . . . the identities and needs that the social welfare system fashions for its recipients are *interpreted* identities and needs. Moreover, they are highly political interpretations and, as such, are in principle subject to dispute. Yet these needs and identities are not always recognized as interpretations. Too often, they simply go without saying and are rendered immune from analysis and critique (Fraser 1989:153–4).

Analysing and critiquing the identities and interpretations of need fashioned for elderly women in the talk and organization of contemporary health and social services has considerable urgency as we witness the rapid erosion of publicly provided long-term care in Canada and an acceleration of the shift from institutionally based care to cheaper, home-based services. The limited attention previously given to elderly women's positioning as receivers of care has been concentrated in institutional settings (Diamond 1992; Evers 1981; Gubrium 1993) and, as a result, our understanding of what it might actually mean to need and receive care in the more private and hidden arena of the home is relatively undeveloped (Barry 1995; Twigg 1997); in Fraser's terms, it 'goes without saying'.

To explore possible interpretations and images of elderly women as care recipients in their own homes or in the vaguely defined 'community', I have drawn on literature in the social sciences as well as on fictional and auto-biographical sources. I have built particularly on material from a sequence of qualitative research and data gathering that I have engaged in on elderly women and the social arrangement of their care. Data are drawn from a study of elderly mothers' experiences of relying on the care of daughters (Aronson 1988, 1990), as well as from subsequent studies of older women's articulation of their needs (Aronson 1992, 1993) and of the work of formal home care (Aronson and Neysmith 1996; Neysmith and Aronson 1997). From this wide-ranging material and base of data, three images of elderly women in need of care are discernible: 'being managed', 'managing', and 'making demands'. 'Being managed' is the image associated with restructur-ing and is embedded in contemporary policy and service organizations. Its discursive focus on the management of low cost, standardized services eclipses elderly care recipients and, in so doing, assigns them very passive and powerless identities. In contrast, the second image, 'managing', cap-tures the possibilities of older women sustaining active senses of selfhood and of striving to stay in charge of everyday life and its challenges. The third interpretation, 'making demands', is also an active image, though with a publicly voiced emphasis; it replaces the narrow framing of elderly women who have service needs with that of citizens demanding resources to overcome collectively experienced obstacles in all areas of their lives.

These three discursive constructions are not fixed categories experienced as distinct realities in older women's lives; individual older women are not stat-ically locked into one or the other. Rather, they can be seen as a range of identities and interpretations that are more or less available to them in contemporary culture. How these competing images and interpretations actu-ally unfold and translate into the material details of older women's daily lives and identities is a key focus of exploration in this chapter. Language, inter-pretation, and imagery do not exist as symbolic, discursive phenomena that float free and abstracted from material realities. Rather, they are grounded in and are constitutive of apparently mundane daily practices and social processes and are therefore a critical site of political struggle. For older women, contested images of 'being managed', 'managing', and 'making demands' translate into quite different senses of themselves and quite differ-ent practical possibilities. They also lead to differences in long-term care poli-cies and service providers' practices. For example, the managerial framing of frail elderly women and their needs that dominates long-term care policies leads to meagre allocations of resources and service practices that objectify and isolate recipients while, in contrast, words and images of older women as inventive individual actors or as an entitled, participating collectivity generate more complex and expansive understandings of and practical responses to their needs.

The character of these three discursive constructions of older women receiving care and their contrasting degrees of development in written or spoken, public or private language are elaborated later. Two aspects of these competing constructions are then explored more closely: the contrasting interpretations of need that underpin them, and the implications of those interpretations for elderly women's efforts to resist 'being managed'. With this conceptual mapping of at least some of the discursive possibilities of needing and receiving care, service use for elderly women is illuminated as a site of disarray and conflict between discourses that are variously privileged or suppressed. Research and analysis that focuses on this area of older women's lives is, of course, also located and shaped amid these conflicting images and vocabularies. In closing, the importance of consciously locating ourselves and our work in this contested discursive context is discussed, with particular emphasis on how knowledge building can be fashioned to explore and make space for more progressive and democratizing discourses and thus to enhance elderly women's welfare as active, entitled citizens.

'Being Managed', 'Managing', and 'Making Demands': Conflicting Images of Elderly Women Receiving Care[1]

The form and language of 'being managed', the dominant interpretation of elderly women's needs, is highly developed; it exists in written and spoken form, in public and private contexts, is communicated by and embedded in the policies and practices of powerful political, health, and welfare institutions, and is commonplace in media representations of governments' battles with deficits and calls for belt-tightening. The combined depictions of population aging and unaffordable health and social programs have generated powerful images of demographic and fiscal crisis over the last twenty years. In long-term care, these images justify shifts from relatively expensive institutional care provision to relatively cheap in-home care provision, emphases on market models of service organization and delivery, and, cumulatively, the diminishment of elderly citizens' entitlements to health and social security (Armstrong and Armstrong 1996; Aronson and Neysmith 1997).

Our knowledge of how this 'master narrative' (Somers and Gibson 1994:74) actually unfolds and finds expression in elderly women's lives is, in contrast to its omnipresence in public discourse, quite lacking. In its expression among elderly women in some of my own research, it is typically brief and unelaborated; sentences are short and the words are spoken with little animation. Elderly women's experiences of what I describe as 'being managed' are captured in defeated statements about their positions and tend to be spoken in very passive terms. For example, in a study of older women reflecting on their frailties and concerns, participants made these kinds of observations about their situations in the community: 'I've just given up; they [home care] will do as they will'; 'When you're an old lady, frail, maybe a little bit helpless, you haven't got the gumption to stand up against a person who's coming in to do a service and saying: "That wasn't good enough." You just let it happen' (Aronson 1992). These crushed observations were accompanied by allusions to the inevitability of their situations because of government cuts and resource constraints: 'There are so many of us now. We're a burden on the younger generation'; 'What else can the government do? This is how it is. They can't take more of us on. I do worry about it.'

The defeat and sense of inevitability framing these elderly women's experiences renders them compliant and uncomplaining; their expectations are lowered, their entitlement undermined, and they are literally more easily managed. Their compliance is accomplished discursively by images of the imperatives of economic restructuring and of government retreat and scarcity that dominate the language of public policy and public debate. In the everyday lives of elderly women needing care, these images assume form in service providers' time and resource constraints; for example, in social workers who are always seen as 'busy' (Opie 1995:208) and in home-support workers who are 'stretched' (Walker and Warren 1996:145).

Receiving care in a way construed as 'managing' is, in contrast, an active process: 'I want to manage'; 'I'm determined to manage. I want to stay here'; 'I'm managing, don't want to give up' (Aronson 1988). The literal opposite of managing is collapsing, failing, falling down, giving up, and pooping out (*Merriam-Webster Thesaurus* 1978). Managing sometimes takes the form of tenacious and creative endurance. For example, older women describe how—against the odds of disability, pain, or discomfort—they use their limited energy judiciously to stay in charge of their everyday lives and to accomplish the activities they value or think necessary (Aronson 1992). In her journals, May Sarton (1988, 1996) chronicles both the joys of living to be old and the determination and work required to resist the limits of ill health and weakness. In *At Eighty-Two* (Sarton 1996:224), she describes the energy required to sustain valued social connections and negotiate the details of daily life: 'So it was a good hour that we had together, but then I was really exhausted. I did not know how to get my supper, but I finally did it as I always do. One manages; that is what one does.' In their study of caring between older couples, Rose and Bruce (1995:124) identify a 'rhetoric of coping' that renders 'situations of unbelievable difficulty manageable'. Examples of this rhetoric are ordinary assertions of endurance: 'I can't really grumble, it could be much worse'; 'I just think of it a day at a time, then I'm alright.' To sustain this kind of determined positioning while still identifying themselves as active and engaged, old women must often involve others in their efforts: 'I pay someone to clean and do the heavy things and the yard work. I couldn't manage here on my own otherwise'; 'I couldn't manage without my niece coming in' (Aronson 1992). The other people who inhabit elderly women's lives and whom they may involve in helping them manage can be complex mixes of family members, social contacts, privately paid helpers, and publicly funded helpers. The complexities of negotiating the conditions of such people's involvement are taken up more fully later.

Our knowledge of the texture and effort of 'managing' and of fending off being a 'burden' or 'being managed' is fairly limited and the language of its expression is relatively muted and private (Aronson 1990). The suppression of this discourse and of attention to the work involved in being cared for is increasingly illuminated by critiques of the literature on caregiving (Barry 1995; Graham 1993; Morris 1993). Among others, Rose and Bruce (1995: 115) note how feminist scholarship has focused so centrally on the caregiver and, ironically, has thus reinforced the image of older women as 'being managed': 'there was a high theoretical and political price of attributing agency to this single valorized group [caregivers], leaving elderly people— both women and men—to be conceptualized as passive objects, and erased, along with those outside dominant culture'.

'Making demands' is an interpretation of elderly women's situations generally found outside or at the margins of the social welfare system and the service and professional enterprises associated with it. It is an image voiced by older people's advocacy organizations and is less focused on individual service receipt than on collective entitlements to well-being in old age. For example, in voicing their concerns about cuts and reorganization in health care and social services, Canadian Pensioners Concerned speaks of older people's entitlement to care and support when needed—an entitlement based on citizenship and on the social settlement established earlier in their lives that promised economic and social security in old age (Canadian Pensioners Concerned, Ontario Division 1998). One of their members articulated this in more personal terms in an interview: 'My husband paid taxes all our lives, he joined up and fought in the war, I did my bit, we raised our kids. . . . [N]ow, we expect to be helped when we need it . . . [I]t's our right, surely.' Similarly, the Older Women's Network, a Toronto-based organization, advocates for 'justice and security for older women'. Recognizing this interpretation of elderly women's needs and identities as part of ongoing struggles to refashion the welfare state opens up different spaces in which to resist and reframe the individualizing and regressive interpretations located in service-giving structures.

The disability rights movement offers a valuable example of comparable efforts to resist individualizing and reductive images of disabled people's expectations and identities. Organizations of disabled people that stand in a political arena outside the frame of health and social services have, for example, concerned themselves not just with demanding better or less meagre services but with resisting their circumscribed positioning as primarily or only service users. They set their sights on much broader social change, concerning themselves not only with better services and more influence in their design but also with more fundamental questions of civil rights and equal opportunities (Croft and Beresford 1995; Morris 1991, 1993, 1996; Oliver and Barnes 1993; Priestley 1995). This focus brings to the foreground the connection between individual needs for support and care and systemic barriers to the participation of people with disabilities as a collectivity.

In summary, these three vocabularies and images of older women—being managed, managing, and making demands—are expressed and recorded with unequal degrees of power and clarity and are not, therefore, equally discernible or accessible. 'Being managed' is the dominant, privileged imagery and language embodied in the practices of policy makers and health and social service organizations. In contrast, the possibilities of 'managing' and 'making demands' are relatively muted and unauthoritative and are found outside the public mainstream. Individual older women may draw on and be affected by all three images simultaneously or successively. Their intersecting and fluid presence means that they often know intimately the clashes and incompatibilities among them and the tensions that, as result, translate into their everyday lives and their senses of themselves. Two areas of particular tension are explored further: struggles involved in older women's efforts to resist meagre managerial definitions of their needs; and the tensions and jeopardies they confront in negotiating the care and assistance of others.

Restructuring Older Women's Needs

Underneath the constructions of 'being managed', 'managing', and 'making demands' lie widely divergent interpretations of elderly women's needs. Elderly women 'being managed' are subject to 'expert needs discourses' that position them as individual cases and generate restrictive definitions of need (Fraser 1989:157). Hochschild (1995:338) writes insightfully about the 'care deficit' and the 'thin' definitions of need generated by changes in the organization of work, gender relations, and the state: 'We legitimate the care deficit by reducing the range of ideas about what a child, wife, husband, aging parent or home "really needs" to thrive. Indeed, the words "thrive" and "happy" go out of fashion, replaced by thinner, more restrictive notions of well-being.' This observation resonates with the kinds of managerial and service practices that we currently see in the everyday delivery of health and social services for elderly people; for example, in decisions to cut home-care workers' time allotments to allow for only practical definitions of their work, and in eliminating supports deemed inessential to all but basic physical survival. In the dominant discourse, such practices are communicated as fiscally responsible inevitabilities—not really decisions at all—and are translated into restrictive and exclusionary programmatic and administrative forms and languages, e.g., admission criteria, assessment protocols, and service priorities (Campbell, Chapter 9 in this volume; Clarke and Newman 1997; Dominelli and Hoogvelt 1996). That they actually represent a reinterpretation and thinning of needs is not made explicit.

Hochschild (1995) notes the complexity of the task required of elderly people under these conditions. Insufficient care resources mean that the 'care deficit' is transformed from a social issue into a psychological issue: 'Can I manage my emotional needs to match the minimalist norms of care?' (Hochschild 1995:340). Qualitative studies of elderly women positioned in this way suggest the privately borne struggles that ensue, the costs of stifling needs for help, the preoccupation with feeling burdensome, and the damage done to identity and self-respect (Aronson 1990). Barry (1995) highlights the sheer work that these processes require of elderly people as they must shape their needs to fit the limits of available care provision, whether it is the physical work involved in struggling to get dressed alone or the emotional and moral work of being properly responsive and appreciative of whatever assistance is provided.

Elderly women resisting rather than succumbing to insufficient care and assistance may strategize and negotiate to assert their own definitions of their needs. For example, Eliasson (1990) describes an elderly woman with very limited mobility who relied on a homemaker to do all her shopping. She was eager to ensure that she got the particular products and brands that she had always liked, but recognized that the homemaker's time was limited. In order to sustain the preferences and small pleasures of a lifetime, she prepared precise lists and maps of shelf arrangements in stores to expedite the home-maker's task. In effect, she successfully strove not to submit to a thin defini-tion of need and, in doing so, transformed the apparently standardized function of shopping into a highly particular and personalized activity.

In contrast to such individual and relatively private ways of resisting 'being managed', the imagery of 'making demands' suggests very different approaches to definitions of need and approaches that are, as noted earlier, publicly articulated and politicized. 'Making demands' coincides with Fraser's (1989:157) identification of oppositional needs discourses and the articulation of runaway needs that unsettle and expand the confines of expert discourses. Elderly women positioned here call attention to identities much more complex than 'service user', 'client', or 'case'. They claim public attention to not just needs for health and social care but for better housing, adequate incomes, and the ability to participate in the broader public culture (Kuhn 1986). Thus, the Older Women's Network seeks 'the inclu-sion of older women in planning health care programs and community support programs to ensure a life of dignity and control'. However, this quest is set in the context of much wider aspirations and objectives to, for instance, 'initiate and support public discussion on issues relating to justice and security for older women' and 'to work with others to create a society free from sexism, ageism and racism . . .' (Older Women's Network pamphlet, undated) . Writing from the UK about parallel initiatives taken by the Association of Greater London Older Women, Curtis captures vividly the importance of thinking beyond health issues and confining definitions of functional need to make demands for more expansive attention to and enrichment of later life:

> We feel we have rightly placed an emphasis on health in pursuing our aim to help older women gain confidence. But, though women are survivors, even they cannot 'live by bread alone'. . . it is imperative that we don't just add years to life but also add life to their years (Curtis 1995:179)!

The expansive visions and activities of groups such as these stand outside the definitions and confines of more regulated forms of senior citizens' invited participation in long-term care policy making and delivery (Aronson 1993). As such, their contributions and their mode of organizing represent crucial sites of struggle and innovation and warrant the kind of careful attention and political support that Reitsma-Street and Neysmith (Chapter 7, this volume) call for in their analysis of restructuring and 'community work'.

The Politics of Receiving Care: The Front Lines of Home Care as a Site of Struggle

'Being managed', 'managing', and 'making demands' embody very different representations of elderly women's abilities to influence how their needs are understood and met and of the power dynamics embedded in encounters between themselves and the individuals and organizations that provide care and assistance.

'Being managed' in the context of the dominant discourse on long-term care represents, as we have noted, a very passive positioning for elderly recipients of care. They are treated as bundles of expertly defined needs to be accorded priority in some standard process of resource rationing, a process that is managed by service providers with little or no discretionary power and who are employed in insecure and straitened working conditions (Aronson, forthcoming; Campbell, Chapter 9, this volume; Opie 1995). Paradoxically, political decisions to reduce public health and social services and to manage them in this way are accompanied and justified by a discourse about consumer empowerment, choice, and participation (Croft and Beresford 1995). The contradiction and deceit underlying this juxtaposition of meagre, standardized responses to thin definitions of need with buoyant images of free choice and consumerism have been elaborated upon by critics in many jurisdictions. For example, writing from New Zealand, Grace (1991:341) observes: 'It is ironic that a discourse articulating a concern to promote health in the name of freedom and "wholeness" functions to alienate people from their capacities to engage in protest and effectively operates to subject them further to the political and economic order.'

In its adherence to thin definitions of need and to narrow, practical definitions of caring work, the dominant construction of elderly people 'being managed' accords little value or significance to the relational context of caregiving and receiving. Ultimately, though, the well-being of elderly people living at home hinges on just such 'small scale solidarities of inter-personal relationships which can be stimulated and encouraged by public policies' (Evers 1993:25). Public policies uncommitted to generating and supporting such conditions jeopardize care receivers and their efforts to manage. If they cannot count on such support, they may be forced to submit to their disentitlement and allow themselves to 'be managed'—to have their needs go unmet, to suffer and make do. Alternatively, they may strive to get their needs met in other ways, for instance, by relying on the discretionary help of paid caregivers (as did the older woman described by Eliasson) or of family members.

Another way of actively managing need definition involves resisting any kind of engagement with service providers and the intrusion of their expert interpretations. Here, 'managing' takes the form of active *dis*engagement from others. For example, Mrs Williams, an elderly woman interviewed in a community survey by Parker (1995), refused and dismissed offers of formal services. She was committed to managing on her own terms, described a lifetime of doing so, and rebuffed the overtures of any 'Bloody Do-Gooding Cow' that came her way. Like Mrs Williams, Maudie Fowler, in Doris Lessing's *The Diaries of Jane Somers* (1983), thwarts the good intentions and expert knowledge of professionals and service providers and hangs tenaciously and furiously to a life of her own defining. Of Maudie and the other frail elderly women in her neighbourhood, the younger female protagonist in Lessing's novel observes:

> Maudie won't have a Home Help, she won't. As she talks, I see that for years this or that social worker has been trying to get Maudie to see reason. The stories Maudie tells about them, you'd think they were a race of sluts and thieves. But now I know a bit more, because I see Annie's Home Help. And Eliza Bates is ill, quite suddenly very ill, almost helpless, and Annie's Home Help is now hers too, though one of the things she had been so proud of all these years is that she has never, ever, asked anyone for anything, ever let her place go, ever been a burden (Lessing 1983:189).

In other words, Mrs Williams and Maudie Fowler simply refused to be subjected to the intrusion of expert interpretations of their needs and resisted the advances of professionals. Hurst Rojiani, a social worker, came to recognize that for Miss K, an elderly woman with whom she worked, the very presence of ostensibly helpful outsiders like herself occasioned fear. Miss K feared the power of their judgements about her competence and the risk of living in her own home. Miss K lumped all these 'others' together as 'the Aging People' and observed: 'I sometimes think they want to help me more than I want to be helped' (Hurst Rojiani 1994:148).

The construction of elderly women 'managing' in the face of disability or illness—whether by resisting thin interpretations of their needs or by refusing to engage with those claiming to want to help them—creates some space for protest and resistance. It is important to recognize, however, that elderly women's tenacious efforts to 'manage' and influence the way their needs are understood and met must be accomplished from a position of systemic subordination and insecurity. Disguised and indirect efforts to obtain help are the resort of the insecure and vulnerable (Baker Miller 1976), and for older women the complexity of such efforts is compounded by the particular sense of shame that typically accompanies neediness (Aronson 1990). These contradictory and difficult conditions set the scene for conflictual and problematic encounters between elderly people in need and the paid and unpaid care providers on whom they rely. The structured inequities in these relationships tend not to be understood as political phenomena but as personal or interpersonal problems. For example, we have well-established cultural images of 'the guilt-inducing mother' and 'the selfish daughter'. Elderly women and caregiving daughters voice tensions from both positions: 'I don't like to ask too much of her'; 'If only she'd just ask directly and *say* what she needed—I'd know where I was' (Aronson 1988). In paid care provision, we hear parallel characterizations of the 'manipulative' or 'demanding' client that, in similar fashion, conceal the underlying dynamics of unmet need and powerlessness. These structurally rooted dynamics tend to be understood exclusively as matters of interpersonal tension and private sorrow rather than also as the unfair manifestations of politically determined divisions of resources, entitlement, value, and work. Ungerson articulates sharply the importance of recognizing that care providers and receivers share common interests and of better understanding the intersections of public/paid and private/unpaid sources of care:

> . . . carers and the people they care for have a joint project: to campaign for the development of support services that allow all of us who wish to remain in our own homes to do so. If such support services are of high enough quality and reliable enough, then the private aspects of care—the parts that contain the love and watchfulness—can flourish within a public framework, underwritten by the collectively guaranteed provision of caring services by the state' (Ungerson 1993:15).

In the absence of such high-quality and reliable public services to buttress informal supports and solidarities, it is important to acknowledge that the strategies and survival tactics of 'managing' at the front lines of home care are not equally accessible to all elderly people in need of care. The elderly woman, described earlier, who helped her homemaker accomplish her shopping in the way she wanted, was successful in influencing how she was cared for (Eliasson 1990). Her success hinged on the fact that she was cognitively and socially able to establish a positive relationship with her care provider who simultaneously was willing to extend herself. Research on the work of home-care workers reveals the significance of just such extra and unofficial activities undertaken to personalize their work with elderly clients and thus to expand official, minimalist definitions of need (Aronson and Neysmith 1996). Such solutions require home-care workers to have goodwill, time, and skill and elderly home-care recipients to present themselves as engaging and deserving. In the absence of these conditions, a very different scenario could result. Instead of being perceived as tenacious and creative and therefore deserving, an older woman with similar needs and strategies could easily be deemed manipulative, fussy, difficult, and therefore undeserving.

The politics of care receiving and caregiving are enacted across differences not only of age, health, and ability but also across differences of class, race, and culture. For example, some elderly people's success at 'managing' may be accomplished by purchasing needed care. Elderly people who can afford to pay for care over and above their public entitlements or the care available in their informal networks are thus able to buy additional resources to meet their needs. This solution is only available to a relatively privileged subset of elderly people and, with the deterioration of publicly provided services and the imposition of fees and other barriers to access, questions of equity loom significantly (Korpi 1995). While recognizing differences in social class and economic status among elderly women, it should be noted that the ability to purchase extra resources and supports does not assure them influence and control. The power of elderly 'consumers' of care is compromised by their dependence and frailty and is not experienced as the free, choice-filled process touted by advocates of privatization and market models of public care (Baldock and Ungerson 1993; Grace 1991).

Paid home-care workers, whether working under private or public auspices, are typically poorly paid women drawn from social groups subordinated in terms of race and class. As elderly people strive to manage and assert thick definitions of their needs, some care receivers may use the class and race privilege that they enjoy in relation to this vulnerable labour force. For example, Barry (1995) records one elderly woman's frustration with the meagre home care she received; she expressed her frustration in clearly class-based terms: 'These home carers need supervising. You should see what they do to help people—it's very upsetting for an elderly woman to be told "I can only give you 20 minutes"—they need an older one to keep an eye on them—like domestic servants—they can't be trusted. . . .' (Barry 1995:370). In parallel, homemakers who are women of colour describe how elderly care recipients who are White can express their frustrations and demands in both classist and racist terms (Neysmith and Aronson 1997). In short, what is meted out and experienced at a local level as demeaning or racist treatment can be more completely understood as the manifestation of broader oppressive structures and as the consequence of a meagrely funded, disentitling system of care that pits different populations of vulnerable people (mostly women) against each other at the point of care delivery and receipt.

The intersections of class, race, gender, and age at the front lines of home care can, of course, also generate alliances and bonds of commonality. Shared culture can stimulate good and informed connections between those who provide and those who receive care. In the case of Mrs Williams, a sense of class- and gender-based alliance with her home help produced a delightful disorganization of managerial approaches to service evaluation and illuminates the complex possibilities of the backstage of home care. Mrs Williams described the home help whose work she actually found unwelcome and unsatisfactory, but whose presence kept 'The Social' at bay:

> A lady came from somewhere and asked me was everything all right, was I satisfied with the home help. I said I was. Well, you have to, don't you when it's somebody's job, you can't complain about them because they might lose it and nobody wants to put somebody out of work do they? I mean not except this Tory government we've got, they enjoy doing that, they're wicked; but nobody else would (Parker 1995:120).

From elderly women's vantage points, these complex dynamics, with their potentials for conflict and connection, are all highly significant in their efforts to manage and establish some control over how their needs are defined and how they feel about themselves. However, all efforts to resist 'being managed' face a range of constraints in a culture that systematically marginalizes the elderly. Socially structured ageism and ableism, together with the disdain held for older women in contemporary culture, will pose particular challenges to elderly women's access to discourses of both 'managing' and 'making demands'. There is sometimes an understandable reluctance in senior citizens' organizations to highlight issues of ill health and disability. In their strategic concern to represent the elderly population as a group with diverse interests, abilities, and aspirations, seniors' organizations have sought to rectify the inaccurate equation of old age with frailty and physical dwindling and to counter the construction of the older population as a drain on the health system and a burden to younger generations. For example, in his study of *Canada's Fighting Seniors*, Gifford (1990:2) explicitly distances the newly emerging movement from the 'view of the over 65s as largely sick, dependent people'.

This resistance to homogenized images of the older population is crucially important, but it may feed into the wider cultural denial of the aging process and the reality that bodies do lose their power and social connections do weaken in later life (MacDonald 1983). Consciousness of these realities and the politicization of disability in old age may be further constrained by our lack of cultural images for what 'independence' and 'participation' might mean for elderly women. For non-elderly people with disabilities, there are now some established ideas (if not always material manifestations) about 'access' and 'equality' in the public domain. Simply being sustained at home is challenged as too limited an objective. For example, Morris quotes a younger woman with a disability who protests limiting definitions of the meaning of independence and the confinement that comes with service receipt: 'They seem to think that community care is about someone being cosy and comfortable, being kept clean. To me that's a step back into the situation of residential care—living in the contained environment of your own home. If you don't broaden it out it isn't independent living' (Morris 1993:161).

In contrast, frail or disabled older women tend to be more readily relegated to a very narrow range of activities and aspirations in the private domain, a relegation that is easily accomplished because the majority of the very old and very frail are women. This cultural and political fragmentation of different groups' experiences and interests is mirrored in divisions in the literature; disability and old age have tended to be explored in isolation so that the intersections and commonalities are poorly understood and gender, which is crucial to understanding both, has also been poorly incorporated (Horowitz, forthcoming; Morris 1996; Parker 1993; Reinharz 1986).

Recognizing the challenges of overcoming these divisions, older women's political initiatives can build upon some of the insights and strategies developed among younger women with disabilities. For example, there is a growing literature on women and disability that articulates the power imbalance between those needing care and those providing it, and to the injustices and diminishment that, subtly and out of public view, unfold in the lives of women who are sick or disabled. In describing what it is like to be assessed for care at home, for instance, Ellie O'Sullivan (1994:16) protests the way she is reduced to only her physical impairments: 'I think of the times when the arthritis is bad, when I struggle to cut the bread or open a tin. I want to tell her [the occupational therapist], though, that I make films—that I can do lots of things, lots of things.' In parallel, Mickey Spencer captures the pain of being reduced by thin definitions of needs, by the stripping of practical from emotional care, and by the erasure of her sense of self in 'Caretaker Nightmares':

Colorless Rigid Empty
I am an infant I am a helpless old woman
I am difficult My needs don't count
I can't comb my hair She is rough
   She gives up and cuts it off
   My long hair is too messy
She hurries me My shirt is on backwards
I need privacy for these struggles

She takes my art tools
  They are only sharp-edged dangers to her
  My materials only mess and junk
She cooks her way   not mine
  Makes my bed the way she wants
  Puts my things where she can reach them
  Changes my life-learned details
    to suit herself
No matter how weak I become
  It is still my life
I put these nightmares on the wall
To demand power over my life (Spencer 1996:91)

These eloquent protests and complaints are rooted in a sense of injustice and cumulatively generate the language and symbols of a social movement for the advancement of the rights of people with disabilities. Politically, their articulation may provide possibilities of language and alliance for older women striving to generate organized resistance to their systemic marginalization and to regressive changes in social welfare.

Building Knowledge About Elderly Women Receiving Care: Making Space for Alternative Voices

Just as elderly women are situated and situate themselves in the contested discursive ground described in this chapter, so do we locate our work as researchers and practitioners. The three images of elderly women explored here—being managed, managing, and making demands—each has direct implications for approaches to knowledge building and practice.

Within the imagery of 'being managed', research and service practices cast elderly women in very confined ways—they appear as 'cases' to be counted and fitted into organizational forms or to be processed in efficient and standardized ways. Service providers' work consists of arranging meagre services and responding to circumscribed definitions of need in ways that allow for the routinization and deskilling of their labour (Aronson, forthcoming; Campbell, Chapter 9, this volume; Opie 1995). Research positioned in accord with this imagery articulates its purposes in the language of the market-place (e.g., consumer satisfaction, quality assurance) and measures very particular, reductive service inputs and outcomes as funders require (Campbell and Ng 1988; Opie 1995).

Practices building on images of elderly women 'managing' require more individualized and skilled responses from service providers, responses for which there is less and less room in delivery organizations that are run on market or market-like principles. Carried out within the confines of the 'managerial state' (Clarke and Newman 1997), the work of service providers committed to helping elderly women manage often requires the evasion or expansion of officially defined care providers' roles; for example, home-care workers 'go beyond the call of duty' to better meet elderly people's needs, and social workers sustain relationships with elderly people ('cases') in the community whom they are officially required to 'close' and manage more efficiently (Aronson, forthcoming; Aronson and Neysmith 1996; Opie 1995). In effect, workers find themselves uncomfortably straddling the discourses of 'being managed' and 'managing'. The risks of over extension and exploitation are obvious. Further, enduring constant tension between commitments to organizational rules and to elderly people's interests and between thin and thick definitions of needs takes its toll in tiredness, frustration, and low morale, all of which ultimately jeopardize elderly women who are striving to manage but are unable to do so alone (Lewis et al. 1997; Pahl 1994; Riffe and Kondrat 1997).

Research and theorizing that are built upon images of elderly people 'managing' and 'making demands' can clarify and contextualize these work and practice processes and elaborate the political character of elderly women 'managing'. While interpretive sociological frameworks and clinically oriented research have often generated rich descriptions of older people 'managing', they have tended to understand the activities of 'managing' quite narrowly as, for example, processes of identity and meaning construction or as the manifestations of particular patterns of biography or personality (e.g., Matthews 1979). In his observational study of life in nursing homes, Diamond (1992:52–3) provides a valuable example of a broader understanding. He underscores the importance of conceptualizing 'nursing home patients not just in terms of their sicknesses but also as social and political beings, and to listen to their world, even its babble, for its social and political significance'. With this conceptualization, he argues, elderly recipients of care are accurately cast as key actors in social policy because it is they—not policy makers—who must live them out.

Developing a broader and more contextualized appreciation of the character of 'managing' means that we do not make the mistake of understanding 'making demands' as the only politicized construction of elderly women needing care. Aptheker (1989) cautions against looking for political resistance only in the form of social movements with public languages and symbols:

> To focus on women's resistance as it exists within the parameters of their daily lives is not to celebrate the confinement or to romanticize the enormity of the damage inflicted. It is to acknowledge the meaning women invest in their daily lives, to acknowledge this work on its own merits, to acknowledge that many women are indeed activists who have participated in the shaping of history. . . . Moreover, it allows us to see the continuity, the connection between women's participation in resistance movements as these

are conventionally defined and women's resistance as it has been invented out of the rigours of daily life (Aptheker 1989:175).

A great deal of research has been inattentive to the political significance of the labours and inventions of older women needing assistance and care as the power of the managerial discourse dominates structures of knowledge building and legitimation. Resisting the dominant discourse and articulating alternative interpretations of older women's experiences and possibilities has been the focus of this chapter. Continued exploration of alternatives can allow us to distinguish what Fraser (1981:181) terms 'better from worse interpretations of people's needs': to elaborate and amplify those interpretations that are reached by relatively democratic and fair processes and that challenge patterns of subordination and inequality. Identifying and critically discriminating between contested interpretations of older women's needs in the context of the changing Canadian welfare state makes particular demands on those of us who are researchers. In her discussion of the possibilities of research challenging relations of dominance, Patti Lather offers direction when she speaks of:

> . . . the need for intellectuals with liberatory intentions to take responsibility for transforming our own practices so that our empirical and pedagogical work can be less towards positioning ourselves as masters of truth and justice and more toward creating a space where those directly involved can act and speak on their own behalf (Lather 1991:164).

Note

1   These images are also developed in: J. Aronson, 'Conflicting Images of Older People Receiving Care: Challenges for Reflexive Practice and Research', in S.M. Neysmith, ed., *Critical Issues for Future Social Work Practice with Aging Persons* (New York: Columbia University Press, forthcoming).

References

Aptheker, B. 1989. *Tapestries of Life: Women's Work, Women's Consciousness, and the Meaning of Daily Experience.* Amherst: University of Massachusetts Press.

Arber, S., and J. Ginn, eds. 1995. *Connecting Gender and Aging: A Sociological Approach.* Buckingham: Open University Press.

Armstrong, P., and H. Armstrong. 1996. *Wasting Away: The Undermining of Canadian Health Care.* Toronto: Oxford University Press.

Aronson, J. 1988. 'Women's Experiences in Giving and Receiving Care: Pathways to Social Change'. Ph.D. dissertation, University of Toronto.

_____. 1990. 'Older Woman's Experiences of Needing Care: Choice or Compulsion?' *Canadian Journal on Aging* 9, no. 3:234–47.

_____. 1992. 'Are We Really Listening? Beyond the Official Discourse on Needs of Old People'. *Canadian Social Work Review* 9, no. 1:73–87.

_____. 1993. 'Giving Consumers a Say in Policy Development: Influencing Policy or Just Being Heard?' *Canadian Public Policy* xix, no. 4:367–78.

_____. Forthcoming. 'Conflicting Images of Older People Receiving Care: Challenges for Reflexive Practice and Research'. In *Critical Issues for Future Social Work Practice with Aging Persons*, edited by S.M. Neysmith. New York: Columbia University Press.

_____, and S.M. Neysmith. 1996. '"You're Not Just in There to Do the Work"': Depersonalizing Policies and the Exploitation of Home Care Workers' Labour'. *Gender and Society* 10, no. 1:59–77.

_____, and S.M. Neysmith. 1997. 'The Retreat of the State and Long-Term Care Provision: Implications for Frail Elderly People, Unpaid Family Carers and Paid Home Care Workers'. *Studies in Political Economy* 53:37–66.

Baker Miller, J. 1976. *Toward a New Psychology of Women*. Boston: Beacon Press.

Baldock, J., and C. Ungerson. 1993. 'Consumer Perceptions of an Emerging Mixed Economy of Care'. In *Balancing Pluralism: New Welfare Mixes in Care for the Elderly*, edited by A. Evers and I. Svetlik, 287–314. Aldershot: Avebury.

Barry, J. 1995. 'Care-Need and Care-Receivers: Views from the Margins'. *Women's Studies International Forum* 18, no. 3:361–74.

Campbell, M., and R. Ng. 1988. 'Programme Evaluation and the Standpoint of Women'. *Canadian Review of Social Policy* 22:41–50.

Canadian Pensioners Concerned, Ontario Division. 1998. *Seniors Viewpoint* 24, no. 4:12–13.

Clarke, J., and J. Newman. 1997. *The Managerial State*. London: Sage Publications.

Croft, S., and P. Beresford. 1995. 'Whose Empowerment? Equalizing the Competing Discourses in Community Care'. In *Empowerment in Community Care*, edited by Raymond Jack, 59–76. London: Chapman and Hall.

Curtis, Z. 1995. 'Gaining Confidence and Speaking Out'. In *Empowerment in Community Care*, edited by Raymond Jack, 170-83. London: Chapman and Hall.

Diamond, T. 1992. *Making Gray Gold: Narratives of Nursing Home Care*. Chicago: University of Chicago Press.

Dill, A.E. 1990. 'Transformations of Home: The Formal and Informal Process of Home Care Planning'. In *The Home Care Experience: Ethnography and Policy*, edited by J. Gubrium and A. Sankar, 227–52. Newbury Park: Sage Publications.

Dominelli, L., and A. Hoogvelt. 1996. 'Globalization and the Technocratization of Social Work'. *Critical Social Policy* 47:45–62.

Eliasson, R. 1990. 'Perspectives and Outlooks on Social Science Research'. In *Science We Trust?*, edited by A. Elzinga, J. Nolin, R. Pranger, and S. Sunesson, 256–71. Lund: Lund University Press.

Evers, A. 1993. 'The Welfare Mix Approach: Understanding the Pluralism of Welfare Systems'. In *Balancing Pluralism: New Welfare Mixes in Care for the Elderly*, edited by A. Evers and I. Svetlik, 3–32. Aldershot: Avebury.

Evers, H. 1981. 'Care or Custody? The Experiences of Women Patients in Long-Stay Geriatric Wards'. In *Controlling Women: The Normal and the Deviant*, edited by B. Hutter and G. Williams, 108–30. London: Croom Helm.

Fraser, N. 1989. *Unruly Practices: Power, Discourse and Gender in Contemporary Social Theory*. Minneapolis: University of Minnesota Press.

Gifford, C.G. 1990. *Canada's Fighting Seniors*. Toronto: James Lorimer.

Grace, V.M. 1991. 'The Marketing of Empowerment and the Construction of the Health Consumer: A Critique of Health Promotion'. *International Journal of Health Services* 21, no. 2:329–43.

Graham, H. 1993. 'Social Divisions in Caring'. *Women's Studies International Forum* 16:461–70.

Gubrium, J.F. 1993. *Speaking of Life: Horizons of Meaning for Nursing Home Patients*. Hawthorne: Aldine deGruyter.

Hochschild, A.R. 1995. 'The Culture of Politics: Traditional, Post-Modern, Cold-Modern and Warm-Modern Ideals of Care'. *Social Politics* 2, no. 3:331–46.

Horowitz, A. Forthcoming. 'Aging and Disability in the New Millennium: Challenges for Social Work Research and Practice'. In *Critical Issues for Future Social Work Practice with Aging Persons*, edited by S.M. Neysmith. New York: Columbia University Press.

Hurst Rojiani, R. 1994. 'Disparities in the Social Construction of Long Term Care'. In *Qualitative Studies in Social Work Research*, edited by C. Kohler Riessman, 139–52. Thousand Oaks: Sage Publications.

Korpi, W. 1995. 'The Position of the Elderly in the Welfare State: Comparative Perspectives on Old-Age Care in Sweden'. *Social Service Review* 69, no. 2:242–73.

Kuhn, M. 1986. 'Social and Political Goals for an Ageing Society'. In *Dependency and Interdependency in Old Age*, edited by C. Phillipson, M. Bernard, and P.A. Strang. London: Croom Helm.

Lather, P. 1991. *Getting Smart: Feminist Research and Pedagogy with/in the Postmodern*. New York: Routledge.

Lessing, D. 1983. *The Diaries of Jane Somers*. London: Michael Joseph.

Lewis, J., with P. Berbstock, V. Bovell, and F. Wookey. 1997. 'Implementing Care Management: Issues in Relation to the New Community Care'. *British Journal of Social Work* 27:5–24.

MacDonald, B., with C. Rich. 1983. *Look Me in the Eye: Old Women, Aging and Ageism.* San Francisco: Spinsters/Aunt Lute.

Matthews, S.H. 1979. *The Social World of Old Women.* Beverly Hills: Sage Publications.

Merriam Webster Thesaurus. 1978. New York: Pocket Books.

Morris, J. 1991. *Pride Against Prejudice: Transforming Attitudes to Disability.* Philadelphia: New Society Publishers.

_____. 1993. *Independent Lives: Community Care and Disabled People.* London: MacMillan.

_____. 1996. *Encounters with Strangers: Feminism and Disability.* London: Women's Press.

National Advisory Council on Aging. 1995. *The NACA Position on Community Services in Health Care for Seniors: Progress and Challenges.* Ottawa: Ministry of Supply and Services.

Neysmith, S.M., and J. Aronson. 1997. 'Working Conditions in Home Care: Negotiating Race and Class Boundaries in Gendered Work'. *International Journal of Health Services* 27, no. 3:479–99.

Older Women's Network. No date. Information pamphlet.

Oliver, M., and C. Barnes. 1993. 'Discrimination, Disability and Welfare: From Needs to Rights'. In *Disabling Barriers—Enabling Environments*, edited by J. Swain, V. Finkelstein, S. French, and M. Oliver, 267–77. London: Sage Publications.

Opie, A. 1995. *Beyond Good Intentions: Support Work with Older People.* Wellington: Institute of Policy Studies, Victoria University of Wellington.

O'Sullivan, E. 1994. 'The Visit'. In *Mustn't Grumble: Writing by Disabled Women*, edited by Lois Keith, 13–17. London: Women's Press.

Pahl, J. 1994. '"Like the Job—But Hate the Organization": Social Workers and Managers in Social Services'. In *Social Policy Review 6*, edited by R. Page and J. Baldock, 190-210. Canterbury: Social Policy Association.

Parker, G. 1993. 'A Four-Way Stretch? The Politics of Disability and Caring'. In *Disabling Barriers—Enabling Environments*, edited by J. Swain, V. Finkelstein, S. French, and M. Oliver, 249–55. London: Sage Publications.

Parker, T. 1995. 'Some Bloody Do-Gooding Cow'. In *Health and Disease*, 2nd edn, edited by B. Davey, A. Gray, and C. Seale, 119–23. Buckingham: Open University Press.

Priestley, M. 1995. 'Dropping "E"s: The Missing Link in Quality Assurance for Disabled People'. *Critical Social Policy* 44–5:7–21.

Reinharz, S. 1986. 'Friends or Foes? Gerontological and Feminist Theory'. *Women's Studies International Forum* 9, no. 5:503–14.

Riffe, H.A., and M.E. Kondrat. 1997. 'Social Worker Alienation and Disempowerment in a Managed Care Setting'. *Journal of Progressive Human Services* 8, no. 1:41–55.

Rose, H., and E. Bruce. 1995. 'Mutual Care But Differential Esteem: Caring Between Older Couples'. In *Connecting Gender and Aging: A Sociological Approach*, edited by S. Arber and J. Ginn, 114–28. Buckingham: Open University Press.

Sarton, M. 1988. *After the Stroke*. New York: Norton.

_____. 1996. *At Eighty-two*. London: Women's Press.

Shapiro, E. 1997. *The Cost of Privatization: A Case Study of Home Care in Manitoba*. Winnipeg: Canadian Centre for Policy Alternatives.

Somers, M.R., and G.D. Gibson. 1994. 'Reclaiming the Epistomological "Other": Narrative and the Social Constitution of Identity'. In *Social Theory and the Politics of Identity*, edited by C. Calhoun, 37–99. Oxford: Blackwell.

Spencer, M. 1996. 'Caretaker Nightmares'. In *Pushing the Limits: Disabled Dykes Produce Culture*, edited by S. Tremain, 91. Toronto: Women's Press.

Thorslund, M., A. Bergmark, and M.G. Parker. 1997. 'Difficult Decisions on Care and Services for Elderly People: The Dilemma of Setting Priorities in the Welfare State'. *Scandinavian Journal of Social Welfare* 7:197–206.

Twigg, J. 1997. 'Deconstructing the "Social Bath": Help with Bathing at Home for Older and Disabled People'. *Journal of Social Policy* 26, no. 2:211–32.

Ungerson, C. 1993. 'Caring and Citizenship: A Complex Relationship'. In *Community Care: A Reader*, edited by J. Bornat, C. Pereira, D. Pilgrim, and F. Williams, 143–51. London: MacMillan.

Walker, A., and L. Warren. 1996. *Changing Services for Older People*. Buckingham: Open University Press.

Chapter 4

Single Mothers and the Press: Rising Tides, Moral Panic, and Restructuring Discourses

Patricia M. Evans and Karen J. Swift[1]

Feminists have revealed the profoundly political character of 'the family' and 'motherhood'. They have pointed to how these socially constructed institutions reflect and shape gender expectations, the relationships between adults and children, and the nature and degree of state involvement. The particular norms of 'good mothering' have varied over time and location and, as Carol Smart (1996) points out, an ideal of motherhood requires the identification of those who fall below the standard. Single mothers, who are frequently viewed as the obverse of the 'good mother', have been subject to particular moral scrutiny and social regulation (see Little 1998; Ursel 1992), processes that are central to the identification and 'manufacture' of bad mothers (Swift 1995).

In the last two decades, family structures and forms have diversified, although these changes have not necessarily diminished the idealization of the nuclear and heterosexual family. In what she calls a 'classic case' of blaming the messenger, Meg Luxton (1997:11) suggests that the New Right has countered the feminist critique of families by claiming that feminists are destroying the family. The emphasis on 'family values', coupled with the free fall of social rights in the 'new' economy, help to increasingly target single mothers as the subjects of 'demonizing' discourses and media reports that amount to 'moral panic' (McIntosh 1996; Silva 1996). These discourses identify single mothers as inadequate and problematic, but also (in a spectacular reversal of power relations) depict them as sufficiently powerful to redefine the social landscape (Silva 1996). Single mothers on social assistance have also been the focus of cutbacks in relation to the levels and conditions of benefits, and they are increasingly viewed as 'workers' rather than 'mothers' (Abramowitz 1996; Duncan and Edwards 1997; Evans 1995). Discourses that configure single mothers as irresponsible adults and ineffective parents also construct them as undeserving of public sympathy and help to legitimize and entrench shrinking public provision and retrenching the welfare state.

Since the early 1990s, the media in Britain and the United States have portrayed single mothers in increasingly problematic ways (Roseneil and Mann 1996). Has the Canadian portrayal of single mothers altered over time and in ways that support a restructuring discourse? Through newspaper articles selected from the early 1980s and the mid-1990s we examine how single mothers are constituted in the press. The general questions we address include: Who is the single mother and what makes her 'newsworthy'? What attention is there to the work she does caring for children? Is she demonized and, if so, in what way? Is there evidence of counterhegemonic images of what is, after all, a growing proportion of the population? Through our analysis of the two time periods and attention to newspaper processes, we explore the changing construction of the single mother 'problem', the range of corresponding 'solutions' that are offered, and the images of single mothers that are created.

Fraser (1997) suggests that attention to discourse can further our understanding of: (1) how social identities are shaped and changed over time; (2) how social groups are formed and unformed under conditions of inequality; (3) how the dominant hegemony is contested and solidified; and (4) the possibilities for emancipatory change and practice. Newspapers are not necessarily the most influential form of media, but they do help to filter and frame our construction of our social world (van Dijk 1988). In so doing, they reflect hegemony—the dominant discourse that shapes and reminds us of the views that we are *supposed* to hold.

A Framework for Analysis

News-making and Hegemony

Gramsci's (1971) ideas of hegemony help us to understand how relations of dominance are achieved and maintained. He proposed that hegemony and the continual reproduction of the relations of power are achieved not only by coercion and the use of explicit power but also through ordinary institutional processes. Educational and legal systems, for example, operate in ways that benefit those who rule by reinforcing the existing sets of social divisions, including gender. However, hegemony is not absolute nor predetermined; rather, it is a dynamic process that is continually negotiated and contested (Fraser 1997). In the present era, the media have taken on a particularly prominent hegemonic voice, partly because of their extension and accessibility to virtually all populations. In a country of relatively high literacy such as Canada, print media are important in shaping people's understandings of how things are and what is really going on. For this reason, news in print form has become an increasingly important source of data for social analysis. Recent examples exploring the relationship between dominant discourse and press coverage include Knight's (1998) analysis of strike-breaking legislative reforms in Quebec and Ontario,

Meyers's (1994) examination of the attempt to repeal the ban on gays and lesbians in the US military, and Callahan and Callahan's (1997) explication of the construction of child welfare disasters as reported in news.

While we may think of news as self-evident, scholars who study news and the media have proposed different ideas about what makes news and why. Chibnall (1977) describes eight 'imperatives' that control or frame journalism: immediacy, dramatization, personalization, simplification, titillation, conventionalism, structured access, and novelty. Van Dijk (1988) concludes that deviance, which satisfies most of these imperatives, receives considerable attention in news. Along similar lines, Knight (1998) argues that 'disruption of the social order' is the main criterion of newsworthiness. His analysis shows how the dominant ideology of society is continually represented, legitimized, and reproduced through the media.

Taras (1990) views Canadian news processes in historically based but overlapping phases. First, he identifies the partisan phase, which lasted roughly from Confederation to the First World War and coincided with the development of political parties. During this time, newspapers were 'seized upon' as crucial vehicles of political propaganda and publishers and politicians often decided together what stories to print and how to shape the story line. This was followed by an 'objective' phase when publishers sought to reflect a range of views and opinions rather than just the views of a specific party. In the third and current 'critical' phase, journalists are expected to analyse as well as report the news. Taras argues that the news media have actually become socially damaging in this role by challenging the ultimate authority of the state. Chomsky, one of the best-known news analysts, argues that the media critique simply reflects debates among dominant élites and does not challenge the ultimate authority of the state. Media, according to Chomsky (1989:11), 'serve the interests of state and corporate power, which are closely inter-linked . . . limiting debate and discussion accordingly'.

Martin (1997) points out that these state and corporate 'interests' are overwhelmingly male. The news, Molotch (1978, quoted in Martin 1997: 239) claimed some years ago, is 'essentially men talking to men'. Martin argues that news serves the 'news needs of men' and ignores or 'relegates to the women's section' reportage of events concerning women. The popular notion of 'hard' and 'soft' news (Tuchman 1978) reflects this gendered division of news. Hard news is usually conceived as 'factual presentations' of daily occurrences deemed newsworthy—political events, wars, and other stories featuring men as key players. Soft news, on the other hand, involves 'human interest' stories, often of struggles or foibles, that are intended to demonstrate the texture of everyday experience. Soft news items need not be 'timely'; they have less immediacy and do not usually have to be run on any particular day. Women are often featured in soft news stories. Also important to notice is what is not considered to be news at all, i.e., what is left out of news coverage altogether (Lowes et al. 1996; van Dijk 1988).

It is not just the content but how news stories are constructed that affects interpretation. Goffman's (1974) idea of the 'frame' is helpful in understanding the construction of social meanings embedded in news stories. Goffman suggested that particular frames are employed to select and organize 'strips' arbitrarily cut from an ongoing stream of activity. For Tuchman (1978), frames enable the news industry to transform occurrences into defined events for news purposes. Strips are also selected to some extent in relation to assumed reader interest. In addition, the presentation of the strip and the attention given to a fact affect the way it is received: placement, tone, number of repetitions, sequence of related facts, and the frame of analysis, often implicit, all instruct readers about its importance.

Analysis of the construction of a text can reveal ideological purposes and meanings. Van Dijk's (1988) analysis of deviance in the news, for instance, shows that dominant definitions of deviance are reproduced and legitimized, while the actual experiences of individuals disappear, along with alternate explanations and theories for human behaviour. Readers, as Smith (1983) makes clear, bring social understandings to their reading of texts, filling in gaps and providing schemes for understanding not only what is explicit in the text but what is implied. Pictures, headlines, and contrasting news items can help to invoke ideological messages and impart particular instructions about how stories are to be understood.

The processes that are used to gather and produce the news also help to reinforce dominant discourse. As newsroom budgets shrink, stories from news wire services become a more viable option for newspapers than expensive investigative reporting. Reporters also have set 'beats' and 'rounds', including news services, which regularly produce news, and they work to establish 'recognized news sources' who are usually occupants of political and bureaucratic offices in socially sanctioned institutions. Relying on major sources makes it easier for reporters to do their jobs by providing facilities for them to gather, furnishing them with advance copies of reports, and giving press conferences. These processes taken together, in effect, subsidize the news industry and also result in homogenization of the news (Herman and Chomsky 1988; Taras 1990). Such regular sources, with their enormous power to shape public thinking, tend to reflect hierarchies in the 'real world'. These various processes mean that socially recognized 'experts' are very often the primary sources of news stories. Most analyses of this 'tiered' structure place business and political leaders as primary sources and union leaders and interest group spokespersons as secondary or reactive sources (Knight 1998). As Martin (1997) points out, there is also a large pool of 'omitted' sources, which includes most women. When women do become secondary sources, she contends, their role is to provide negative emotional reaction, or the 'fear and loathing' angle (Voumvakis 1984, quoted in Martin 1997:244).

Although various theorists may disagree about the media's role in sustaining relations of power, there is growing consensus that media and the creation of news cannot be understood without examining the power sources and relations that finance and drive the news industry. Corporate power is particularly apparent in Canada where newspaper ownership is much more concentrated than in the United States. Three major companies (Black/Southam, Thomson Corp., and the Toronto Sun) account for two-thirds of newspaper readership, almost half of which is controlled by Conrad Black (Lowes et al. 1996). In an era of globalization and the rapid spread of technology, however, newspapers are increasingly challenged to maintain their traditionally high profit levels in the face of the competition provided by twenty-four-hour immediate television coverage. The new 'corporate journalism' invests in marketing and packaging rather than improving information. As a result, the jobs in the newsroom are cut and stories are shorter, less well researched, and increasingly designed to grab the reader's attention (Miller 1998). Chomsky (1989:10) argues that in 700 words, it is impossible to present either unfamiliar or surprising ideas in any credible way, while 'regurgitation of welcome pieties' faces no such problem. Print media have also become heavily reliant on advertisers since they can no longer sell enough papers to support themselves; advertising represents 75 per cent of the revenue of daily Canadian newspapers (Lowes et al. 1996).

Some analysts contend that these developments in the news industry have accentuated the 'male' criteria of news presentation (Martin 1997). Thus, real or 'hard' news increasingly involves the male world of political and military action, while the female world, traditionally unfamiliar as news, becomes even less accessible and interesting. Presentation of a narrow set of victims, Herman and Chomsky (1988:xv) argue, 'raises public self-esteem and patriotism, as it demonstrates the essential humanity of country and people'. Women, of course, are prominent among this set of victims, at least in certain contexts. Far from bringing women forward as primary news, the development of a 'women's section' in fact reinforces the idea that women's reality is not the 'real life' depicted in the hard stories that appear on page one (Martin 1997).

(Re)Searching the News

Our analysis of newspaper articles on single mothers examines their particular meanings and ideological messages. It covers two time periods, 1982–4 and 1994–6, and spans a period that encompasses significant social, economic, and political changes. For example, although the proportion of the unemployed was similarly high in both periods (11 per cent in 1982 and 10 per cent during 1994–6), double-digit unemployment occurred in 1982 for the first time in more than forty years. By the mid-1990s, however, the unemployment statistics, while high, were falling rather than increasing.

Single mothers in the 1990s appeared particularly vulnerable to the ups and downs in the economy, and did not share in the gains that have been characteristic of married women's employment.[2] But perhaps the most important difference between these two periods is the emergence and apparent entrenchment in the 1990s of a 'restructuring discourse' that 'seeks to radically shrink the realm of political negotiation by increasing the autonomy of market forces and of the family' (Brodie 1995:49). Indeed, by the mid-1990s, the neoliberal perspective on the deficit was the dominant discourse, welfare state retrenchment was well underway, and 'family values' rhetoric on the increase (Cohen 1997; Luxton 1997).

We used the Canadian News Index (CNI), which indexes articles from eight major Canadian newspapers to construct two systematic samples, using every third article in which the term 'single parents' or 'single-parent families' occurred.[3] This method produced a final sample of fifteen articles for the earlier period and twenty articles for the 1994–6 period, after excluding articles that focused on single fathers rather than single mothers.[4] In our analysis of the articles, we paid particular attention to placement, type of article (hard/soft), length, the verifying sources, and the use of language.

What Makes News? Shifts in the Single Mother 'Problem'

Our examination of the press portrayal of single mothers attempts to unravel one thread in the weaving of a public discourse that supports and justifies the shrinking of the Canadian welfare state. In this section we identify the themes that characterize the differences we found in the press coverage of single mothers in two periods, the early 1980s and mid-1990s. These include a diminished public presence in the reporting on single mothers, an increased reliance on an 'expert discourse', a growth in the use of statistical data, and a shift in the depiction of single mothers from 'helpless' to 'bad'.

A Diminished Public Presence

News, as we suggested earlier, is often categorized into the 'soft' news stories that can appear at any time and include feature articles with 'human interest' appeal, general background articles and columns, and the 'hard' news stories that provide information, background, and reaction to what are deemed to be 'newsworthy' occurrences or events. Using this simple classification, it appears that single mothers and their concerns were considered to be more newsworthy in the earlier period. The majority (eight out of fifteen) of articles from the early 1980s were classified as hard news and *all* eight of these articles were prompted by changes or problems that resulted directly from some form of state action involving one of the three levels of government. The range of policy issues that were thought to be sufficiently interesting to create news included government cutbacks to university grants to single mothers, tax changes, welfare investigations, and child-support issues. The headlines chosen to accompany the articles suggested a degree of concern: single mothers were 'targets' of a 'crackdown'; welfare workers may be 'barging' into bedrooms. While the majority of sources were male and official, two of the eight articles were prompted by press releases from antipoverty groups that featured women spokespersons who were critical of the methods used in 'man in the house' investigations and the inadequacy of child-support collection.

The articles from the later period make a striking contrast. First, there were considerably fewer articles (five out of twenty) that could be regarded as 'hard' news. Secondly, rather than reflecting a range of issues, as was the case in the earlier period, *all* of the articles from the 1990s related to one issue, which was child support. Three articles were prompted by the court challenge of Suzanne Thibaudeau, a single mother, to the right of fathers to claim the tax deduction for child support; the other two articles focused on problems of collection and arrears. It is not surprising that the Thibaudeau case received significant coverage; it became a *cause célèbre* and wound its way up to the Supreme Court. However, it is surprising, and we think it is significant that child support, a highly privatized and individualized source of income support, was the *only* policy issue that captured attention as 'news' in our mid-1990s collection.

Articles from the earlier sample were also more likely to connect economic conditions and lack of structural supports with the problems that single mothers face. They comment, for example, on the 'slumping economy' in Vancouver, the 'housing crisis' in Halifax, cuts to education grants in Alberta, the need to improve workplace flexibility, and the take-home pay of single mothers. A 1996 article contrasting incomes in one- and two-parent families does refer to 'slow job growth and paltry wage gains', but it also includes the subtitle, 'Togetherness pays', leaving the reader in no doubt about the lesson to be drawn. An article from 1994 headlines the lack of government responsibility and quotes a spokesperson from the Vanier Institute of the Family: 'What you now hear in Canada is something you would not have heard 40 years ago which is, "You had the children; they're your problem."' This view is certainly supported by our analysis, which suggests that by the mid-1990s, the government is seen to have very little role in either ameliorating or exacerbating the conditions in which single mothers and their children live. The state, quite simply, is less apparent in the news coverage on single mothers and is less implicated in how well or how poorly they are doing. This is a stance that is highly consistent with a restructuring discourse and a retreat from public responsibility.

Constructing the 'Expert' Discourse

In our analysis, we quickly uncovered the presence of a group of articles that did not fall easily into either the hard or soft news categories. These are articles triggered by the release of a report or the delivery of a conference paper reported in a hard news and fact-oriented manner. The presentation of the articles tends to mask the considerable discretion that is used in choosing which conference paper or report to cover, as well as how to cover it. We have found this middle category to be extremely helpful in our analysis and it emerged as an important difference in the coverage of the news in our two periods.

The later articles were notable for the prevalence of 'expert discourse' in media stories about single mothers. Fully half of the stories from 1994–6 sprang from the release of studies or reports about single mothers and/or from interviews with an expert concerning data about single mothers. In contrast, only one-quarter of the articles from the earlier period reflected an 'expert' discourse, discourses that tell us that single mothers are 'stigmatized', 'schools must adjust', and that single mothers need 'help to reshape their lives'. The general direction of the 'news' in the 1990s is captured in words appearing in story headlines: The number of single mothers is 'soaring', and this is seen as a 'troubling increase'. Single mothers 'rarely enjoy' success, they are 'out of luck', they are in a 'plight', they are 'adrift', and their job prospects are 'bleak'. Their children suffer 'stress', have high 'problem rates', 'face troubles', and are 'at great risk'. Even the appeal court's decision ordering the non-custodial parent to pay tax on child-support payments is a 'shallow win' for single mothers. In short, single mothers and their children are a problem population, one that readers certainly would not wish to join. Two of twenty story headlines slightly mitigate this picture, one 'vindicating' single mothers, the other 'praising' them.

These powerfully negative images of single mothers and their children are portrayed through the expert opinions of people. In a significant number of stories, expertise is invoked early in the story through the use of generic terms, such as 'the agency', the 'Foundation', 'some lawyers', or 'the government'. Also used to invoke the facticity of the story are frequent references to unidentified 'data', 'statistics', or 'research', as well as general references to unspecified social researchers and experts, who are assumed to know about or can explain certain phenomena. For example, one article suggests: 'Social researchers have long known that growing up in poverty puts children at increased risk for problems such as hyperactivity, emotional distress or failing a grade at school.' This authoritative statement tells readers outright that they need not doubt the veracity of the facts to follow. The story establishes that single-parent families, on average, were far poorer than two parent families. This element of the story completes what Smith (1983) refers to as a 'schema'. That is, the reader accepts single mothers as poor and poverty as the cause of problems; it follows, then, that single mothers are the cause of their children's problems.

Another story reporting on the same study includes interviews with various people commenting on findings. These individuals are introduced not as experts or even as researchers but as 'social observers', a term offering less assurance of expertise: 'Social observers finger a variety of reasons for the problems some children in single-mother families are having.' This introductory statement is followed by 'strips' from interviews with several individuals who provide explanations of problems experienced by the children of single mothers, including 'family insecurity related to the workplace'. The use of the word 'finger' helps to detract from the importance of the statements these interviewees make, since this verb is unusual and most often used in relation to the criminal world. These methods of structuring and word choice, as van Dijk (1988) points out, can subtly add weight to or delegitimize the information provided in the text. In this case, explanations of children's problems related to structural features of the economy, while mentioned, carry little weight in the story. Individual 'experts' in our news stories are given titles or labels that embody ideas of expertise, such as analysts, officials, professors, lawyers, doctors, researchers, psychologists, and directors of various projects or departments. Also, the institutional attachments of most experts are explicitly mentioned, adding the weight of legitimized social organization to their credibility. One expert in fact informs us that the single-parent family is unnatural: '"It's the order of nature to have two parents", says Dr. Aminufu Harvey, associate professor at the University of Maryland.'

Because full names are generally provided in news stories, it is possible to determine that the overwhelming majority of experts in our sample are male. In fact, in only one item were as many as two female expert sources used. Perhaps not coincidentally, this was a story reporting the findings of a study 'vindicating' single mothers as the cause of children's problems, pointing instead to poverty as 'the culprit when it comes to health and welfare of children'.

It would be misleading to suggest that the reason so many news items cover research on single mothers is because a vast number of such studies have recently been done. Rather, our sample suggests that several stories were picked up through news services, provided with a slight local variation, trimmed to suit available space, and published as hard news. At times this apparently hard news story appeared days or weeks after the actual release of the study in question, a fact masked by simply failing to refer to the release date. The first three items in the 1990s sample related to the same study that found high 'problem rates' among children of single mothers; these articles appeared, for instance, in slightly different versions in the *Winnipeg Free Press,* the *Globe and Mail,* and the *Montreal Gazette.* Another report, focusing on 'bleak job prospects' for single mothers, is featured in two stories from the sample in June 1994, and information from this report is picked up in a much later item published in September 1996.

This pattern demonstrates how selected strips of information enter discourse through repetition, while other strips are deselected and sidelined.

An example of the latter is the story citing research that vindicated single mothers, blaming poverty instead for children's problems. An 'expert' quoted in the story said the study was so significant that had it been conducted in the United States, it 'would have been splashed all over Time and Newsweek'. However, not a single fact or quote from this study was repeated elsewhere in our sample, substantiating Chibnall's (1977) idea that conventionality is one of the characteristics of readable news. Use of the word 'vindicate' in the headline of this article is apparently an effort to create readability through drama. However, based on the number of stories in our sample representing single mothers as problems, it would appear that conventionality is considered the more readable characteristic of news about this group.

Statistics and Their Power over Women

In total, fifteen of the twenty articles from the 1990s employed statistics on single mothers to bolster the main story line; this was the case for only two articles from the 1980s. In fact, perhaps the most striking feature of stories from the later era is the substantial use of statistics to describe and explain the situation of single mothers. The importance of the numbers is underlined by language used in the stories themselves. Phrases such as 'massive survey', 'mountains of data', and 'most comprehensive' study instruct readers quite explicitly to regard information about the risks of single motherhood as true.

Comparisons between single mothers and married mothers are a frequently used technique to underline the seriousness of 'the problem' of the single mother. For example, the article we mentioned earlier entitled 'Togetherness pays' compares the income levels of two-parent and single-parent families in 1980 and 1994, finding that the earnings from work and savings of single-parent families fell a 'staggering' 40 per cent in that time, while two-parent families 'have done better'. Charts, graphs, and tables are also used to highlight particular information featured in the story. Another story compares two groups of single mothers, the 'never married' and the separated or divorced, with married mothers' success in finding paid jobs. This study finds the problems for the never-married group 'critical'. The expert quoted for this story tells us this group may have 'fallen so far behind that perhaps they won't be able to catch up'. In contrast, married mothers, according to a prominently featured chart, are employed in far greater numbers than either group of single mothers. The juxtaposition of graph lines in this chart reproduces a powerful visual image of hierarchy for the reader: married women on top, separated and divorced women along the midline, and the line representing the never-married mothers sagging lower along the bottom as time goes on.

What kinds of 'facts' about single mothers are considered worth studying and reporting? A survey of the twenty items in our second set reveals the

following main categories: single parents as a percentage of Canadian families; income, education, and employment levels of single mothers; numbers
of births to unmarried mothers; numbers of young mothers keeping and
raising babies; types and extent of problems experienced by children of
single mothers; and information about welfare and child-welfare service to
single mothers. Statistics in the first three categories were by far the most
dominant and included a bewildering number and kinds of comparisons
made and trends cited.

The overwhelming effect of data provided about 'these people', as single
mothers are sometimes referred to in articles, is that they and their children
are leading exceedingly difficult and problematic lives, and that the future is
likely to be worse. A second effect is that this undoubtedly diverse population of women comes to be seen as homogeneous—poor, young, uneducated, unemployed, and on welfare. This is a group who are social burdens,
in receipt of 'ever higher payments from government', whose ranks no one
would willingly join. It is also important to note that the sources producing
information, statistics, and studies are limited to a relatively few. Data from
Statistics Canada, for instance, figured prominently in eight of the seventeen
stories relying on research. The reliance on data from this source points to
the importance of women being aware of research done with them and
about them. It also illustrates our earlier discussion of the importance of the
'beat' or 'regular news source' as central to understanding what is likely to
become news.

From 'Hapless' to 'Bad'

The previous discussion has identified ways in which the discourse about
single mothers has altered. Issues related to single mothers are less likely to
make the time-sensitive, event-driven news, and the news about them is
increasingly constructed through a reliance on experts and the use of statistics. These processes are important components in a critical change in the
overall image of single mothers portrayed in our two time periods.

In the early 1980s single mothers are typically portrayed as hapless,
meaning unfortunate, or, as one dictionary suggests, 'ill-starred'. Teenage
single mothers become pregnant because of an immature and mistaken
search for love and fulfilment. Two very different types of articles deliver
this message. The first article reports the 'preliminary results' of a study
that finds the following differences between the young mothers who keep
their babies and those who place them for adoption: 'The young women
who keep their babies seem to depend on the infants to fill a void in their
lives. . . . They say, "This baby will love me."' In contrast, those who gave
their babies up were 'thinking ahead about themselves and about what their
children really need'. The second article features an eighteen-year-old Manitoba mother who is caring for her baby while serving a term in prison. It is
the violent nature of her crime, her youth, and the fact that she is Native

that become the 'strips' selected to tell the story while the pain she has experienced and the difficulties she has inevitably encountered in caring for her baby in a prison environment are excluded. Also obliterated is her voice in the decision to keep her baby with her; this is presented simply as a decision of the prison authorities. The single quote from the young woman that is incorporated into this story is that her daughter 'keeps me company. . . . I'm not as lonely as before.'

A second theme in the depiction of single mothers as 'hapless' in the early collection of articles is their struggle to cope, a struggle that is understood to be generally unsuccessful. In one article, a woman who is executive director of a children's centre explains why many single mothers need help: 'Keeping routines and managing bedtimes are just too difficult for some parents. There's not really much fun having dinner with a two-year-old, so pretty soon you quit cooking dinner.' An article headlined 'Strengths of Single Moms' is newsworthy precisely because it is designed to surprise the reader with the unexpected slant that single mothers have strengths. It begins with a blocked-off and highlighted description of the stereotype: 'Her house is a shambles, the TV is blaring, the children have dripping noses—and the mother herself, hair a mess and clothes askew, is distraught.' 'Does such a mother exist?' the reader is asked. The answer is given: 'Perhaps, but she doesn't have to live that way. . . .' Interviews with two single mothers provide the material for human interest and contrast. One suggests that 'A single mother *can* cope and can achieve her goals if she really sets her mind to it' while the other advises, 'A lot of single mothers give up. . . . They should turn frustration and anger into positive, productive action.' Thus, one part of the message is that a single mother's life is indeed complicated and difficult; the other part of the message is that she requires and 'ought' to possess a reservoir of personal resources including extra amounts of determination, energy, and organization to help her 'manage'.

Under the rather positive-sounding headline 'Town Will Help Single Mothers' from the *Halifax Chronicle Herald* in 1983 appears the only truly 'demonizing' article from the early years. It contains a number of overtly hostile quotes from municipal politicians debating whether or not to grant interim benefits to single mothers who are cut off from provincial assistance because they are living with a man (they decide to award the benefits). They describe the mothers as 'using their children as leverage' and 'setting a bad example'. One councillor suggested that the 'Children's Aid Society should be requested to "take the children from that unwholesome family atmosphere".' In this early period, the characterization of 'bad mothers' is reserved for those who engage in sexual relationships with men who are not the fathers of their children and make 'fraudulent' claims for assistance.

Single mothers in the 1990s are not so much portrayed as helpless, immature, or disorganized; they are targets of blame—they are 'bad' mothers and represent an important drain on scarce public resources.

Almost half (eight) of the headlines from the twenty articles in the mid-1990s either concern the emotional and behavioural problems of children from single-mother families or they focus on the 'troubling' increase, the 'soar' in the numbers of single mothers. In a particularly powerful and negative image, a *Globe and Mail* columnist condemns both the present and future prospects of the children of young, single mothers: 'They're born in a deep hole, and they never climb out.' In sharp contrast, *none* of the articles from the early 1980s headlined the problems of children and only two featured the increase of single mothers.

The overall growth in single-mother families certainly does not explain the 'rising tides' discourse so evident in the 1990s, bolstered by the 'expert' discourse and the use of statistical data. In 1981 13.7 per cent of families with children were headed by a single mother (Lindsay 1992) and by 1996, this had increased to 16.5 per cent (calculated from Statistics Canada 1997). Although this amounts to a 20 per cent increase, it is important to note that between 1976 and 1981 single-parent families increased by 28 per cent (Lindsay 1992). Clearly, the simple rate of growth in the numbers of single mothers is not an adequate explanation for the increased attention it receives in the press.

Time frames are frequently invoked to establish that the problems cited do indeed constitute a 'rising tide'. Comparisons between the 1950s and the 1980s are used in our later sample to document that the birth rates among single mothers are 'soaring'. However, a comparison between the 1990s and the 1930s, contained in a small story from February 1994, shows that the percentage of single parents in 1991 is actually slightly lower than in 1931—13 per cent as opposed to 14 per cent.

Not only is the increase in single mothers 'troubling' in the 1990s but single motherhood is seen to represent a greater degree of 'choice'. The number of single mothers is increasing, we are told in two articles, because the stigma that once constrained their behaviour has disappeared. Margaret Wente, a *Globe and Mail* columnist, dismisses the usefulness of child support, job training, contraception as possible routes to contain the numbers she is concerned about, and instead favours stigma. She comments, 'I suspect we'll spend the next 25 years trying to put the fear and guilt back into young girls. It's a dreadful thing to do to them. But the alternatives are worse.' Stigma is also identified in two of the articles from the earlier period, but in both of these articles it is framed as a problem that needs to be reduced or eliminated because it increases the difficulties that single mothers experience.

A second element of a single mother's 'choice' is also evident in the 1990s. The dichotomization between the 'unwed' mother, who is almost always a teenager, and the older separated or divorced woman has given way to a new type of single mother. 'Murphy Brown' has arrived on the scene as the older single mother with professional qualifications who chooses to mother on her own. She appears relatively rarely and is understood to represent a small proportion of those who are single mothers, but she is nonetheless portrayed as highly problematic. Two articles, for example, are careful to note a higher incidence of behavioural problems among the children of 'well-off' single mothers when compared to poor two-parent families. Single mothers 'by choice', especially if they use alternative methods of reproduction such as sperm banks, represent a powerful challenge to the conventional image of single motherhood as well as to the importance of men as fathers. In an article entitled 'Ms. Conceptions Will Have 'em Talking', these single mothers are depicted as trading in 'Mr Right' for 'Mr Anonymous'. The fact that a proportion of women using alternative reproductive methods are in lesbian partnerships is also obliterated. They, too, are subsumed into the category of 'single' mothers, revealing the heterosexist use of the term.[5]

Coverage of single mothers had changed in significant ways from the 1980s to the 1990s, ways that help to reinforce a construction of single mothers as 'bad' mothers and the single-mother family as extremely problematic. The single mother is no longer viewed, however patronizingly, as stressed and overburdened. While sympathetic articles are in evidence in the 1990s, the overwhelming nature of the news on single mothers is that they are growing at a frightening rate, and they are increasingly problematic to their children, former partners, and society at large. In the early 1980s single mothers were objects of pity, but by the 1990s they were to be blamed and feared.

What News Does Not Change?

We have outlined the notable differences in reporting that we found in our two time periods, but there are also stubborn similarities. In both periods it became clear from the content what is not there, what is left unreported. For example, it was equally difficult in both periods to find positive images of single mothers as 'mothers' engaged in the work of caring for their children. Much more prominent are the images of single mothers in relation to the paid workforce, either as 'workers' or as 'non-workers'. The few positive images that we found of single mothers caring for their children were also problematic, giving little attention to the difficulties they experience, and relying on an individualistically situated remedy of self-sacrifice.

In a 1983 soft news feature headlined 'Strengths of Single Moms', only fifteen of the 300 story lines involve the caring work of single mothers. This is particularly remarkable given the fact that caring work must have figured very prominently in the lives of one of the two featured single mothers who, we are told in passing, has an eight-year-old child who is an amputee with a spinal disorder. All fifteen of these lines depict the 'good' single mother as the cheerful provider of cheap and healthy family activities, such as gardening and swimming. One single mother is quoted as saying, 'The cheapest and best things in life are things you do with your kids—even if it's only a special candlelight dinner of hot dogs.' Once again the message is clear in the 'strips' provided. Good single mothers manage their inadequate incomes well and without complaint; they also strive to achieve a 'normal' life for themselves and their children while, at the same time, understanding their marginalized position in relation to mainstream society. The message is all the more telling because the lessons are taught by single mothers themselves who are portrayed in the articles as 'exemplars'.

The mid-1990s sample contained a feature article with a similar message on 'good' single mothering. In an article headlined 'In Praise of Single Mothers', the single mothers featured are certainly not depicted as typical: they are the mothers of Black US basketball stars. The remarkable success of their sons is, in part, attributed to the sacrifices their mothers made, such as working overtime, giving up holidays to provide extras for their children, worrying about them, and (in keeping with racial stereotypes) being vigilant in discouraging them from activities that may lead to crime. Their vigilance and sacrifice, we are told, compensated for the many problems that beset sons raised without a father in the home. However, even when the intention is to provide extremely positive images of the care these mothers have given to their children, the reader is directed not to think that single mothering can be 'as good as' the 'natural' family. A quote from a friend of one of the stars is selected for use in the article to remind the reader of the intrinsic obstacles that confront all sons of single mothers, no matter how successful: 'He is learning manhood on his own. When you are raised without boundaries, you have to find them for yourself.'

When the caring role of single mothers is reported, the news, at best, is not very good. They must be managers and copers, and even with unstinting levels of self-sacrifice, their children are at a significant disadvantage. Caring labour is never portrayed in the context of a contradictory, complex meaningful life experience; the needs of single mothers are submerged and are not revealed as separate, or possibly competing with, the needs of their children.

The general lack of attention to the single mother's caring role might be considered remarkable, given that children are an essential and defining characteristic of the single mother. At the same time, the work women do in caring for others is typically invisible and undervalued (for discussion and a range of examples, see Baines, Evans, and Neysmith 1998). The neglect of the single mother's work in caring for her children did not emerge as a time-sensitive aspect of our analysis. Instead, the inattention to caring issues is a stubbornly persistent feature in covering the news about single mothers. The image of single mothers caring for their children does not provide drama or deviance, criteria that constitute journalistic 'imperatives' (Chibnall 1977). But the relative absence of positive images, and the narrow parameters of the positive images that are drawn, help to ensure that the construction of the single mother in the press is overwhelmingly problematic.

Conclusion

Our analysis suggests that the construction of single mothers that had emerged by the mid-1990s in the press was highly congruent with a restructuring discourse and what Luxton (1997:21) refers to as the 'reassertion of the legitimacy of inequality'. Over the time span we examined, the depiction of single mothers shifted. In the early period, they were generally viewed as helpless or hapless—they faced difficult circumstances not entirely of their own making and required, in addition to considerable personal resources, some structural supports in order to overcome them. By the mid-1990s, however, the dominant discourse surrounding single mothers had constituted them as problematic to their children and a threat to social well-being. In the 1990s the poverty of single mothers is no longer viewed as a result of inadequate social assistance and/or low wages, but had become a more or less inevitable fact of life. Because single mothering was constructed as a reflection of individual choice or an indication of a general disregard for the welfare of their children, poverty becomes an expected and not unacceptable outcome. Government, as a player in the lives of single mothers, had virtually disappeared, except as an agent to collect child support, but the ideological construction of the single mother in the 1990s extends beyond the concerns of the public purse. The single mothers who are not dependent upon social assistance, the 'Murphy Browns', are also portrayed as a danger to the social fabric woven with visions of the idealized 'family'.

We identified processes that appear to contribute to the changing construction of the 'problem' single mothers. First, evident in the later collection of articles is the increased reliance on 'experts' to provide authoritative verification of the 'problem'. Second, the authorative view of single mothers is also supported by a veritable barrage of statistical data, much less in view in the earlier period. These processes do not occur in isolation but appear to relate to the perceived imperatives of the news industry in the 'new economy'. They include an increasing emphasis on profits, a growing concentration of corporate power, and less investigative, 'primary' reporting. As this occurs, content becomes more uniform and space for alternative views and diverse voices shrinks (Carter, Branston, and Allan 1998).

There were also elements in the news construction of single mothers that did not appear to change over time. In both periods, the work of caring for children receives little attention. The complexities and ambiguities, the rewards and demands of caring labour are reduced to a simple message that single mothers must always do more because they can never do enough. This discourse allows little space for agency, and in both periods there was little recognition of single mothers as a diverse group of women who use a variety of skills and considerable efforts to ensure the safety and security of their children and themselves.

The images of single mothers in print media clearly reinforce traditional notions of women's social roles: mothers and, by implication, all women should be self-sacrificing, regardless of personal cost. Silences about the labour involved in caring for children alone powerfully reinforce this message. In addition, our two samples demonstrate how images of single mothers have changed along with the power dynamics in the social order. As the restructuring discourse has taken hold during the 1990s, single mothers have increasingly been 'conscripted' to play a role in proving the need for reduced social costs and the recasting of citizens as 'workers'. Portrayal of this group *as a group* is in itself an important part of this mechanism; portraying all single mothers as alike reinforces the sense of threat to the public purse and the social and economic fabric. The schema that equates the problems of children with family structure rather than low income, along with an emphasis on the 'rising tides', help to construct the single mother 'problem' as seemingly enormous and never-ending and invites 'moral panic'. The effect of these portrayals is to strengthen hegemonic discourses posing the proper role of the state not as support but as control, reshaping and repositioning 'problematic' social groups.

What are the practical implications of our analysis? Although we expected changes in the ways single mothers were constructed in the news over time, we were surprised by the nature and extent of some of these changes we found, and the power of the images that were created. We were also surprised at the number of times images could slip by us as 'normal' in the initial readings, serving as a constant reminder that a critical perspective does not provide immunity from the powerful influence of hegemonic discourse.

Attending to discourse should increase the awareness of how hegemonic images are produced, reproduced, and maintained and provide some ideas for providing alternative versions. Academics are frequently called upon as 'experts' to comment on their own and others' research and we are generally pleased and flattered to do so. Our analysis suggests that we are increasingly asked to take on this role and we need to engage much more carefully with the press. This may mean, for example, articulating very consciously, clearly, and briefly 'alternative' versions that are often absent or poorly represented. This makes reporting the 'other' side a more attractive option for the reporter and minimizes the chances of out-of-context quotations that support rather than oppose the hegemonic perspective. What does seem to us as important is participation and contestation, however limited it may be, in news construction.

Our analysis of the time periods suggested a decline in the 'voice' of antipoverty/social justice groups, a likely reflection of the decreasing space available for alternative views. However, it is important that groups continue their attempts to engage with the press. Nancy Fraser (1997:154) underlines the role of contestation and conflict in the disruption of hegemony. At the broader level, the feminist project must also develop strategies that effectively challenge hegemonic discourse and interpretations. Newspapers constitute only one site among many where damaging images are created, but, we suggest, it does not need to be a site that is surrendered by default and without a struggle.

Notes

1   The authors are listed alphabetically; this was in every sense, a collaborative effort. We would like to thank Tracy Clemenger for her very able and energetic research assistance, as well as the members of the network and the reviewers for their helpful comments. Thanks are also due to SSHRC for the financial assistance provided through the network grant, 816-94-0003.

2   Crompton (1994) suggests that the influx of older and generally better-educated married mothers into the labour market has created an employment pool in which single mothers are disadvantaged.

3   The CNI includes the *Vancouver Sun, Calgary Herald, Edmonton Journal, Winnipeg Free Press, Toronto Star, Globe and Mail, Montreal Gazette*, and the *Halifax Chronicle Herald*. A rough estimate of readership suggests that these eight newspapers reach 34 per cent of the households in these major cities.

4   In the earlier period there were sixty-one articles, giving us a final sample of fifteen articles, after excluding five that focused on single fathers. In the later period, the same search produced seventy-four articles, providing a final sample of twenty articles, after excluding three on single fathers.

5   Paralleling this concern of the challenge to the 'family ethic' that alternative methods of reproduction generate is the challenge to the 'work ethic'. During the mid-1990s, considerable coverage and controversy accompanied a divorced woman's decision to give up her job as a social worker with Metro Toronto in order to go on welfare. See 'The Making of an Angry Woman', *Toronto Life* (Summer 1994):56–62.

References

Abramowitz, M. 1996. *Under Attack, Fighting Back: Women and Welfare in the United States*. New York: Cornerstone Books.

Baines, C., P. Evans, and S. Neysmith, eds. 1998. *Women's Caring: Feminist Perspectives on Social Welfare*, 2nd edn. Toronto: Oxford University Press.

Brodie, J. 1995. *Politics on the Margins: Restructuring and the Canadian Women's Movement*. Halifax: Fernwood.

Callahan, M., and K. Callahan. 1997. 'Victims and Villains: Scandals, the Press and Policy-making in Child Welfare'. In *Child and Family Policies: Struggles, Strategies and Options*, edited by J. Pulkingham and G. Ternowetsky, 40–57. Halifax: Fernwood.

Carter, C., G. Branston, and S. Allan. 1998. 'Setting New(s) Agendas: An Introduction'. In *News, Gender and Power*, edited by C. Carter, G. Branston, and S. Allan, 1–16. London and New York: Routledge.

Chibnall, S. 1977. *Law and Order News*. London: Tavistock.

Chomsky, N. 1989. *Necessary Illusions: Thought Control in Democratic Societies*. Montreal: CBC Enterprises.

Cohen, M. 1997. 'From the Welfare State to Vampire Capitalism'. In *Women and the Canadian Welfare State: Challenges and Change*, edited by P. Evans and G. Wekerle, 28–67. Toronto: University of Toronto Press.

Crompton, S. 1994. 'Left Behind: Lone Mothers in the Labour Market'. *Perspectives* (Summer):23–8.

Duncan, S., and R. Edwards, eds. 1997. *Single Mothers in International Context: Mothers or Workers?* Bristol: Taylor & Francis.

Evans, P. 1995. 'Single Mothers and Ontario's Welfare Policy: Restructuring the Debate'. In *Women and Public Policy*, edited by J. Brodie, 151–71. Toronto: Harcourt Brace.

Fraser, N. 1997. *Justice Interruptus: Critical Reflections on the 'Postsocialist' Condition*. New York: Routledge.

Goffman, E. 1974. *Frame Analysis*. Philadelphia: University of Pennsylvania Press.

Gramsci, A. 1971. *Prison Notebooks*. New York: International Publishers.

Griffith, A. 1986. 'Reporting the Facts: Media Accounts of Single Parent Families'. *Resources for Feminist Research* 15, no. 1 (March):32–3.

Herman, E., and N. Chomsky. 1988. *Manufacturing Consent*. New York: Pantheon.

Knight, G. 1998. 'Hegemony, the Press and Business Discourse: News Coverage of Strike-Breaker Reform in Quebec and Ontario'. *Studies in Political Economy* 55 (Spring):93–125.

Lindsay, C. 1992. *Lone-Parent Families in Canada: Target Groups Project*. Catalogue no. 89–522. Ottawa: Statistics Canada.

Little, M. 1998. *'No Car, No Radio, No Liquor Permit': The Moral Regulation of Single Mothers in Ontario, 1920–1997*. Toronto: Oxford University Press.

Lowes, M., R. Hackett, J. Winter, D. Gutstein, and R. Gruneau. 1996. *Project Censored Canada: Blindspots in the News Agenda? 1996 Yearbook*. Vancouver: Simon Fraser University.

Luxton, M. 1997. 'Feminism and Families: The Challenge of Neo-conservatism'. In *Feminism and Families: Critical Policies and Changing Practices*, edited by M. Luxton, 10–26. Halifax: Fernwood.

McIntosh, M. 1996. 'Social Anxieties About Lone Motherhood and Ideologies of the Family: Two Sides of the Same Coin'. In *Good Enough Mothering? Feminist Perspectives on Lone Motherhood*, edited by E. Silva, 148–56. New York: Routledge.

Martin, M. 1997. *Communication and Mass Media: Culture, Domination and Opposition.* Scarborough: Prentice-Hall Canada.

Meyers, M. 1994. 'Defining Homosexuality: News Coverage of the "Repeal the Ban" Controversy'. *Discourse & Society 5*, no. 3:321–44.

Miller, J. 1998. *Yesterday's News: Why Canada's Daily Newspapers Are Failing Us.* Halifax: Fernwood.

Roseneil, S., and K. Mann. 1996. 'Unpalatable Choices and Inadequate Families: Lone Mothers and the Underclass Debate'. In *Good Enough Mothering? Feminist Perspectives on Lone Motherhood*, edited by E. Silva, 191–210. New York: Routledge.

Silva, E. 1996. 'Introduction'. In *Good Enough Mothering? Feminist Perspectives on Lone Motherhood*, edited by E. Silva, 1–9. New York: Routledge.

Smart, C. 1996. 'Deconstructing Motherhood'. In *Good Enough Mothering? Feminist Perspectives on Lone Motherhood*, edited by E. Silva, 37–57. New York: Routledge.

Smith, D.E. 1983. 'No One Commits Suicide: Textual Analysis of Ideological Practices'. *Human Studies* 6:309–59.

Statistics Canada. 1997. *Annual Demographic Statistics 1996.* Catalogue no. 91-213-XPB. Ottawa: Minister of Industry.

Swift, K. 1995. *Manufacturing 'Bad Mothers': Critical Perspectives on Child Neglect.* Toronto: University of Toronto Press.

Taras, D. 1990. *The Newsmakers: The Media's Influence on Canadian Politics.* Scarborough: Nelson Canada.

Tuchman, G. 1978. *Making News: A Study in the Construction of Reality.* New York: Free Press.

Ursel, J. 1992. *Private Lives, Public Policy: 100 Years of State Intervention in the Family.* Toronto: Women's Press.

van Dijk, T. 1988. *News as Discourse.* Hillsdale: Lawrence Erlbaum Associates.

Chapter 5

Location, Location, Location: Restructuring and the Everyday Lives of 'Welfare Moms'[1]

Karen J. Swift and Michael Birmingham

Globalization and restructuring are becoming commonplace terms, often used to describe our social and economic condition as the new millennium begins. We are aware that people's lives are affected by these processes, becoming geared to large forces outside their own control. Feminists suggest that women in fact will bear much of the cost of these changes in how we both acquire and spend money (Bakker 1996). However, so far little has been written about the effects of these processes on everyday life.

Single mothers on assistance are one of the populations most clearly affected by restructuring of the social safety net. The attention of both policy makers and the public has focused on this group as one that could and should be relocated to mesh better—and more cheaply—with our new restructured direction. Some changes in their situation have already been made, and others are on the drawing board, changes designed to relocate these women and their children in relation to the job market and the welfare state. These changes are publicly justified through images of 'welfare moms' as unemployed, unproductive people outside the mainstream of public life.

Our research interest was in exploring the experiences of these mothers in the contemporary context, with special attention to contradictions between popular discourse and their accounts of their own everyday lives. In this chapter, we examine some aspects of the social and economic context in which these women care for their children, some of their daily experiences as reported in focus groups organized as part of the research, and we conclude with some observations about the implications for social policy of their everyday lives.

As part of our research, three focus groups were organized in Ottawa to explore the experiences and perceptions of single mothers on welfare. The women in all three groups were asked to discuss their perceptions of what they and their children need, the labour involved in trying to meet these needs, and their relationships to welfare and the larger society. The sample is limited in that only one geographic location is represented. Furthermore, our sample is relatively small and self-selected. Consequently, we make no effort to generalize findings. Rather, we employ the open-ended discussion with these mothers to make visible specific aspects of caring labour. Certainly, their personal and financial situations are typical of some common experiences for this group across Canada and the United States, an assertion supported by reference to literature concerning single mothers on assistance (Davis and Hagen 1994; Ellwood 1988; Kitchen and Popham 1998; Lindsey 1996; Mosher, Chapter 2, this volume; Ozawa 1994; Rank 1994). Mothers' understanding of their situation reflects common issues, problems, solutions, and possibilities for women in similar circumstances.

In order to explore some differences among women in this population, we selected groups of women located differently in relation to the state, the market economy, and social service programs. Two groups involved women who are citizens of Canada. One group lives in rental housing. They were hit especially hard by Ontario's 21 per cent welfare reduction in 1995 because the cost of their housing remains fixed. These women, most of whom had one child and none more than three children at the time of our group meeting, now spend substantial time making ends meet, searching for and comparing various small sources of support. The tone of their meeting was often angry as they reminisced about men they saw as hurting and misusing them and as they compared themselves to other single mothers whom they see as faring better in the distribution of scarce resources, including jobs.

The second group lives in subsidized, non-profit housing. For these women, the welfare cuts, although hard to absorb, have been more manageable than for women in the first group because their housing costs were reduced to some extent along with their income. This group, the smallest of the three, had between two and four children at the time of the group meeting. Women in this group focused much discussion on volunteer and community activity. Several spoke of previous experience in the paid labour force and various skills and credentials they hoped would assist them in obtaining a job when their child-caring responsibilities would permit.

The third group was constituted of mothers born in Somalia who came to Canada as refugees and were awaiting more permanent status in the country. Their group discussion, conducted in their mother tongue, placed considerable importance on Canada's immigration laws, which they saw as preventing reunification with their husbands. All these women had more children than their Canadian counterparts in our groups—between four and seven. The number of children is an important criterion in determining eligibility for subsidized housing; these mothers were well positioned to qualify, and in fact all who came to the focus group had this benefit. Their position in relation to the labour market, however, is tenuous because of their child-caring responsibilities and language limitations. These women share a concern about their status in the country, not only for themselves but for their children, who they feel may be marginalized from jobs and postsecondary education by virtue of their status in the country.

Women in all three groups were aware of other subgroups of single mothers and how they were differently 'privileged' and located in relation to the labour market and to various services. For those with the fewest benefits, these differences were a source of considerable resentment. These expressions of hostility both call attention to and challenge the concept of 'single mothers on assistance' as an identifiable and homogeneous group. We will examine how this categorization affects the self-concept of its 'members', helping to foster dissatisfaction with themselves and with others in this category. We will also explore differences among these three groups of women. Our intent is to reveal how the concept of 'welfare moms' helps to produce and maintain the power relations required for a 'globalizing' economy.

In analysing our data, we relied not only on the accounts of the women themselves but on placing these accounts of experience within a specific social context. Scott (1992) has argued that satisfactory evidence of experience is not constituted simply of personal accounts of individual experience. Rather, this kind of evidence should be based on questions about how experience is historically established, how it operates within its social context, and in what ways it comes to constitute subjects whose experience is articulated. This kind of analysis does not question the veracity of the speakers but interrogates the social origins and meanings of what they have to say. Experience, to quote Scott (1992:38), 'is not the origin of our explanation, but that which we want to explain'. A further goal of research based on accounts of experience is to understand the processes by which social identities are 'ascribed, resisted or embraced' (Scott 1992:33). Unexamined, such processes retain powerful social effects; through explication of them, social identities such as 'welfare mom' can be questioned, challenged, and changed. Certainly, the mothers in our sample did not readily accept their assignment into this social grouping, and in various ways sought to challenge and escape it. Generally speaking, however, they saw it as a valid social category to which other women might rightfully belong. In our analysis we try to respect the voices of the women in our groups, but challenge the validity of the social category of which they are all 'members'.

The Social and Economic Context of Caring

During the 1990s, the Canadian public became convinced that the country suffered from a huge deficit that could only be reduced through drastic cuts to social programs. The recession affecting much of Canada that began in the early part of the decade brought some of the highest unemployment rates since the Great Depression. Simultaneously, the globalization of the world economy brought a rhetoric about increasing the 'productivity' of the labour force in order to enhance Canada's competitive position in world markets. A primary strategy proposed for achieving this goal is to get people off welfare and into paying jobs.

Globalization refers to the ability of transnational corporations to move capital and jobs around the world to sites of greatest profitability. It is generally recognized that the framework in place to shape and drive the globalization of capital and labour has been put in place by the world's superpowers, particularly the United States (Clark 1997). Some have argued that as globalization occurs, the state is becoming less powerful as a regulator of social and economic processes. However, an alternate and supportable argument is that nation-states, particularly of the more powerful countries, are more likely shifting their energies from the supportive functions of the welfare state to functions that facilitate corporate interests. It is in fact this shift that we refer to as 'restructuring'. This direction is generally explained and legitimized, especially in neoliberal discourse, as a way to create economic conditions from which everyone can benefit. However, it is widely acknowledged that the benefits of globalization are very unevenly distributed. This is true among countries, with Western nations reaping substantial benefits at the expense of extracting resources, skills, and cheap labour from Third World countries. It is also true among groups within countries, with some groups enjoying large profits while many others are losing ground in the labour market.

As part of the restructuring process, attacks on social spending, including welfare programs, have been gaining strength and momentum (O'Neill 1998). As Fraser (1989) has pointed out, this 'welfare war' is largely about—and perhaps against—women. In fact, women's needs are among the principal stakes in battles over social spending. Critiques of the basic idea and structure of welfare programs have been made from various viewpoints. Ellwood (1988), for instance, argues that welfare has not solved the problem of poverty because it addresses mere symptoms, not causes. Ozawa (1994) has convincingly argued that while families on welfare represent a diverse population, current programs do not address this diversity. Neoconservative ideas, symbolized in the 1990s by the American Newt Gingrich, are expressive of a much stronger view. Gingrich (1995) charges, for example, that welfare programs actually 'subsidize idleness' and are therefore un-American. His antidote for idleness is straightforward—those who don't work, don't eat. 'The vision of the merciless', as Ignatieff (1984) has said, 'does have a certain clarity'. While most Canadian policy makers are not willing to go to the lengths of American neoconservatives, there has been a sharp shift in Canadian policy directions regarding vulnerable populations, including single mothers. This shift towards neoliberal politics recommends lowering payments and reducing programs and benefits, while increasing pressure on women to consider 'moving from welfare to work'.

For single mothers on social assistance, these developments have resulted in decreasing entitlements, resources, and security along with a return to closer scrutiny of their social contributions, labour, and personal lives. Policy proposals such as 'workfare' and various training programs suggest that these women should no longer be seen as automatically entitled to financial support during child-rearing years but rather should be viewed as currently unproductive people who are potential recruits for the labour market, an idea captured in the phrase 'moving women from welfare to work'.

At the same time, important shifts in Canada's employment picture have occurred. Recently reported figures from Statistics Canada show the jobless rate continuing at high but declining levels—8 per cent at year end 1998, down from 8.6 per cent at the end of 1997. According to the *Globe and Mail* (9 January 1999), these figures represent the best year in a decade for Canada's job creation overall, amounting to a 3.2 per cent increase over the course of 1998. Prior to 1998, employment prospects for women appeared particularly unpromising. Many of the jobs that disappeared over the past few years were full-time jobs. Perhaps most distressing for women has been the loss of jobs, especially full-time jobs, in traditional women's areas—for instance teaching and nursing. Statistics Canada reported that in 1996 women gained relatively few jobs compared to men (*Toronto Star*, 8 March 1997). Further, Armstrong (1996) argues that men have recently been getting 'more than their share' of both full-time and part-time jobs in traditional women's areas.

At the end of 1998, however, there were shifts in some of these trends. Not only did job creation apparently improve but many of these jobs were filled by women, who reportedly were 'flooding' into the health and social service sectors. Furthermore, almost two-thirds of job gains for women were in full-time employment (*Globe and Mail*, 9 January 1999). However, a note of caution should be sounded. Since low-wage, contract work characterizes the 'new economy' (Korten 1995), it can be expected that although many of the new jobs are full time, they will be at low wage levels and will not be permanent. Furthermore, those 'good jobs' that are created are unlikely to benefit women most in need of income and security. Undoubtedly, the benefits of job creation will be unevenly distributed, with poor women continuing to be poor.

Another significant trend affecting women is the devolvement of labour from areas of full-time paid work to 'the community' (Shields and Evans 1998). Announcements of massive hospital closings and school restructurings quite commonly include vague suggestions that 'community care', 'home care', volunteerism, personal involvement, and 'family care' are superior ways to deliver most services requiring caring labour. Some of this care will undoubtedly be assumed by lower-paid, lower-skilled workers, mostly women, as home-care workers, homemakers, nurses' aides, tutors, etc. Clearly, much of the work of personal care now being deinstitutionalized and de-budgeted will also devolve onto the shoulders of unpaid women in the private home. As Margaret Wente argues, tongue in cheek, 'my mother is the answer to Mike Harris's prayers for how to deliver community care. My mother is a one-woman voluntary social service agency—a combination of Wheel-Trans, Meals-on-Wheels, social worker, community advocate, grief counsellor and financial advisor all rolled up into one' (*Globe and Mail*, 8 March 1997). Women in our focus groups echoed this sentiment, describing considerable labour done by low-income women who supposedly have no skills and are 'not working'.

As the war on welfare has gained momentum, so negative discourse about single mothers has intensified (see Chapter 4). As Davis and Hagen (1996:319) argue, 'in the debate on welfare reform, stereotypes of women on welfare have resurfaced, and most proposals for reform are designed to modify and regulate women's behaviours'. Discourse concerning single mothers generally suggests in strong terms that this family form is a threat to the social fabric. Furthermore, children of these mothers are often perceived as having the potential for serious and expensive social problems. The images presented through discourse tend towards vilification of those in receipt of social assistance. These women are typically characterized as lazy since they are 'not working', and as undeserving of public resources since they make 'no contribution' to society.

It is true that Canadian single mothers and their children are at high risk of poverty in the 1990s. Female lone parents represent nearly half (47 per cent) of poor non-elderly families with children, but constitute only 20 per cent of this population (Hunsley 1996). It is widely known that Canada has for several years, and again in 1998, been rated as the number one country in the world for quality of life by the United Nations (United Nations Development Programme 1998). However, first-class quality of life does not extend to all of Canada's citizens and residents. Canada is in fact among the three highest Western countries in its poverty rate for single mothers, along with Australia and the United States. Although less than 10 per cent of single mothers in some European countries are poor (Freiler and Cerny 1998), recent figures show that 61.4 per cent of Canadian single mothers with children under eighteen live in poverty. This translates into 390,000 families. In the under twenty-five age group, the percentage in poverty rises to an unacceptable 91.3 (National Council of Welfare 1998). As Hunsley (1996) notes, these mothers often find themselves in the lower strata of the poor. Of course, single mothers are not the only Canadian women at risk of poverty. As United Nations reports show (United Nations Development Programme 1998), Canadian women, along with women in many countries, generally are at a serious economic disadvantage in relation to men at all ages, and many more women than men live below the poverty line. Such circumstances as childbearing, responsibility for the care of others, and dislocation (for instance, through immigration) intensify the already serious economic problems that women face.

In Canada, mothers on welfare are guaranteed poverty since benefits for them and for all welfare recipients are below the poverty line. Depending on the province, single mothers on assistance receive from 48 to 69 per cent of the official low income cut-off, figures that, although quite low, were reduced even further in Alberta and Ontario (Conway 1997; Freiler and Cerny 1998). To address the 'problem' of single mothers on welfare, two policy directions are in various stages of implementation. The first is to restrict both access to and levels of social assistance to this group. In both Ontario and Alberta, for instance, welfare rates have been substantially reduced. In some jurisdictions, the 'man in the house' rule, which renders ineligible for assistance a woman cohabiting with a man, has been reinstated, as Janet Mosher discusses in Chapter 2. The second part of this strategy to reduce welfare costs and 'increase productivity' is 'workfare', which requires that those 'able' to enter the paid labour force, including single mothers, provide 'approved' labour in return for social assistance payments. Critics of this approach are legion, of course. Schragge (1997:33) views workfare as a 'punitive response to wider changes in the structures of the economy and in work . . . [promoted] partly in an attempt to prove that work remains a possibility'. From an entitlement point of view, Pascal (1993) forcefully argues against the notion that rights imply duties, including caregiving duties, noting that in this scenario mere redefinition of duty can cost women their entitlements. Taken to its logical conclusion, even the most basic needs of 'able-bodied' adults and their dependent children might then not constitute legitimate claims for entitlement.

The second main approach to reducing welfare in Canada is the proposed National Child Benefit. Through this policy, federal and provincial income security programs would be integrated, becoming a single benefit paid to all low-income families with dependent children. Three main objectives for the benefit are claimed. These include 'preventing and reducing the depth of child poverty, promoting attachment to the workforce . . ., and reducing overlap and duplication of child-related benefits' (Battle and Mendelson 1997). The model is promoted by prominent social policy experts as an important first step in alleviating poverty and equalizing benefits among low-income families. Among its advantages are that it simplifies income support, that it will be income rather than needs tested, and that it will provide portability so that families moving into low-wage jobs from welfare will not lose the benefit. Proponents of this policy shift note that it is designed to reduce rather than 'cure' poverty (Battle and Mendelson 1997:2), and that it will reduce the 'fairness' gap between families on assistance and the working poor, whose children at present may be even more poverty-stricken than those whose parents receive welfare (Caledon Institute of Social Policy 1997). It is clear, however, that part of the rationale for this approach is the reduction of disincentives to labour force participation by women on welfare. In other words, this proposal is intended to take down the 'welfare wall' that supposedly stands between individuals and the paid labour force. As we have argued elsewhere (Swift and Birmingham 1999), this proposal also provides subsidies to corporate interests through the encouragement of low-wage contract jobs that offer no benefits or security—the kinds of jobs favoured by the new transnational corporations that are central to the restructured economy. In addition, this approach separates the interests of mothers and children, deeming children's needs worthy of public attention, while their mothers' needs are not.

To summarize, women are already at an economic disadvantage relative to men, and single mothers receiving assistance are increasingly vulnerable. Both material support and entitlements of this population are under threat, and these women are frequently urged to improve their position by 'getting back to work'. Current policy proposals rely on this approach in an attempt to simultaneously cut public costs while reconfiguring welfare in ways that mesh with the new economy. At the same time, much work in the paid labour force is being deskilled, devalued, and devolved. At home, women will be expected to take on more caring labour, some of it the relatively skilled labour previously done by paid professionals. Missing from these discussions is the question of how the most vulnerable women, including single mothers, are to support and provide care for themselves and their dependants in this developing scenario. Also far in the background are alternate explanations of the underlying sources of the problems confronting this population. Class, race, and gender-based inequalities that characterize both the past and the 'new' economic structures in Canada are glossed over by categorizing these women as 'welfare moms'.

Caring and Need

The idea of caring has been developed primarily by feminists in order to fully conceptualize elements of relational life as experienced by women (see Chapter 1 for an in-depth discussion of this concept). The notion of caring labour is closely related to and in fact rooted in 'need' (Fisher and Tronto 1990). Ideas concerning need come mostly from male-dominated domains such as philosophy and public policy and centre upon differentiating what is essential to us from what we merely desire. This distinction is important in the public world because need distinguishes which of our desires entitles us to the resources of others; simple desire, on the other hand, is 'capricious' (Thompson 1987:98) and unfettered by social obligations (Ignatieff 1984).

The discourse of need also addresses itself to defining different kinds of need, distinguishing for instance between survival needs from the need to flourish (Doyal and Gough 1991; Ignatieff 1984). Marx differentiated between 'natural needs', those physical needs required to be met for continued existence, and 'necessary needs', which are natural needs plus a sense of normalcy (Heller 1976). Recently, the notion of needs as 'thick' and 'thin' has been described by Fraser (1989), one of an emerging group of women contributing to conceptions of need. A thin need is conceptualized as objective and universal, while thick needs are understood and interpreted in cultural context and relate to the quest for development and fulfilment. The idea of 'thick' needs echoes Marx's conceptualization of need as multifaceted and positive. Marx in fact spoke of need as wealth—a person 'rich in needs' was a 'human being in need of a totality of human manifestations of life' (quoted in Heller 1976:143–4). In 1990s Canada, however, discussions of need are far from this conception. Increasingly in the social and political domain, 'need' is limited to 'natural' need—the most basic requirements of survival. This narrow or neoliberal definition of need justifies minimal claims on the public purse and therefore fits the agenda of deficit reduction. Currently at issue is whether needs to 'flourish', to be fulfilled, or to feel socially 'normal' constitute any claims on the public purse.

Contemporary social policy debates centre upon determining not only what will qualify as needs but also on determining systems of obligation for meeting various needs. The development of the Keynesian welfare state represented an attempt to increase society's obligation to meet the needs of its members, and to move some obligations from individual families and the community to the social whole. The very existence of the welfare state normalizes the condition of need and tends to reduce moral judgements of the needs expressed by individuals and families. With the shift to neoliberal politics, however, the obligation for meeting need is devolving back from the state to family and community. As the liberal welfare state has dwindled, social claims are being reduced to 'natural' or survival need as the only legitimate social claim: 'Sure you try to make your food last', one mother told us. 'I eat, but I don't eat as much as I used to because I can't afford it.'

The experiences articulated by women in our focus groups of caring for children in circumstances of small and shrinking resources stands in substantial contradiction with neoliberal conceptions of need. There is in fact little in contemporary discourse that adequately captures mothers' attempts to meet needs with minimal resources. The labour involved in determining and meeting the needs of children is considerably more immediate, complex, contradictory, 'messy', and painful than suggested by most contemporary ideology and discourse. Mothers describe a barrage of different, often conflicting, upsetting and impossible demands conveyed to them by their children and by others in contact with their children. They describe children screaming, demanding, and even leaving home over their own inability to provide for their children's needs and wants. Mothers also describe considerable labour and emotional costs of meeting needs, including their own. These mothers eat less, put off buying clothes for themselves—even winter coats—beg from friends and lovers, are regularly upset by what they cannot provide in their needs-meeting efforts: 'I cry myself to sleep at night', said one.

In general, women in our focus groups stated the needs of their families in strikingly modest terms: 'I want my kid to be able to open the fridge door and have whatever he wants.' Of course, mothers on assistance must understand and address themselves to the crucial problem of meeting survival or necessary needs: 'Food is my first priority, bills are my second priority. Then I have to worry about boots and coats for winter', said one mother. Another 'decided not to pay the [Hydro] bill and concentrate on food'. However, statements suggest that what might be construed in the neoliberal context as mere desire are often perceived by mothers as essential to the well-being of their children, or 'thick' needs: 'I had to borrow a dollar to put under his pillow [for the tooth fairy].'

Discourses of need, and especially neoliberal views, generally focus on the individual as the unit of need. This is not surprising, given our history as a liberal society, and in fact we may unthinkingly accept this idea. A complaint by one mother about resource shortages and her attempts to solve them, for instance, demonstrates acceptance that her child's needs are synonymous with her own: 'Sometimes I have to call the baby's father and say I need diapers and bread and he brings it to me.' This common form of expression merges children's needs with those of mothers, providing additional strength to neoliberal claims that welfare mothers are a drain on social resources.

Certainly, the children of these mothers do not accept the neoliberal view of need as mere survival. As several mothers pointed out, children and adolescents form their perception of needs through constant comparisons to their peers. They 'see their peers wearing better clothes, [eating] better school lunches and some have tutors who teach them at home'. Another mother agreed: 'Teenage children like to wear good clothes because they want to have what other teenagers have. We [single mothers] can't afford to buy what they need anymore.' Some mothers are afraid their older children may leave home prematurely, searching for what their mothers cannot provide.

Since Ontario's 21 per cent reduction in welfare benefits, the labour of feeding and clothing their children has increased for all of these mothers, especially for those in market rental housing, since their rent now consumes a much larger portion of their total income. Shopping takes longer, in order to 'shop the specials'. More trips to food banks and clothing depots were reported, and considerably more time is spent juggling different bills, trying to figure out how much to pay on each without incurring too much penalty. These mothers also spend considerable time and effort to find information about benefits they might be able to qualify for and on making comparisons of different kinds of benefits available to various subgroups of mothers on welfare. Our focus groups, in fact, provided an occasion for some of this information to be shared.

Caring Labour: The 24/7 Shift

Embedded in current policies exhorting 'welfare mothers' to increase their attachment to the paid labour force are several assumptions about work. The most basic of these is that the care of children is not real work. At best, it is assumed that mothers on welfare caring for children provide unskilled and sporadically executed labour. Such assumptions are not grounded in actual research on mothers and their labour processes but on traditional and gendered understandings of the idea of 'work'. The well-known 'work ethic' is, of course, deeply rooted in the West and has been recently re-emphasized in neoliberal discourse. This approach is based on a view of human nature, drawn from the thinking of Hume and Smith, that only the most desperate need to survive will drive people to labour. Those who overcome their basic nature in order to meet need are judged as morally worthy. Vellekoop-Baldock (1990) further explores how a separation between home and work, or private and public, developed in relation to capitalist modes of production. As women became increasingly consigned to the private sphere, labour performed in the home became invisible and thus excluded from the idea of a 'productive' process. This dichotomy has, of course, continued, as has the moral value attached to paid work. Processes through which paid work is distributed are hidden, as is the entire arena of unpaid caring labour, which involves acts of concern for others not accounted for in the 'work ethic' model. Ironically, the view of paid work as overcoming 'natural' instincts, coupled with the distribution of paid work to the male, produced a confirmation of male superiority—men who laboured were morally superior for doing so. Women at home were presumably not labouring but simply doing what came naturally, an unskilled pursuit carrying no special moral value.

Following from this logic, the tasks involved in caring for children have come to be seen as 'not working'. Even women in our focus group sample, after outlining a prodigious amount of labour done in the home, lamented the fact that they were 'not working'. In addition, many of them felt shamed by their lack of paid employment. This contradiction has, of course, been taken up by feminists, especially in explorations of 'caring labour' done by women in the private home (see Baines, Evans, and Neysmith 1991, 1998).

While generally undervaluing their own efforts, mothers in our focus groups nevertheless described to us a substantial amount of labour involved in meeting needs of their children at home. This labour was captured in the phrase '24/7', meaning they see themselves as being on duty twenty-four hours a day, seven days a week. As one mother reasonably pointed out, 'There's no one else to do it.' Strenuous efforts and labour are involved in attempts to meet children's material needs: mothers try to extract resources from various government programs, make trips across town to more generous food banks, engage in political action to change laws, take small jobs, trade child care, organize community suppers, skip meals, plan purchases to take advantage of bulk rates, borrow food and money, make personal and legal approaches to fathers of their children, and budget their money many months in advance.

The labour carried out by these mothers runs at least partly by the 'preindustrial clock', as Abel and Nelson (1990:8) explain, dictated largely by human needs rather than by bureaucratic or political imperatives. Of course, this labour has been socially assigned to women; it would not necessarily be their choice to do it otherwise. As well these mothers must coordinate their labour with extra local work organization. Institutions like the school system (Griffith and Smith 1987) and local norms of behaviour (Duncan and Edwards 1996) influence labour performed in the private home, with attendant effects of routinizing and homogenizing a mother's labour. A related characteristic of this labour is that it is not fully 'Taylorized'; that is, planning of this labour is not effectively and fully separated from the doing of the work. Certainly many barriers prevent completion of planned and hoped for tasks. Nevertheless, mothers caring full time for children maintain at least a modicum of control over planning time, allocation of resources, and type and distribution of tasks involved in their labour. This is a point that may help to explain the persistent public resentment of these mothers, now fuelled by neoliberal rhetoric. Images of single welfare mothers planning and executing an unsupervised labour process flies in the face of social beliefs in the need for close and constant supervision of labourers. To acknowledge that this work is for the most part carried out reasonably well would be to suggest that even some of the economically worst off in society do not need managers or surveillance to function effectively. The persistent image of welfare mothers as lazy operates to counter this subversive idea, providing the rationale for additional rules, supervision, and coercion now being put in place.

The reward system for labour carried out by the full-time single mother is different from rewards for members of the paid labour force. Unlike assumptions buried in the work ethic, which suggest that financial rewards will increase in tandem with 'productivity', these mothers operate on an inverse equation: their labour increases as their income decreases. In opposition to assumptions of job choice embedded in labour market thinking, these women do not consider resigning regardless of the decreasing quality of life they report. Their personal rewards are on the emotional level:

- 'Emotionally I get very big satisfaction when my kid comes to me and says "Mom, I really love you".'
- '[S]ometimes when you do a lot of volunteer work within the community itself you get appreciation from other people and it makes you feel good.'
- 'I think I get a lot of personal strengthening. If I can do this, I could run the country.'

Socially acceptable rewards are class based, however. Through its emphasis on 'family values', the neoliberal agenda now promotes this emotional reward system for economically 'independent' mothers; that is, those who can afford to remain both out of the paid labour force and off public assistance during crucial child-rearing years. Popular discourse, supported by 'experts' in the field, insists that full-time parenting is a rewarding endeavour that produces healthier, happier children. However, social policy encourages mothers on assistance in an entirely different direction. For them, a pay cheque, however small and unpredictable, is promoted as the best reward.

Since caring for children is not cast as labour, it may be readily assumed that no particular skills are involved. Mothers in our focus groups, however, did not for the most part accept the notion that they are unskilled in relation to the norms of the paid labour force. This is important for, as Vellekoop-Baldock (1990) notes, both specialization and training mark and enhance the social and economic worth of paid labour. The idea of caring as unskilled is reinforced by various stereotypes of mothers as lazy, uneducated, and unwilling to work. In fact, women in our groups spontaneously mentioned 'roles' they take on as part of their caring labour, including the following: doctor, nurse, accountant, speech therapist, counsellor, cook, mediator, social worker, public speaker, therapist, and psychiatrist. Some women were adamant that their skills were no different from those of professionals paid to do the same work. One mother described her work as a 'speech therapist' for her son: 'Speech pathologist(s) make a lot of money. I'm . . . doing the exact same things as what they're doing and what they're telling me to do with my son; it's the same thing. I think that the work that single mothers do at home is the same as any professional out there working.' Another described how she approaches 'therapy' with her child when he is under stress: 'Once you get them past the anger and you start really going down deep into their feelings, you have to focus on them, you have to talk to them. It may take you ten minutes, it may take you hours . . . with my son . . . other kids pick on him about his weight. . . . If he went to a therapist or whatever, this hour session would cost something like $100.00.'

In addition, many of the women mentioned education, skill training, and experience in various kinds of paid employment, including child care, mediation, and recreation. Also striking were the kinds and extent of volunteer activities reported by all three groups of mothers, including advocacy work, public speaking on behalf of social and economic issues, planning and execution of needs assessment surveys, and program development and coordination. Similar to the findings reported in chapters 6 and 7, we found that volunteer activity was the source of considerable esteem-building for some women:

- 'When we did the park, I coordinated the whole child-care part. I had two assistants with me. I never thought I could pull it through. I couldn't believe that I did it. I said to myself: "Hey, I did this!"'
- 'Our complaint is how to get family reunification, support and help for [our] children. I took this matter to the newspapers. . . . I even met with [politicians].'

Caring Commodified

It is in the very nature of capitalism that new needs and thus new markets are continually created. Canadians are encouraged and taught that spending and purchasing spurs economic growth, based on the assumption that 'when a dollar changes hands, economic growth occurs' (Hawken 1997: 48). In capitalist economies, and no less in a globalizing world economy, it becomes almost a citizen's duty to purchase up-to-date goods and services. In fact, contemporary discourse suggesting economic growth as required for a healthy, vibrant country virtually equates the citizen with the consumer. Seldom are the social value and benefits of goods and services questioned in this discourse. Mothers, including single mothers, accept the idea that they should be 'proper' consumers on behalf of their children. Children themselves become advocates for new and trendy products and pressure their mothers to meet their 'need' to be like their peers. Mothers express the contradictory pressures on them to be proper consumers with the substantially reduced resources available to them: 'I'd love to go out and take my son to McDonalds, but I can't afford to. . . . It tears my heart out to tell that little boy, "No, mommy can't afford it".'

Because of intense social focus on mothers and motherhood, the caring of mothers for their children has special social meanings. Mothers who cannot care for their children adequately are often perceived as not caring about their children (Swift 1995). It is the labour of caring, in other words, that often comes to symbolize the quality of feeling a mother has for her children. For single mothers on assistance, this way of assessing affection is especially problematic because they have limited resources to provide for their children. In failing to meet socially recognized needs of their children, the levels of affection felt by these mothers comes into question, feeding stereotypes of the lazy, disinterested welfare mom. Children also adopt this way of thinking. Mothers in all three groups spoke about their anxieties and disappointments in not being able to provide materially for their children satisfactorily. One mother expressed her guilty feelings for leaving an abusive relationship, which had allowed her child to have some of the 'normal' possessions of a Canadian child: 'He had a Nintendo, he had two bikes. Because I couldn't live with the abuse anymore, I took my kid away from this and he doesn't have this anymore. If I stayed there and got beat up every day, my kid would still have everything.' This mother is caught in the painfully contradictory situation of choosing between materially supported violence and materially impoverished peace. 'I'd rather be at home with my children alone', another woman said, 'than to be a statistic buried in the cemetery', expressing the potential result of making the opposite decision. Another mother suggested that older children see clearly they will not have a good start in life. The social assistance cuts, she maintained, have created 'confrontation between the mother and the child'. This mother does not have the choice to buy more consumer goods, but, she implies, she would gladly become a better consumer if the opportunity were available. Low-income mothers in a capitalist society, in other words, are under constant pressure to view what neoliberals sometimes construe as 'desires' as normal needs of children growing up in a capitalist economy. It is the tension created by this contradiction that is intended to drive them off welfare and into the paid labour force.

Caring and the Public Domain

The stereotype of single moms on welfare is one of 'sitting at home and waiting for the cheque', an image well known to mothers in our groups and in fact articulated by several of them. The stereotype, of course, invokes the most 'dangerous' images of the private home, where women, if not scrutinized and organized, will fall into torpor and inactivity. This stereotype also evokes the private sphere as a place where nothing of importance occurs, and by implication invokes a contrasting image of the presumed productivity of public life. Work in the public sphere, it is suggested, is certainly not a site where anyone is sitting around and waiting for a cheque. Underlying this idea is an apparent justification for moving mothers off welfare and into the labour market: they are a social cost and a group that makes no social contribution. Since many single mothers do not want 'to work', welfare benefits should be stigmatized, and shaming practices are appropriate policy tools to help push them into the paid labour force.

However, the single mothers in our groups belie these images. For one thing, they are not sitting at home; rather, a constant flow between public and private spheres characterizes the lives of both the mothers and their children. Mothers conduct aspects of their caring labour in the world of commercial enterprise, as well as in government offices, schools and classrooms, community centres, and recreation sites:

- 'I take care of the medical appointments, meetings with the teachers, and also do the shopping.'
- 'We have to go to different stores for the savings, which takes longer.'
- 'I go to ESL [English as a second language] classes and my youngest goes to daycare there.'

Not only are these mothers performing labour with and on behalf of their children in the public sphere, they also spend money; participate in the exchange and distribution of goods; create networks and facilitate connections with other community members; provide direct and unpaid care for friends, relatives, and neighbours; build and sustain volunteer services, and provide and receive all kinds of services:

- 'I work for a group that sends people to camp. I go to the camp when it's my week; I was part of organizing this.'
- 'My sister calls and says "Can I drop off my two? They've got chicken pox."'
- 'We're trying to start this food basket program. . . . Right now we're going door to door to find out how many people in the area want to get involved in this.'

In short, they help to create and sustain the social and economic fabric. In addition, mothers perform valuable reproductive labour in socializing their children to become punctual, educated, and appropriate workers. The labour performed by these mothers, as by any other consumers, acts to stimulate the economy, helping to create and sustain employment in for-profit businesses as well as non-profit services.

Furthermore, transfer payments are not a one-way benefit. Rather, they are tools commonly used to affect the economy. Justifications for the National Child Benefit clearly demonstrate how this works: 'Because the new National Child Benefit is geared to income, more will go to families whose income is falling in bad economic times, and they will spend the income, helping the economy to recover. Conversely, when the economy improves, incomes should go up and child benefits to low-income families should in total decrease relative to the economy as a whole, thereby decreasing demand for goods and services and helping to cool off the economy' (Battle and Mendelson 1997:21). This rationale acknowledges that welfare recipients are not simply receivers of the public purse. In fact, low-income populations and the social programs they access for support are necessary economic tools that can be and are used to adjust economic trends in a globalizing economy.

Of course, as a number of studies have shown (Harris 1993; Hershey and Pavetti 1997), many mothers on welfare have been in the paid labour force, some many times, and many look forward to future paid jobs. A number of women in the first two groups fit this description, and several expressed strong desires to re-enter the paid workforce. Mothers in all groups indicated they would like the opportunity to 'work': 'I'd sooner have a full-time job than to stay home.' Some compared domestic labour quite unfavourably with paid labour, noting that the former offers no vacations, no breaks, and little recognition.

Labour force participation appears fraught with many barriers, however. One mother put herself in the position of an employer, demonstrating why a paid job is unlikely for her: 'If I'm an employer and I've got a single mother who's got two kids and I've got a woman [with no kids], who am I going to hire?' Another described her attempts to hold down a child-care job:

> Where I worked it was a before and after school day-care and I worked split-shift. I had to travel to two shifts. I was there from 7:30 to 9:00, go home, come back and be at work from 3:30 to 6:00 p.m. I would have to pay a sitter for six hours in order to work four. If I work til 6 and my child has to be picked up by six . . . I can't do it. It's not that I don't want to work; right now it's just not feasible.

Entry into the paid labour force, although expressed as desirable, is viewed as impossible by the Somali mothers in our sample. This is because of the amount of child-care responsibility they carry. These many barriers, some of which are particular to subgroups of this population, are well known to policy makers but frequently overlooked in policy proposals. In general, both discourse and policy seem better suited to devaluing the 'private' activity of caring for children, while failing to develop genuinely accessible choices and strategies for full and satisfying public participation by these women.

Caring and (Dis)Entitlement

The neoliberal agenda has eclipsed both the liberal vision and the feminist critique, and has brought moral judgement of women back to the forefront of debates about entitlement. This agenda is well served through invocation of the social meanings attached to 'welfare mothers'. Such an approach seems increasingly directed towards denial of full entitlement to those not engaged in the prescribed forms of 'work', a group that may be increasing in size and diversity. Taken to its logical extremes, full citizenship may soon be reserved for a relatively small number of people.

Women in all three groups clearly recognized the stigma attached to welfare, and were extremely concerned about the possibility of their children being shamed and marginalized as welfare recipients. Comparisons of discussions on the question of stigma suggest that Canadian women are well versed in the 'proper' amount of shame to be felt because they are on welfare. The Canadian women saw entitlement as based on both individual duty and formal Canadian citizenship. They described being treated differently at the bank and by private companies such as the telephone company. At times, their humiliations were quite public and hurtful. Canadian women in our groups had clearly internalized the stigma of being on welfare in a way their Somali counterparts had not. 'I hate it', said one. The group in rental housing in particular had a heightened awareness of and sensitivity to the issue of 'earning' entitlements. They felt that many groups, for example, immigrant women, were less entitled than they were, yet were getting more in benefits. One woman in our study expressed the feeling this way: 'It's so disrespected that you're a single parent at home. . . . People see me as one of the deadbeats out there who's on social assistance. . . . Well, I'm sorry. I'm degraded. I just try to hold up my head and walk straight and do my daily thing.'

The Somali women, in contrast, expressed a strong sense of entitlement, based on the fact that not just Somalis but other cultural groups in Canada receive welfare: 'I think we have the right to take it because not only Somalis are living in Canada. [People from] about seventy countries speaking seventy languages live here and take welfare.' One also expressed the idea of welfare as a fundamental human right: 'Everybody has the right to take welfare if not working. It is a humanitarian thing. You need something to eat and a safe place to live and the whole world knows [this].' Implicit in these statements, although not articulated, is the displacement of millions of people in the Third World created by processes of globalization and restructuring. Many people, particularly but not only refugees, now living in Western host countries such as Canada have been driven here by severe social and economic dislocations instigated or at least facilitated by the contemporary transnational corporate agenda. Women in our Somali focus group represent some of the consequences of these social processes. Their new social location as refugees places them in a position different from that occupied by the Canadian women. They are recognizable victims of formidable global processes; this being the case, it is appropriate that they receive assistance based on precepts of human rights. They are located, in other words, at a site of resistance unavailable to Canadians.

Exploited and Excluded—What Happens to Entitlement?

Processes of restructuring enter into and reorganize people's lives and their location in relation to the state and the market. At least three levels of these effects can be seen in this chapter. One level is the 'private' relationship between mothers and their children. In a restructuring capitalist society, mothers are pressured not only through advertising but by their own children to increase their consumption capacities. Failure to rise to this challenge can lead to shame, blame, loss of authority over children, and even loss of the children themselves. Second, subgroups of single mothers on assistance are positioned to compete with each other for scarce but needed resources such as subsidized housing. Their children are also positioned competitively in terms of citizenship and resources. Different groups of mothers struggle to feel sufficiently 'worthy' and energetic to claim legitimate resources.

Finally, and perhaps most conspicuously, the labour of poor single mothers is increasingly cast as valueless, even as the caring labour of middle-class mothers is encouraged and professionalized (Swift 1995). Current policy recommendations account for none of these effects. Typically, single mothers on assistance are spoken of as a heterogeneous group upon whom all policy proposals will have the same effects. Also typically, relationships between mothers on assistance and other women are not drawn. The evidence and analysis supports the need for research-based policy proposals that begin with and account for the variable experiences of women providing caring labour. Otherwise, policies can only be seen as expressions of neoliberal ideology designed to reposition women for further exploitation.

Demonstrated throughout the chapter are many contradictions embedded in current policies relevant to single mothers on welfare. Current neoliberal rhetoric about mothers 'not working' alternately ignores and devalues the caring labour actually done by these women on an all day, every day basis. This rhetoric also ignores the realities of the job market, in which women's employment is an uncertain element. Neoliberals would like to persuade mothers that with a paid job they could provide more and better material care for their children. Given the substantial barriers present for many mothers' entry into the paid labour force, together with the lack of adequate jobs and the absence of replacements to do the labour they currently perform at home, the policy of urging women to meet the needs of their families through paid labour makes little sense. Experience in other Western countries demonstrates that labour force participation does not help many single mothers stay out of poverty (Freiler and Cerny 1998). In Canada, many employed single mothers, like their counterparts on welfare, can expect to be poor, since they earn on average only 38 per cent of incomes that two-parent families earn (Hunsley 1996). Moreover, some American analysts are suggesting that 'workfare' policies could further erode wages for the poorest third of the population, which certainly includes many single mothers (Swanson 1998).

Attacks on welfare mothers serve the interests of ruling élites. Governments at both federal and provincial levels appear fiscally responsible when they demand that recipients become more 'self sufficient'. Governments also seem to be attending to restructuring and the requirements of the 'new economy' by promoting policies such as workfare and the new Child Benefit that permit some women to take advantage of short-term labour force opportunities without losing all welfare benefits. Some mothers will no doubt benefit from these policies and become 'good examples' of the new independence being encouraged. As our discussions with a variety of mothers demonstrate, however, many other welfare mothers are in no position to 'move from welfare to work'. The position of single mothers in the paid labour force appears to be changing in the current economic context of restructuring and job loss, although the directions are unclear at present. Some single mothers may be, as Lindsey (1994) has suggested, no longer exploited but actually excluded from the developing economy—many of them may become a reserve pool of labour in an era that no longer requires reserves. On the other hand, some single mothers living on substantially reduced assistance or forced off assistance altogether may be candidates for the new and apparently growing 'service industry' of McJobs offering low-wage, part-time, and insecure work. Others continue trying to make ends meet on scant social assistance payments. All of these mothers continue to do caring labour, which remains largely invisible, which is not viewed as 'productive' labour, and which seems to be connected to reduced or threatened entitlements.

The idea of welfare is itself in a contradictory state. It is payment for labour rendered in current 'workfare' terms, but an entitlement in terms of the old welfare state. Furthermore, there are contradictions between need as mere survival for public purposes and need for economic purposes to afford the continual flow of 'necessary' new products and services. This contradiction presents substantial labour for low-income mothers as they attempt to mediate socially produced consumption needs with a public view of need as mere survival. In today's social and economic climate, the pressure is on single mothers on assistance to see themselves as unproductive in the home. Other women, focusing on the myths of welfare laziness, may not see that their own behaviour is also increasingly subject to scrutiny and control.

It is clear we cannot count on a return to the welfare state as it was before the 1990s. In fact, feminist and other critiques of the welfare state remind us of its flaws and the inequities built into it for marginalized groups. The directions of neoliberalism hold even less promise for the most oppressed and vulnerable populations. Recent proposals for new relationships among economic, public, and civil spheres point in the direction of validating and valorizing work in the 'third' or voluntary sector (Rifkin 1995). Findings from our study point to recommendations that are similar in a number of ways to recommendations in emerging third sector discourse: recognition and visibility of a wide range of human needs; visibility and valuing of caring labour in all its painful, rewarding, and complex forms; entitlements for mothers as for other citizens. However, it is absolutely critical to distinguish this direction from apparently similar proposals based on propping up capitalism and facilitating globalizing trends. Instead, we suggest genuine valuing of caring labour as one element needed to build a completely different kind of society.

Our chapter points to the importance of social locations in the shifting terrain of restructuring and globalization. Neoliberal and even more centrist discourse attempts to locate mothers on assistance as a central cause of contemporary social and economic problems. Through this mechanism, the variable experiences, contributions, and problems of these women are effectively hidden. The category itself is thus flawed: it does not explain experience as it purports to do, but rather operates ideologically in support of corporate agendas. It will be crucial for feminists in both the immediate and long-term future that more accurate and complete accounts of women's experience, from actual social locations of gender, race, and class, be explicated and communicated. At present many women are experiencing both the effects of restructuring and their own resistance to it. Also important for feminists, then, will be to facilitate understanding among women of the possibilities of resistance, challenge, and change available to us, possibilities that may vary by social location but that have common aims of valuing and supporting caring labour and human need.

Note

1 Portions of this chapter first appeared in K. Swift and M. Birmingham, 'Caring in a Globalizing Economy: Single Mothers on Assistance', in D. Durst, ed., *Canada's National Child Benefit: Phoenix or Fizzle?* (Halifax: Fernwood, 1999):84–102.

References

Abel, E., and M. Nelson. 1990. 'Circles of Care: An Introductory Essay'. In *Circles of Care: Work and Identity in Women's Lives*, edited by E.K. Abel and M.D. Nelson, 4–34. Albany: State University of New York Press.

Armstrong, P. 1996. 'The Feminization of the Labour Force: Harmonizing Down in a Global Economy'. In *Rethinking Restructuring*, edited by I. Bakker, 29–54. Toronto: University of Toronto Press.

Baines, C., P. Evans, and S. Neysmith. 1991. *Women's Caring: A Feminist Perspective on Social Welfare*. Toronto: McClelland & Stewart.

_____, P. Evans, and S. Neysmith. 1998. *Women's Caring: A Feminist Perspective on Social Welfare*, 2nd edn. Toronto: Oxford University Press.

Bakker, I., ed. 1996. *Rethinking Restructuring*. Toronto: University of Toronto Press.

Battle, K., and M. Mendelson. 1997. 'Child Benefit Reform in Canada: An Evaluative Framework and Future Directions'. Ottawa: Caledon Institute of Social Policy.

Caledon Institute of Social Policy. 1997. 'The Down Payment Budget'. Ottawa: Renouf Publishing Company.

Clark, I. 1997. *Globalization and Fragmentation: International Relations in the Twentieth Century*. New York: Oxford University Press.

Conway, J. 1997. *The Canadian Family in Crisis*, 3rd edn. Toronto: James Lorimer & Company.

Davis, L., and J. Hagen. 1996.'Stereotypes and Stigma: What's Changed for Welfare Mothers'. *Affilia* 11, no. 3:319–37.

Doyal, L., and I. Gough. 1991. *A Theory of Need*. London: Macmillan.

Duncan, S., and R. Edwards. 1996. 'Lone Mothers and Paid Work: Neighborhoods, Local Labor Markets, and Welfare State Regimes'. *Social Politics* 3, no. 43:195–222.

Ellwood, D.T. 1988. *Poor Support*. New York: Basic Books.

Fisher, B., and J. Tronto. 1990. 'Toward a Feminist Theory of Caring'. In *Circles of Care: Work and Identity in Women's Lives*, edited by E.K. Abel and M.D. Nelson, 35–62. Albany: State University of New York Press.

Fraser, N. 1989. *Unruly Practices: Power, Discourse and Gender in Contemporary Social Theory*. Minneapolis: University of Minnesota Press.

Freiler, C., and J. Cerny. 1998. *Benefiting Canada's Children: Perspectives on Gender and Social Responsibility*. Ottawa: Status of Women Canada.

Griffith, A., and D. Smith. 1987. 'Constructing Cultural Knowledge: Mothering as Discourse'. In *Women and Education*, edited by J. Gaskel and A. McLaren, 87–103. Calgary: Detselig Enterprises.

Gingrich, N. 1995. *To Renew America*. New York: HarperCollins.

Harris, K. 1993. 'Work and Welfare Among Single Mothers in Poverty'. *American Journal of Sociology* 99, no. 2:317–52.

Hawken, P. 1997. 'Natural Capitalism'. *Mother Jones* (April):40-53, 59–62.

Heller, A. 1976. *The Theory of Need in Marx*. New York: St Martin's Press.

Hershey, A., and L. Pavetti. 1997. 'Turning Job Finders into Job Keepers'. *Future of Children* 7, no. 1:74–86.

Hunsley, T. 1996. *Incomes and Outcomes: Lone Parents and Social Policy in Ten Countries*. Kingston: Queen's University School of Policy Studies.

Ignatieff, M. 1984. *The Needs of Strangers*. London: The Hogarth Press.

Kitchen, B., and R. Popham. 1998. 'The Attack on Motherwork in Ontario'. In *Confronting the Cuts*, edited by L. Ricciutelli, J. Larkin, and E. O'Neill, 45–56. Toronto: Inanna Publications.

Korten, D. 1995. *When Corporations Rule the World*. West Hartford: Kumarian Press.

Lindsey, D. 1994. *The Welfare of Children*. New York: Oxford University Press.

National Council of Welfare. 1998. *Poverty Profile 1996*. Ottawa: National Council of Welfare.

O'Neill, E. 1998. 'From Global Economies to Local Cuts: Globalization and Structural Change in Our Own Backyard'. In *Confronting the Cuts*, edited by L. Ricciutelli, J. Larkin, and E. O'Neill, 3–11. Toronto: Inanna Publications.

Ozawa, M. 1994. *Women, Children, and Welfare Reform*. *Affilia* 9, no. 4:338–59.

Pascal, G. 1993. 'Citizenship: A Feminist Analysis'. In *Welfare Theory*, edited by G. Drover and P. Kerans, 113–26. Aldershot: Edward Elgar Publishing.

Popkin, S. 1990. 'Welfare: Views from the Bottom'. *Social Problems* 37:64–79.

Rank, M.R. 1994. *Living on the Edge: The Realities of Welfare in America*. New York: Columbia University Press.

Rifkin, J. 1995. *The End of Work*. New York: Putnam.

Schragge, E. 1997. 'Workfare: An Overview'. In *Workfare: Ideology for a New Under-Class*, edited by E. Schragge, 17–34. Toronto: Garamond Press.

Scott, J. 1992. 'Experience'. In *Feminists Theorize the Political*, edited by J. Butler and J. Scott, 22–40. New York: Routledge.

Shields, J., and B. Evans. 1998. *Shrinking the State*. Halifax: Fernwood.

Statistics Canada. 1997. *Canadian Economic Observer* (January). Catalogue no. 11-010-XPB. Ottawa: Statistics Canada.

Swanson, J. 1998. 'Child Poverty Focus Brings Policies That Push Down Wages'. *NAPO News* no. 64:2–3.

Swift, K. 1995. *Manufacturing 'Bad Mothers': A Critical Perspective on Child Neglect*. Toronto: University of Toronto Press.

_____, and M. Birmingham. 1999. 'Caring in a Globalizing Economy: Single Mothers on Assistance'. In *Canada's National Child Benefit: Phoenix or Fizzle?*, edited by D. Durst, 84–112. Halifax: Fernwood.

Thompson, G. 1987. *Needs*. London: Routledge and Kegan Paul.

United Nations Development Programme. 1998. *Human Development Report*. New York: Oxford University Press.

Vellekoop-Baldock, C. 1990. 'Volunteerism and the Caring Role of Women'. In *Volunteers in Welfare*, edited by C. Vellekoop-Baldock, 118–33. Sydney: Allen and Unwin.

Part 2

Of Time, Work, and Voluntary Action

Chapter 6

Volunteerism, Gender, and the Changing Welfare State: A Case-study in Child Daycare

Susan Prentice and Evelyn Ferguson

Understanding parent volunteerism in child daycare centres requires the untangling of a complex knot of issues, both contemporary and historical.[1] These issues include individual parent choice, local centre policy and practice, provincial regulations, the norms of the early childhood profession, as well as past and current public policy environments.

Although parent involvement has long been a feature of child-care provision in Canada, it has assumed increasing importance in recent years as the Canadian welfare state has undergone deficit-driven restructuring. As the interventionist and redistributive welfare state is restructured, public and political discourse has emphasized a renewed promotion of philanthropy, volunteering, and self-help. Neoconservatives advocate the downsizing or full elimination of state provision of social welfare, hailing what they see as the moral superiority and less costly nature of volunteer activity; welfare pluralists applaud decentralization; and progressives promote the benefits of participation and direct democracy presumed to flow from services delivered by the voluntary sector (Browne 1985; Rekart 1993). Meanwhile, the norms of the early childhood profession continue to encourage its members to 'work with' parents, often in a project of skill transfer. As public funding is withdrawn, parents experience increased pressure to assist their centres, largely to maintain or enhance the quality of care their children receive. At a personal level, many parents—usually mothers—are motivated to participate in their children's centres for reasons that vary by gender, class, ethnicity, and other forms of social stratification. Throughout all of these changes, the distinction between 'public' and 'private' fades, drawing our attention to what some have called the 'blurring of boundaries' between the state and other spheres of life (Little 1995).

As a study about child care and volunteerism, this chapter is necessarily a study about women and gender relations. Child care is one of the most 'feminized' social services. Licensed child-care service is provided as a substitute for full-time, home-based care, overwhelmingly in order to facilitate maternal employment (Ferguson 1989, 1991). Most child-care providers are women, and child care is publicly identified as a 'women's issue', debated through a discourse of women's rights and responsibilities. Finally, many or most volunteers in child-care centres, whether on boards of directors or as helpers in daily care, are women.[2]

Caring is central to most women's lives. The imperatives of caring shape women's opportunities, having significant costs and consequences for women (Baines, Evans, and Neysmith 1998). This social fact is rarely recognized in mainstream discussion or delivery of welfare services. Instead, a purportedly neutral (but really masculine) conception of citizenship is built into the welfare state. It is this aspect of citizenship 'under the guise of gender neutrality' that poses the real problem for the exercise of civil, political, and social citizenship rights for women, especially the majority of women with care-giving responsibilities (O'Connor 1996). In many arenas, feminists and social critics have pointed out these contradictions to elaborate the negative meaning they have for women and others. Julia O'Connor points out that feminist debates on the welfare state are increasingly focusing on care-giving work and its allocation between state, market, and family, women and men (O'Connor 1996). Yet the literature on parent involvement in the child-care field has remained remarkably insulated from this challenge.

Our chapter begins to remedy this gap. Through a case-study of mothers' participation in Winnipeg daycare centres, we highlight the continuity that child care shares with other social services, as well as emphasizing its distinctiveness. In this chapter we examine one aspect of volunteerism in child care: how and why mothers volunteer in the delivery and administration of child care at the individual centre. We find that volunteering is a contradictory experience for mothers: a 'labour of love', but also a discharging of duty, both overt and covert, shaped by the institution of motherhood and the motherhood mandate. Volunteering is also classed: affluent and low-income mothers have different and unequal experiences of volunteering.

Our findings push us to ask when and under what conditions is volunteer labour a freely chosen and empowering act, and when is it an intensification of social inequality? We use the findings from our study of mothers' involvement to consider larger issues surrounding volunteerism in the changing welfare state. Our research highlights the reliance upon and pervasiveness of gender and class relations in welfare state restructuring.

Volunteerism and the Welfare State

That Canada's welfare state is characterized by a mixed economy is a well-known and long-standing feature of social welfare in this country (Valverde

1995).[3] Since well before Confederation, benevolent and charitable associations delivered services. Even with the postwar establishment of statutory services, philanthropic good works continued. Historical analysis increasingly reveals significant continuities between the policies and practices of welfare administration and service delivery before and after the emergence of the postwar welfare state. Mariana Valverde points to the many services, administrative practices, and political philosophies that link prewelfare state services to today's postwelfare state (Valverde 1995:36). In particular, she highlights the crucial and continuing involvement of charities and volunteers (Valverde 1995:37). Others have pointed to the pervasive, although rarely acknowledged, influence that government has always had on the activities of the volunteer sector; especially the collaborative role of the state in funding and regulating services nominally delivered by the voluntary sector. In Canada today, for example, well over half (58 per cent) of the budgets of registered charities are supplied by government grants, and most service-delivering agencies participate in a complicated partnership with the state through purchase of service agreements and regulations, a partnership that considerably complicates our idea of an arms-length non-governmental sector.

The image of volunteerism is largely shaped by notions of 'do-gooders', and the *nobless oblige* of the socially privileged élite, particularly its women (Browne 1985:10; Rekart 1993:148). Historically, working-class, ethnocultural, and other marginalized communities played (and continue to play) an active role in self-help and community development. In sharp contrast with the 'discharging of duties of rank, station and wealth' that often legitimated the charitable work of the prosperous, working men and women formed trade unions, mutual-assistance groups, friendly societies, and cooperative associations to provide material aid such as sickness, funeral, and death benefits, as well as programs for education and moral advancement such as libraries, schools, and adult education.[4] Chapters 7 and 8 in this volume demonstrate that the two traditions of volunteerism—the community development, self-help approach, as well as traditional charitable/philanthropic work—have continued to the present day.

Yet curiously, the non-profit sector as a whole has scarcely been studied in Canada, although some research has analysed how certain sectors of non-governmental social services are linked to the state. Minimal attention has been paid to the gendered nature of volunteerism in Canada, particularly as it intersects with class (Browne 1985:10). What little is known empirically about volunteerism nationally is largely derived from Statistics Canada's 1987 Survey of Volunteer Activity.[5] It estimated that 5.38 million Canadians performed formal volunteer work over the twelve-month period in 1986–7, and millions more undertook informal volunteer work (Vaillancourt 1994).[6] Formal volunteering for organizations totalled over 1 billion hours, at an average of 191 hours per volunteer (Day and Devlin 1996:x,

1–2; Duschesne 1989:60). If the 3.7 hours per week that the average formal volunteer freely gave were remunerated at the average service sector wage, the volunteer labour would have been valued at $12 billion in 1987, or 2 per cent of the GDP. Out-of-pocket expenses paid by volunteers during the same period totalled $841 million, or an average of $158 per volunteer, the equivalent of 38 per cent of all charitable donations in 1987.[7] The national study revealed that the participation rates of volunteers rises with education (especially of women) and household income (Day and Devlin 1996:x). Men with full-time employment volunteer more hours than men working part-time; for women, the reverse is true. Despite these differences, the overall participation rate for women as volunteers is higher than that of men. Francois Vaillancourt concludes decisively that 'men participate less in volunteer work than women (Vaillancourt 1994).'

Why do people volunteer? Despite the neoconservative insistence that volunteer activity is a ramp to labour force participation, volunteers themselves indicated that enhancing employability was generally 'not at all important' to them. According to the Statistics Canada 1987 Survey of Volunteer Activity, participants far more commonly explained their involvement as being important to them, as helping others, assisting a cause they believed in, doing something they liked to do, and feeling they had accomplished something. For nine out of ten volunteers, each of these reasons was at least 'somewhat important (Duschesne 1989:32).'

Some commentators have labelled the physical, emotional, intellectual, and social recharging that volunteers experience as a 'helper's high'. They argue that people volunteer because they feel it benefits society, because they wish to 'express gratitude to others by doing so, because it helps them to integrate into the community, because it is a way of meeting people and developing relationships' (Duschesne 1989:32). In sum, most volunteers define volunteering as helping, giving, and being with others. Only one in ten volunteers reports a sense of obligation or duty as motivation for contributing.

In the context of the fiscal crisis of the welfare state, volunteerism has assumed increased importance (Duschesne 1989:33; O'Connor 1973). Volunteerism is often presented positively as one solution to spiralling costs and bureaucratic unresponsiveness. Social welfare pluralists have made this argument extensively. Simultaneously, social movement participants, welfare professionals, and the social welfare community have advocated a role for volunteers and client-controlled social services. Volunteerism is particularly important for women since women make up a majority of unpaid volunteers and often find themselves making private arrangements to cope with the loss or erosion of public services (Ferguson 1998; Rekart 1993). The crucial role women play in supporting social welfare becomes even more apparent when we closely examine the kinds of volunteer work women tend to undertake in contrast to men. Women's volunteer activity tends to mirror traditionally 'feminine' caring work, whereas men's volunteer activity tends to replicate traditional masculine power. According to the 1987 national survey, 77 per cent of volunteers in health, 65 per cent of volunteers in education and youth development, and 66 per cent of volunteers in social services are women (Dacks, Green, and Trimble 1995). An additional 7 million women, comprising some two-thirds of the adult female population, volunteer on an informal basis (Duschesne 1989:Table 14). In this work, women are very likely to help relatives and children (Duschesne 1989:Table 14). This phenomenon is not unique to Canada: crossnational evidence demonstrates that women are overrepresented in both informal and formal care networks (O'Connor 1996:17).

Volunteerism is applauded from all sides of the political spectrum. Right-wing support for restructuring the welfare state is 'virtually indistinguishable' from support from the left, according to Josephine Rekart: both advocate a larger role for the voluntary sector, the importance of pluralism, self-help, and mutual aid (Rekart 1993:xi). She points out that although quite different philosophies underlie this apparent consensus, the overlap suggests that a return to greater reliance on the voluntary sector for social service delivery has wide political appeal (Rekart 1993:xii). Within the feminist literature on women and caring, some have argued that volunteering—as an exercise in citizenship and solidarity—is a tool for the empowerment of women. Conversely, other feminists have argued that volunteerism works against women's social empowerment by exploiting their unpaid labour, and that demands for volunteer work are yet another burden in a double- or triple-shift day. These observations converge to raise important theoretical and practical questions about the restructuring of the social welfare state.

Child Care and the Changing Liberal Welfare State

Child care provides an ideal case-study in which to examine the contradictions of volunteerism, gender, and the state. Child care is an essential precondition for the labour force participation of mothers and hence women's economic security and independence. A crucial aspect of strengthening women's position in society involves strengthening women's economic security and promoting their financial independence. Child care is directly linked to changing women's current inability to participate fully in Canadian social and economic life.

Throughout the 1970s and 1980s, federal and provincial governments were pressured by women's groups to address the profound social and economic disadvantages faced by women. Governments responded with task forces, public consultations, and the creation of status of women offices. Although many of these measures were largely symbolic or bureaucratic, issues such as violence against women and the feminization of poverty nevertheless began to be debated as matters of public policy. Government responses to women's demands included direct provision of, funding for, or regulation of services traditionally provided by women in the unpaid sphere of domestic work, such as child care, nursing homes for the elderly, and home care for the sick. Such services have helped women move into the paid labour force, thanks to the provision of public services, and often in their direct employ. Feminists across Canada have claimed such services as a necessary foundation for women's full social, political, and economic equality.

Among needed services, child care has often assumed a critical place. Judge Rosie Abella, head of the Royal Commission on Equality in Employment, gave it a prime role, declaring that 'childcare is the ramp that provides equal access to the workforce for mothers' (Abella 1984:178). In the decade since Abella declared child care an essential ramp, the federal government has cut back its spending on child-care services. Federal child-care service funding fell by 33.5 per cent from 1993–8, an enormous reduction in an underfunded system. The federal government's withdrawal has gone beyond spending cuts. With the replacement of the Canada Assistance Plan by the Canada Health and Social Transfer (CHST), the grounds for federal involvement in child care have virtually been eliminated. Sandra Bach and Susan Phillips argue that child care is the 'first fatality' in efforts to construct what has been called a new social union (Bach and Phillips 1997:236). This new social union is characterized by a shift from public to private service provision, from direct state funding of services to reliance on the tax system, and from moderate federal involvement alongside the more visible primacy of provinces. Across Canada, this move has exacerbated long-standing variation in access, the degree of public funding, quality, and the supply and type of child-care services. As a result, parents confront even more widely varying options, unequal accessibility, uneven quality, and lack of uniform standards. As different provinces react to the withdrawal of federal funds, inequity across the country grows.

Under the new CHST, it will be much more difficult for the federal government and the provinces to both finance and agree upon a new shared-cost program such as child care. Any new shared-cost program must win the consent of a majority of the provinces—an increasingly unlikely prospect as the different jurisdictions adjust to the shock of massive cuts to transfer payments. As Prime Minister Chrétien has acknowledged, the changes introduced by the CHST mark 'the first time any Federal government has undertaken formally to restrict its use of the spending power outside a constitutional negotiation' (Bach and Phillips 1997:245). In effect, through increased reliance on regressive and indirect tax-based spending, responsibility has devolved not merely from federal to provincial governments but from the public to parents as private consumers. In this context, fragile child-care services will be even more threatened.

Canada's fragile child-care 'system' is comprised of a collection of privately delivered services, the vast majority of which are delivered in the unlicensed informal sector. Canada's licensed and regulated child-care services are provided by the private market, primarily through the voluntary and commercial sectors. Only the governments of Ontario and Quebec directly operate service: a total of less than 5 per cent of the nation's licensed spaces (Childcare Resource and Research Unit 1997). Aside from this exception, the role of provincial/territorial governments is strictly limited to regulating and inspecting licensed services (ascertaining that standards for child/staff ratios, group size, physical and safety requirements, and staff training, among others, are met).

Public financing of child care is restricted to federal tax assistance measures, some narrowly targeted welfare-oriented fee subsidies, and a dwindling program of provincial grants, including start-up, capital, and other special operating supports. At their own discretion, child-care centres may accept and enrol children who meet the restrictive criteria for fee subsidy. A very small number of daycare centres (mainly commercial centres) receive no public grants and enrol no subsidized children. In most centres, however, public funding of child care means that nominally independent daycare centres are part of the broader public sector. Child care is therefore a quintessential example of a service that blurs the boundaries between the formally private and the formally public sector.

Child-care delivery also blurs the boundaries. In some provinces, statutory regulations compel parents to volunteer in their daycare centres. In Manitoba, for example, all non-profit centres (comprising 90 per cent of the province's licensed spaces) must have a board of directors on which parents must hold a minimum of 20 per cent of the seats and on which staff cannot hold more than 20 per cent of the seats. Other provinces have some requirements for parental involvement. Parental involvement is widely presumed to improve the quality of services offered to children, although the exact mechanism for this is rarely explained. Whatever effect parent involvement may or may not have on the quality of care, it is certainly true that parent involvement requirements are a disincentive to commercial daycare operators, who are generally unwilling to concede input to parents. Provinces with strong requirements for parent volunteerism, therefore, tend to have a smaller supply of commercial daycare than provinces, which are silent on this aspect of delivery (Ferguson and Prentice 1999). Despite the many benefits of limiting the free-enterprise sector, child care is one of the few social services in which client participation is made mandatory by provincial regulations. Although client involvement may be encouraged or desired in fields such as mental health, elder care and health, the insistence that (some) parents must volunteer in child care is inextricably linked to the long Western history of seeing the parent/child relationship as one of private property in which parents must assume responsibility.

As a consequence of the view that children are their parents' full responsibility, child care in Canada has developed as a private service in the private market. Extremely restricted public funds may be directed to parents as private consumers; provinces have full discretion over if and what kinds of formal child-care services they will license and/or fund. The vast majority of child-care centres therefore operate independently; they are administered and staffed as nominally stand-alone services. Within each centre, individual parents may or may not choose to volunteer.

In most of Canada's 4,000 licensed child-care centres, as well as in an additional unknown number of unregulated facilities, parents volunteer to support their children's out-of-home care (Ferguson and Prentice 1999). Parent participation varies enormously—in some centres, parent boards of directors meet biweekly to exercise their full authority over financial, administrative, and policy issues; in other centres, 'parent advisory' meetings may be called less than once a year. Parents may accompany field trips, undertake fundraising campaigns, or organize potlucks and social events. Some parents help out in the daily program of care. In non-profit parent-run cooperatives, parent volunteerism is a formal expectation; in other settings, such as commercial centres, parent control may be discouraged even if parent volunteer hours or cash are welcomed.

Volunteerism in Child Care: Observations from a Winnipeg Case-study

Do the summary generalizations about volunteerism hold true for participation in the child-care sector? Do mothers volunteer in order to help, give, and be with others as part of the helper's high? While we see some manifestations of these motivations in our data, we also find there are significant differences between involvement in daycare centres and other benevolent activities.

The essence of this difference, we argue, stems from two related sources. The first is the 'institution of motherhood' underpinning a service that is designed to replace the care of children traditionally provided by mothers at home. Related to this, we find that mothers' volunteerism in child care is a manifestation of caring labour: 'the mental, emotional and physical effort involved in looking after, responding to, and supporting others' (Ferguson and Prentice 1999:11). This kind of volunteer work, which blends both instrumental and affective labour, is particularistic, done in the context of individual relationships between parents (usually mothers), children, staff/teachers, and other parents. Thus, child care is an especially complex site of service and a contradictory experience for mothers.

We made these discoveries in the course of a study of how and why mothers participate in their child-care centres.[8] Through our study of Winnipeg mothers using licensed preschool child care, we found that mothers volunteer in order to make their child-care centres 'caring places' for their children. 'Making the centre a caring place' involves both practical and emotional labour. Mothers' labour and emotional work are directed towards ensuring that their child-care centres are comfortable and interesting, characterized by warmth, security, personal attention, and a minimum of conflict. Mothers' commitment to making the child-care centre a caring place is more than a simple personal choice, since it has deep roots in those social expectations known as 'the motherhood mandate' (Russo 1979). The motherhood mandate, that potent combination of personal and social conviction that mothers above all else are responsible for their children, shapes how and why mothers volunteer in their child-care centres.

The Motherhood Mandate

We believe it is impossible to understand how and why mothers voluntarily participate in their child-care centres without appreciating how motherhood influences women's lives. In her pioneering work, Adrienne Rich has shown that motherhood is both a personal experience and a social institution (Rich 1976). As a result, a woman's identity as a mother is simultaneously subjective and individual, yet created through social expectations and normative standards. When motherhood is grasped this way, it becomes easier to see that women's involvement in activities that affect their children, such as participation in a child-care centre, cannot be separated from the doubled reality of motherhood.

When mothers offer their unpaid labour as volunteers in their child-care centres, they experience contradiction. As volunteers, they negotiate their relationship to organizational expectations, which may include fundraising, board membership, attendance at social gatherings, and/or help in the daily care of children. Women with young children, however, are not just volunteers playing a role that they are free to accept or reject. Women with young children are shaped by the ideology of intensive mothering and the many expectations associated with the institution of motherhood (Hays 1996).

The 'motherhood mandate' manifests itself in a number of different ways. Seventy-one per cent of our sample of mothers reported that their child-care centre was the most important organization with which they were involved, while another 22 per cent said it was somewhat important. When asked why it was so important, mothers' responses were particularly revealing. Women spoke repeatedly about the importance of their children in their lives and its logical consequence: the daycare centre could not be other than critically important. Four different voices make this clear:

- 'The kids are my world; the kids come first. If I can do something to make them happier or better, then in any way that's what I want to be doing.'
- 'The daycare is essential to our well-being. Other groups would be optional, things I do more for my entertainment.'

- 'My kids come before my community and before myself.'
- 'My child takes priority more than something I would do for myself.'

Much of the child development literature has traditionally assumed that the 'mother at home' model of child care is superior to other settings (Maynard 1985; White 1985). This message is difficult and painful for many mothers who must work to support their families. For those women who want to work, such expert opinion may raise fears that they are providing inadequate care for their children. Whether out of fear, for ideological reasons, or from personal desire, many mothers we interviewed expressed a strong wish to spend more time with their children. One mother reported that 'I wish I could be there every day, but I can't.' Another mother explained that 'because I work, I can't offer any help for any of that. It's really hard. . . .'

From this perspective, we can begin to understand the apparently contradictory comments and feelings expressed by mothers when interviewed about parent involvement or volunteerism in their child-care centre. At all times, for whatever volunteer capacity they are discussing, whether stated or not, women presuppose their responsibilities because they are mothers. At times they state this clearly and poignantly, and at other times the message is more subtle and implied. Often mothers' comments are strongly influenced by their feelings that they 'should' be involved in one capacity or another. Mothers regularly express feelings of guilt, regret, and longing when they are unable to meet expectations.

The Priority of Child Care

Researchers claim that only about one in ten volunteers in Canada report that they volunteer in order to have an influence in community affairs or political life.[9] However, over two-thirds of volunteers report that they want to do work that benefits their own children, family, or self. Although we may question these dichotomies of public and private, political and personal, these findings orient us towards some important differences in the motivations volunteers bring to their tasks. The mothers we interviewed generally expressed the desire to enhance their children's or family's lives.

The motherhood mandate is manifested in how mothers express a desire for greater involvement in their child-care centre. While two-thirds of the mothers we interviewed report that they are satisfied with their level of involvement in the daycare centre, most say greater involvement would make them happier. Over one-half said that they would be more satisfied if they had more time for the centre. Not one of the mothers we interviewed said she wanted to do less for her centre, and a great many expressed the wish to do more.

Even mothers who are very active volunteers (such as board members) report that they wish they could do more for the centre. For example, the chairperson of one board of directors, a single mother, explains how she always searches for ways to spend more time at the centre: 'I think I've been able so far to be as involved as my time will allow, it's flexible that way. There's always something that can be done at the centre, so when I have a bit more free time, then I can offer that time to the centre.'

Mothers see involvement with the centre as a means to remain connected to their children during their absence, reporting that they feel better and are more satisfied with the centre when they are making a contribution of time and energy. In addition to sitting on the board of directors, they attend meetings, volunteer for fundraising activities, give feedback to daycare workers, write and distribute newsletters, organize and attend social events (such as family nights, plays, and parties), volunteer to assist staff on field trips, help out with daily care, donate special skills, and more. Sometimes there is a formal expectation, such as with a parent cooperative, which requires a minimum number of hours per month of parental involvement; outside of cooperatives, involvement is a personal and individual decision.

Parent Volunteerism as an Antidote to Professionalism

The tension between professionalism and parental input has long been documented in the child care and early childhood education literature (Mayfield 1990; Shimoni and Ferguson 1992). The professional version of 'parent education' (which has been defined as professionals educating parents about child development, child behaviour techniques, and communication patterns, etc.) assumes a professional expertise that has not always been welcomed by parents (Galinsky 1987). Working with parents of children in daycare is a widely accepted and seldom disputed element of the early childhood educator's job; in fact, a mandate to 'bring about collaboration between home and school' is featured in the Code of Ethics of the National Association for the Education of Young Children (Shimoni and Ferguson 1992:105).

Child care has an ambiguous identity: it is alternately positioned as 'education' (and hence affiliated with universal entitlement) and 'custodial care' (and hence linked to a residual model of service for the deserving). In particular, in this respect, child care has been identified as a rich opportunity for 'parent education'—a broad cluster of approaches, united by professionals' efforts to upgrade the child-care practices of parents in the home (Schlossman 1976:437). In this paradigm, child-care staff are positioned as early childhood educators: they are professionals and experts by way of training and experience. In this scenario, the early childhood education field argues that it has an obligation to act on professional knowledge in work with parents. Whether to ensure the continuity of care or to improve parenting practices, this model of care positions staff as the experts and parents (not just their children) as the clients. As the experts, professionals have greater power than the parents themselves in defining how and when parents should volunteer. For example, our findings indicate that a high percentage of parental and board member time goes towards fundraising; many parents indicate this is the most burdensome volunteer activity.

Many parents resist moves to professionalize child care. The continued popularity of informal and home-based child care may be parental preference for what is perceived as a more nurturing and homelike environment.[10] On the whole, the mothers we interviewed expressed respect for the staff in their centres. However, as their comments demonstrate, mothers also see parental input as a way of compensating for the perceived drawbacks associated with professional expertise.

One of the most commonly expressed reasons for involvement was the parent's desire to balance or complement the professionalism that mothers saw dominating their centres. When arguing for parental input in the hiring of a director, one mother stated: 'All the education in the world doesn't make you qualified. A lot of people can go on their gut instinct too. . . .' Another argued that it was important for parents to have the majority of seats on the board: 'Yes, definitely. I don't see any point in having a bunch of people that know nothing about, well that's not very nice to say, but do you know what I mean, a bunch of people with a paper education background. . . .' Still another stated: 'Sometimes I think they need more of an outside opinion on what . . . you think we need to do, just to get some suggestions. . . .' When asked whether parents needed to know anything in particular in order to be an effective board member, a number of mothers argued that no special background was necessary. In the words of one mother, 'You don't need anything special, you just need to have a willingness to sit there and listen and be able to participate in whatever's needed and have some opinions.' According to another, 'with parents involved, it doesn't get too bureaucratic'.

'A More Caring Place'

We conclude that mothers participate in large part to 'make the centre a more caring place', less 'institutional' and more like a home. Some of the earliest criticisms of group daycare postulated that children were damaged in institutional settings (Bowlby 1951). While much of this wartime research conflated orphanages with daycare centres, it has created a public perception that daycare is simply the 'warehousing' of children in an impersonal institutional environment (Maynard 1985; Riley 1983; White 1985). Less ideologically conservative research demonstrates that size, setting, and culture of each environment determines the experience of children who use the centre. Nevertheless, the image of cold, impersonal institutions exists in both conservative and left-wing form. For example, the progressive cooperative daycare movement of the late 1970s strongly resisted the domination of professionals (New and David 1985).

As a way of making the centre more caring and attentive to individual children, many mothers report that they want to participate in the daily care of the children. For instance, when asked about doing volunteer jobs, one mother stated: 'If we can help out in any way we can for the daycare, why not? I mean, our children have to live in that environment while we're at work. And to make it more cheerful. A cheerful daycare centre. . . .' Another mother commented: 'And anyone should chip in to make it a better place. After all, your child is there most of the time, and it would be like their second home.' About a quarter of the mothers we sampled said being able to help with daily care would make them more satisfied with their centre. Sometimes this was a clear acknowledgement that more care-takers improved the quality of the care for all children. One single mother said: 'During the day, the more parental involvement you have the better. The more parents you have, the more outings you can go on, the more children you can take on the outings. . . .' Still others were helping out to spend more time with their own children: 'When you're picking up, you just kind of chip in while you are there. I usually stay for about a half hour in the mornings, and I might help out a little bit, but I'm mostly dealing with my own child.'

Planning and attending social events were other ways that mothers sought to make the centre a more caring place. Social events included potlucks, social evenings, family nights, child performances, information sessions, and other events, many of which also had a fundraising component, such as fashion shows and teas. These events offered an opportunity for parents to meet each other and their children's friends. One of the benefits of volunteerism is the opportunity to socialize and feel supported. 'Whenever they have meetings, I always go', said one mother. 'They allow you to bring kids. . . . It's nice to meet other parents and kids too.' Social events are a way to mitigate social isolation and share dilemmas with other parents: 'I've talked, you know, at birthday parties, at groups events. We'll sit around and the president is always there, and we'll talk about our problems we have collectively. . . .'

The Fundraising Dilemma

Fundraising is a topic much discussed by our mothers, as with most volunteers, since it is the single most common activity reported by volunteers. Over half of all of Canada's fundraisers are women (Duschesne 1989:44, 47). 'They're always fundraising', said one mother. 'We've done so many it's hard to remember them all', sighed another. Certainly, the creativity and ingenuity are impressive: wine raffles; romantic weekend getaways; selling things of all kinds—wrapping paper, chocolates and nuts, household cleaning supplies, fridge stickers and magnets, silk flowers, books of discount coupons; donating goods for garage sales and buying other goods; compiling recipes for cookbooks, which are then sold to other parents; organizing fashion shows, spring teas, socials, and silent auctions; donating labour performed at home such as cookie dough for bake sales, cross-stitched crafts for the raffle; obtaining sponsors for various jog-a-thons, hop-a-thons, etc.

Fundraising is definitely seen as one way that parents can make a direct financial contribution to the quality of the centre and contribute to special outings, toys, or programs. One mother reported that her centre raised $4,000 for a summer program. When asked about the importance of fundraising, she stated: 'Very important because without fundraising, the children wouldn't get to go to Tinkertown, they wouldn't get to go to the zoo, they wouldn't get to go on . . . restaurant jaunts, like Pizza Hut. . . .'

However, fundraising was also problematic. It was the one form of involvement in which our mothers reported feeling external pressure to participate and the most explicit example of duty motivating participation. When asked whether they had ever felt pressured by anyone in the daycare centre to be more involved, one mother responded: 'Yeah, by fundraising people.' She described how the pressure was experienced: 'It was the guilt thing . . . a bunch of mothers would be sitting around and someone would comment, "How many Treasure Books have you sold?" That kind of thing. And it's more joking, like no one's ever really made me feel bad, but. . . .' Mothers are exquisitely attuned to the contributions of other mothers. 'I feel bad that I'm not doing very much', said one. 'I know other mothers do more', said another. Nor are all mothers convinced that this form of involvement is necessary. One unpartnered, fully subsidized mother reflected that:

> If fundraising meant cheaper fees, I would say it would be very important, but I don't think fundraising is a concern of mine. Usually you only have fundraising to buy more toys or as far as I know that's what they'd use fundraising for. And I guess whether they had me to help them or not, they'd still get their new toys. But if it were to help keep the daycare fees down, there would be more people.

A middle-class mother noted:

> And I have a problem with the fundraising thing anyway. These kids, most of the people my child goes to daycare with, come from good homes and people have enough money to afford to buy toys for the daycare, or pay a little more, because I don't know if we need to do as much fundraising as we are, but I've never brought that up with any of them before.

Managing Conflict within the Centre

Another dilemma parents confront is the management of conflict within a centre. Conflict is a potentially difficult issue within a child-care setting and maternal participation is often carefully monitored to minimize it. Always conscious that their children might bear the consequences of conflict with centre staff, mothers are careful about expressing even indirect resentment about policies. In some crucial respects, staff and parents confront each other as antagonists. Certainly in a fee-for-service arrangement, the financial interests of parents and staff diverge as parents need to keep fees affordable, whereas staff need 'worthy wages'. In other ways, child-care services are organized in such a way as to create conflict between mother and worker. The common enemy of both parents and staff—public policies at the provincial and national level, including meagre services, funding, and access—escapes examination at the everyday level of the centre.[11]

Mothers are generally reluctant to complain, despite their concerns. Some key issues of maternal concern and conflict management were late pick-up policy, sick child rules, and scheduling around centre closure. Late pick-up rules are, at least overtly, designed to respect worker rights to a known departure time. Because of the realities of many mothers' work schedules, fixed pick-up times can be difficult to meet and mothers may be late at the centre for reasons beyond their control. Some centres seemed to have more punitive and rigid rules than others. One mother recounted the painful story of her attempt to amend her centre's late policy rule, an attempt that left her stigmatized as a complainer and resulted in an even more punitive rule. In her words, 'I just feel powerless in the whole process, and I try and counteract that and take steps and, you know, I just feel now things are worse off. It's almost like a punishment somehow by bringing something out in the open, talking about it.' In her case the conflict is with other parents on the board of the daycare: 'I think perhaps the board does hold more power than is fair. I mean they have the discretion to have the children withdrawn, and I just found this absolutely ridiculous. Are these parents all of a sudden now your equals, or are they all of a sudden your superiors?'

Rules about how sick a child must be before she or he must be kept at home were another source of conflict for mothers. One respondent stated: 'I think sometimes they go overboard when they say your child is sick and they have a slight fever and you need to take them home. Meanwhile, you lose your wages and you still have to pay to keep them [during] the day or not.' Likewise, scheduling decisions do not always make the mothers' needs central and mothers express their displeasure. One mother explains how a holiday was arranged at her centre:

> Recently they were closed an extra day. I guess it was over the Easter break, and I needed daycare on Monday. I had school and they were closed. I actually didn't take any action on it. I had called the [provincial] daycare office and they told me that it had to be put to all the parents, to be given the opportunity to vote. If it was more than 50 per cent, the centre should've been open. But I never took action and nobody else seemed to question it, so nothing was changed.

This mother's reluctance to complain is particularly noteworthy as she was the chairperson of her board.

It is not surprising that mothers minimize conflict in their attempt to make child-care settings more comfortable and caring for their children. Children are the most vulnerable players in a service designed to meet the needs of parents, children, and professionals and no one is more aware of this fact than their mothers. Nor do mothers particularly want to remove their child, should they be unhappy with the service.

Parents and the Consumer Model

In the larger discussion surrounding privatization and the welfare state, it is often posited that consumers are able to effect change through their purchasing ability and their power to switch allegiance. We propose that this confidence is misplaced: certainly, it fails to hold true for child care, and we suspect it fails for many other of the personal social services. There is an additional problem with the consumer model. Parents who use child-care services may pay the full fees or they may receive a full or partial government subsidy to cover the cost of the care their children receive. These two kinds of parents, we discovered, have subtly different experiences as purchasers and users of care: some mothers are 'consumers' while others are just 'clients'. In this characterization, we are borrowing Nancy Fraser's categorization of entitlement and access to service (Fraser 1989).

While the market model postulates the potential to 'act with your feet' if you are an unhappy purchaser, this is not always possible or viable in a child-care setting. For all mothers, removing their child means disrupting the stability of care their child is receiving. Both the child-care literature and evidence from parents suggest that turnover of staff and changing caregivers is not generally in the best interests of children (Ferguson 1992; Leach 1987; Shimoni 1992).

Not only do parents often wish to maintain stability for their children, but many mothers really have very few options. Subsidized mothers in particular cannot simply choose from the full range of market choices. They must use services for which a subsidy is available, and demand for subsidy exceeds supply all across the country. Consequently, many subsidized mothers feel lucky to have both a space and a subsidy, and tolerate a great deal of unhappiness before they would remove their child.

From this perspective, it is important to note two findings in our study. First, we found that subsidized, low-income parents—often single mothers (the 'clients') volunteered substantially more time than higher-income, partnered mothers, participating in the centre once or twice a week compared to unsubsidized mothers (the 'consumers'), who generally volunteered only once a month. This was initially surprising to us, as volunteering has usually been understood as more of an upper- or middle-class activity and common sense would indicate that partnered mothers might have more time available for volunteering. Certainly, the 1987 Survey of Volunteer Activity indicates that high socio-economic status and marriage are associated with higher rates of volunteering.

Socially privileged mothers ('consumers') seem to be happier with their daycare centres than 'client' mothers. For instance, one professional, higher-income, partnered mother, when asked whether she would consider sitting on the board, responded: 'I probably would be more likely to consider it if I had concerns about the board or the running of the daycare, but I don't have concerns at our daycare.' Similarly, another unsubsidized, less involved consumer mother stated: 'I guess part of my problem with this is. I feel my daycare's doing a good job, so I really have a hard time imagining what I'd do if they weren't and how much input if things weren't going the way I want.'

In contrast, other mothers who are unhappy with the running of the centre or who have concerns about their children said they want more involvement. For instance, one subsidized single mother, when asked if she had a problem with the running of the daycare stated: 'Have I had a problem? I have lots of problems. I'd like to change everything around.' Later, when asked about the amount of time available for the daycare, she said: 'I would say if I was able to get involved with what I'd like to get involved with, I'd say two times a week or more if it was possible. But then it would probably change as soon as my child would come out of there.' Similar concerns were also raised by another single subsidized mother who said she was involved once a week. This is the same mother who attempted to change the late policy in her daycare:

> I'm not happy because I have to say that I feel that there's prejudice because my family unit is not at all 'normal'. . . . I'm not even so sure that they're very aware that something doesn't sit right with them because whenever there's a difficulty, like Kevin's behaviour isn't good for whatever reason, they're not happy and it always comes back to me and his father and our communication, and there's no problem with our communication.

It is clear from these examples that some mothers want to be involved with their centre out of concern for their children, and this concern is felt more often by subsidized, single-parent mothers. The fact that heightened concern experienced by 'client' mothers influences their level of involvement is generally neither known nor understood in the child-care field. The literature has long documented the discrimination and stigma experienced by low-income, single-parent families in daycare and other social services (Finch 1984; National Survey on Volunteer Activity 1987). Our findings strongly suggest that class is an important factor in parental involvement in child care. The fact that subsidized 'client' mothers volunteered substantially more than unsubsidized 'consumer' mothers also raises interesting questions about mothers' different experiences of the motherhood mandate (Fraser 1989; Handler 1973; Wineman 1984).

While all mothers feel the pressure to be good mothers, this data suggests that low-income mothers may experience the pressure to participate more than their more affluent counterparts. Untangling the reasons for these findings is complicated and must be speculative. In addition to 'client' mothers' greater concern for their children, we suggest that they might have fewer market choices from which to choose, more trouble in switching centres should trouble arise, less trust in middle-class professional child-rearing norms, and more desire to make the centre less institutional and professional. Alternatively they may feel less entitled to their child-care space due to their subsidy and believe that they should contribute a 'shadow payment' to their centre. While 'consumer' mothers who buy their spaces may feel they can choose limited involvement as long as they feel their children are safe and happy, 'client' mothers may have less power to resist the pressure to participate. Whatever the reasons, our data show that while all mothers experience the motherhood mandate, they do so differently. While the specifics of their own personal situations no doubt influence them, our data suggest that class is a major factor.

Conclusions

As we have demonstrated, and as we continue to explore in our ongoing work, child care is both a complex site of volunteerism and a complicated experience for mothers. Volunteerism in child care is, in many respects, qualitatively different from volunteerism in other sectors. First, it is irreducibly and quintessentially gendered. This gendering has several dimensions: child care itself is a gendered service because it is a substitute for mother care. Second, volunteerism itself produces and reproduces this gendering as mothers disproportionately assume the labour of supporting child-care centres. Volunteerism is not merely gendered but also classed (and probably raced) as both 'consumer' and 'client' mothers, in different ways, are compelled by guilt and coaxed by love in their struggles to meet the insatiable demands of the motherhood mandate.[12] In this context, it is understandable that mothers are readily available to meet the professional expectations of early childhood educators that they 'ought' to be involved. Likewise, mothers willingly accord to public policy demands in those jurisdictions that have mandatory volunteerism.

The expectations of parent volunteers in child care are enormous: they are called upon to run agencies and centres, to fundraise, to develop policies, to manage and supervise staff, to participate in daily care, to show in myriad ways that they care and that they are taking responsibility. In our comparative reading, we have found no other social service that has such high expectations, where the costs of volunteerism are so unacknowledged, and where the gendered quality of both are so ignored.

When and under what conditions is volunteer labour a freely chosen and empowering act? When and under what conditions is volunteer labour an intensification of social inequality? This chapter has attempted to provide some responses to these questions. Mothers are never entirely free of the motherhood mandate and the social expectation that they ought at all times to make their children their first priority. Thus, identifying when mothers' volunteer participation is 'freely' chosen is a bit like chasing a chimera. Nevertheless, there are clear indications that some mothers do volunteer in their child-care centre as an act of solidarity, an exercise in agency. For other mothers, participation is subtly coerced, extracted through a potent mix of social and personal expectations and reinforced by practices of professionalism, status, and public policies. In many respects, therefore, maternal volunteerism in child care cannot be considered freely offered. To the contrary, it is largely the discharging of duty, both overt and covert. Under these circumstances, mothers' volunteerism is hardly to be held up as an example of the moral superiority and excellence of the non-profit sector in a changing welfare state.

These observations leave us with some troubling conclusions. As feminists, researchers, and mothers committed to high-quality child care, we have identified ourselves publicly as advocates of a universally accessible, high-quality, non-profit child-care system. Such a system currently relies on parents to administer their own individual non-profit services. Yet, as a society, we do not expect citizens to individually operate health care, clinics, and hospitals, nor do we demand that school administration be the unpaid responsibility of parents. Child care, by contrast, does carry these requirements.

In the absence of a national system of provision, and in the face of the very real threat of poor quality commercial daycare, non-profit, parent-delivered services seem to keep the worst devils at bay. They provide some measure of client-controlled direct democracy, and they do permit the cost-effective and economic delivery of a badly needed service. As feminists, mothers, and child-care activists, we find ourselves caught in a classic contradiction that so often characterizes welfare state policies directed at women. Participation has been the hue and cry of advocates around most programs. However, the responsibility for participation often falls inequitably on women, often the poorest and most vulnerable women. Such participation is laudable in principle, but is frequently reduced to an imposition in practice.

What women as mothers lack is a publicly delivered system in which volunteerism could be freely given or withheld. As long as private services are fragile, parental volunteerism cannot be withdrawn without jeopardizing badly needed services. Since the 1970 Report of the Royal Commission on the Status of Women, feminists have lobbied for a national child-care system. Under the terms of the current new social union, a publicly delivered child-care system is more remote than ever. In the contemporary climate of welfare state restructuring and offloading to the private sector, the prognosis for Canadian children and women grows even more bleak. Under the 'new social union', we can predict that the structural conditions that make parental volunteerism so necessary will only continue to grow.

Notes

1 Support for this project has been generously provided. We thank the University of Manitoba SSHRC Small Grants Program for start-up assistance; the SSHRC Women and Caring Network for conceptual/theoretical development; and the SSHRC Women and Change Strategic Grant (8197006) for additional support. We thank research assistants Alex Morga-Haskiewicz, Wendy Singleton, and Jodi Lee.

2 Little national research has been undertaken specifically on the sex composition of volunteers in child care. According to the Childcare Resource and Research Unit of the University of Toronto, there are no national data on child-care volunteerism by sex. However, the national 1987 survey of volunteers determined that women were more likely than men to volunteer, and that women predominate among education, youth, and social services, the sectors where early childhood education and child care are situated. Thus, this claim is plausible. See Duschesne (1989).

3 For a liberal interpretation, see Guest (1985) and Splane (1965). For a political economy historical analysis, see Moscovitch and Albert (1987), Moscovitch and Drover (1982), and Rekart (1993).

4 Feminist historians have challenged the perception that women's supposedly 'natural' goodness and feminine morality led them to do charitable and benevolent work. Critical reviews include: Marks (1995) and Ginzberg (1990).

5 A rich American literature on volunteerism exists and focuses on the experiences of Black American women who were important players in the War on Poverty in the 1960s. Canadian historiography has been less race sensitive. We predict that some Canadian parallels will be found among Aboriginal peoples, and in our current project we are exploring First Nations and other racialized child-care users' experiences of volunteerism.

6 The average number of annual volunteer hours reported by Day and Devlin (1996:17) is 178, with a median of 81.

7 Charitable donations are only one marker of volunteer activity. The state authorizes these tax expenditures to encourage philanthropic giving. An enormous portion of Canada's total volunteer activity, however, is conducted outside of registered charities with tax credit capacity. Thus, these figures should be treated with caution. See Ross (1996:17).

8 These findings are derived from a 1994 University of Manitoba SSHRC-funded pilot study of forty-nine mothers using licensed preschool group daycare centres in Manitoba who were interviewed in the spring of 1994. Data for this

paper are from these interviews. We used three methods of analysis: quantitative analysis of close-ended questions; content analysis of open-ended questions; and discourse analysis of a subsample of transcribed interviews. We have benefited from the input of our talented and generous colleagues in the Women and Change Network. We are continuing our research in parent involvement under our current grant.

9   Only 11 per cent, according to Duschesne (1989:32).

10 The vast majority of Canadian families using non-parental care use informal, unregulated care. See Ferguson (1998).

11 We are grateful to Sheila Neysmith for drawing our attention to this aspect of ruling relations. For a similar point, Ferguson (1998) has elaborated how 'horizontal hostilities' allow the overall picture to go unaddressed.

12 Our small pilot study (on which this article is based) was unable to collect sufficient data to enable us to analyse the impact of race on volunteerism. We are trying to remedy this gap in our current SSHRC-funded research project.

References

Abella, R. 1984. *Equality in Employment: A Royal Commission Report*. Ottawa: Commission on Equality and Employment.

Bach, S., and S. Phillips. 1997. 'Constructing a New Social Union: Child Care Beyond Infancy'. In *How Ottawa Spends, 1997/1998: Seeing Red: A Liberal Report Card*, edited by G. Simmer, 235–58. Ottawa: Carleton University Press.

Baines, C., P. Evans, and S. Neysmith. 1998. 'Women's Caring: Work Expanding, State Contracting'. In *Women's Caring: Feminist Perspectives on Social Welfare*, 2nd edn, edited by C. Baines, P. Evans, and S. Neysmith, 3–22. Toronto: Oxford University Press.

Bowlby, J. 1951. *Maternal Care and Mental Health*. Geneva: World Health Organization.

Browne, A. 1985. 'The Market Sphere: Private Response to the Need for Daycare'. *Child Welfare League of America* LXIV, no. 4:367–81.

Childcare Resource and Research Unit. 1997. 'Child Care in Canada: Provinces and Territories'. Toronto: Childcare Resource and Research Unit.

Dacks, G., J. Green, and L. Trimble. 1995. 'Road Kill: Women in Alberta's Drive Toward Deficit Elimination'. In *The Trojan Horse: Alberta and the Future of Canada*, edited by G. Laxer and T. Harrison, 270–85. Montreal: Black Rose Books.

Day, K.M., and R.A. Devlin. 1996. 'Volunteerism and Crowding Out: Canadian Econometric Evidence'. *Canadian Journal of Economics* XXIX:37–53.

Duschesne, D. 1989. *Giving Freely: Volunteers in Canada*. Labour Analytic Report no. 4. Catalogue no. 71–535. Ottawa: Supply and Services Canada.

Esping-Anderson, G. 1989. 'The Three Political Economies of the Welfare State'. *Canadian Review of Sociology and Anthropology* 26, no. 1:10–36.

Ferguson, E. 1989. 'Private or Public? Profit or Non-profit? The Preferences of a Sample of Day Care Consumers in Ontario'. Paper presented at the National Conference on Social Welfare Policy, Toronto, 24–7 October.

_____. 1991. 'The Child Care Crisis: The Realities of Women's Caring'. In *Women's Caring: Feminist Perspectives on Social Welfare*, edited by C. Baines, P. Evans, and S. Neysmith, 73–105. Toronto: McClelland & Stewart.

_____. 1998. 'The Child Care Debate: Fading Hopes and Shifting Sands'. In *Women's Caring: Feminist Perspectives on Social Welfare*, 2nd edn, edited by C. Baines, P. Evans, and S. Neysmith, 191–217.

_____, and S. Prentice. 1999. 'Exploring Parental Involvement in Canada: An Ideological Maze'. In *Landscapes in Early Childhood Services: Crossnational Perspectives on Empowerment and Restraint*, edited by J. Haydon. Sydney: Peter Lang Publishing.

Finch, J. 1984. 'The Deceit of Self-Help: Pre-school Playgroups and Working Class Women'. *Journal of Social Policy* 13, no. 1:5–18.

Fitzgerald, M., Connie Guberman, and Margie Wolfe, eds. 1982. *Still Ain't Satisfied: Canadian Feminism Today*. Toronto: Women's Press.

Fraser, N., ed. 1989. *Unruly Practices*. Minneapolis: University of Minnesota Press.

Friendly, M. 1994. *Child Care Policy in Canada: Putting the Pieces Together*. Toronto: Addison Wesley.

Galinsky, E. 1987. *The Six Stages of Parenthood*. Reading: Addison Wesley.

Ginzberg, L. 1990. *Women and the Work of Benevolence: Morality, Politics and Class in the Nineteenth Century United States*. New Haven: London.

Guest, D. 1985. *The Rise of Social Security in Canada*. Vancouver: UBC Press.

Handler, E. 1973. 'The Expectation of Daycare Parents'. *The Social Service Review* 47, no. 3:266–7.

Hays, S. 1996. *The Cultural Contradictions of Motherhood*. New Haven and London: Yale University Press.

Leach, P. 1987. *Your Baby and Child: From Birth to Age Five*. New York: Alfred A. Knopf.

Li, P., and D. Currie. 1992. 'Gender Differences in Work Interruptions as Unequal Effects of Marriage and Child Rearing: Findings from a Canadian National Survey'. *Journal of Comparative Family Studies* XXII, no. 2:217–29.

Little, M. 1995. 'The Blurring of Boundaries: Private and Public Welfare for Single Mothers in Ontario'. *Studies in Political Economy* 47:89–110.

Marks, L. 1995. 'Indigent Committees and Ladies' Benevolent Societies: Intersections of Public and Private Poor Relief in Late Nineteenth Century Small Town Ontario'. *Studies in Political Economy* 47:61–87.

Mayfield, M. 1990. 'Parent Involvement in Early Childhood Programs'. In *Child Care and Education: Canadian Dimensions*, edited by I. Dovey, 240–54. Toronto: Nelson Canada.

Maynard, F. 1985. *The Child Care Crisis: The Real Costs of Daycare for You and Your Child*. Markham: Viking Penguin.

Moscovitch, A., and J. Albert. 1987. *The Benevolent State: The Growth of Welfare in Canada*. Toronto: Garamond Press.

_____, and G. Drover, eds. 1982. *Inequality: Essays on the Political Economy of Social Welfare*. Toronto: University of Toronto Press.

National Survey on Volunteer Activity. 1987. *National Survey on Volunteer Activity*. Ottawa: Supply and Services.

New, C., and M. David. 1985. *For the Children's Sake: Making Childcare More Than Women's Business*. London: Penguin.

O'Connor, J. 1973. *Fiscal Crisis of the State*. New York: St Martin's Press.

_____. 1996. 'From Women in the Welfare State to Gendering Welfare Stage Regimes'. *Current Sociology* 44, no. 2:1–130.

Prentice, S. 1997. 'The Deficiencies of Commercial Day Care'. *Policy Options* (January-February):42–6.

_____, and E. Ferguson. 1997. 'Involvement and Control: Mothers' Views of Daycare Delivery'. In *Rethinking Child and Family Policy: Struggles, Strategies and Options*, edited by J. Pulkingham and G. Ternowetsky, 188–202. Halifax: Fernwood.

Rekart, J. 1993. *Public Funds, Private Provision: the Role of the Voluntary Sector*. Vancouver: UBC Press.

Rich, A. 1976. *Of Woman Born: Motherhood as Experience and Institution*. New York: Norton.

Riley, D. 1983. *War in the Nursery: Theories of Mother and Child*. London: Virago.

Ross, D. 1996. 'How Valuable Is Volunteering?' *Perception* 14, no. 4:17–18.

Russo, N.F. 1979. 'Overview: Sex Roles, Fertility, and the Motherhood Mandate'. *Psychology of Women Quarterly* 4:7–15.

Schlossman, S. 1976. 'Before Home Start: Notes Toward a History of Parent Education in America, 1897–1929'. *Harvard Educational Review* 46, no. 3:436–67.

Shimoni, R. 1992. 'Parent Involvement in Early Childhood Education and Day Care'. *Sociological Studies of Child Development* 5:73–95.

_____, and B. Ferguson. 1992. 'Rethinking Parent Involvement in Child Care Programs'. *Child and Youth Care Forum* 21:105–18.

Splane, R. 1965. *Social Welfare in Ontario, 1791–1893*. Toronto: University of Toronto Press.

Vaillancourt, R. 1994. 'To Volunteer or Not: Canada 1987'. *Canadian Journal of Economics* XXVII:813–26.

Valverde, M. 1995. 'The Mixed Social Economy as a Canadian Tradition'. *Studies in Political Economy* 47:33–60.

White, B. 1985. *The First Three Years of Life*. New York: Prentice Hall.

Wineman, S. 1984. *The Politics of Human Services*. Montreal: Black Rose.

Chapter 7

Restructuring and Community Work: The Case of Community Resource Centres for Families in Poor Urban Neighbourhoods

Marge Reitsma-Street and Sheila M. Neysmith

> Kids are off the street. They have a place to go. Without no volunteers, there
> would be no place. If we can't help, they can't survive.
>
> —Participant in focus group from one community
> resource centre, November 1996

This chapter examines the nature of community work and the spectres
haunting it. Our work is intended to contribute to debates on community
work, unpaid time, and volunteerism. The examination draws upon a study
of the unpaid work that is done in three community resource centres for
children and their families in poor urban neighbourhoods in Ontario. Study
sources include interviews, focus groups, several years of participant observations, official documents, and descriptive statistics.[1]

Following a description of the context of community work in early intervention initiatives for children, the debates about the nature of this work
are presented. Next is an exploration of the actual work done in selected
resource centres. Community resource centres, like family resource centres
(Kyle 1993), are non-profit organizations sponsored by community-government partnerships. They are open weekdays, have a geographic hub, and
offer support services to member families and citizens in a community.
Services include, for example, before- and after-school programs, play
groups, parenting classes, community theatre and festivals, group food
buying, and community kitchens. Unlike many family resource centres,
services in the centres that are the focus of this study are free, accessible to
all who live in the neighbourhood, and there are no waiting lists.

In the last part of the chapter, we start to uncover tensions that threaten
community work, especially in poor communities. Two metaphors help
capture the tensions: the 'hoax' and the 'scary dance'. The 'hoax' metaphor
captures the betrayal and pain associated with the 1990s drastic cuts in
welfare and other services, and the involuntary nature of volunteering in

community placements made obligatory in legislation such as the Ontario Works Act (Ontario 1997). By the end of our study, the spectre of 'involuntary volunteering' (MacDonald 1996:28) had moved from the wings and onto the stage of people's lives within the study's community centres. The 'scary dance' metaphor captures the dynamics of a situation wherein individuals from very different social locations agree to cooperate to develop alternatives. The choreography is enticing because it offers possibilities for new, meaningful expressions of community life, but the moves can be dangerous because the partnerships are usually unequal. What happens to community work when one partner is not as free or strong as the other to decide the movements of the dance? In a community-government partnership, what are the implications if there are differences in the power of the various partners to determine how the volunteer, unpaid, community work gets done and for whom?

The Context of Community Work in Early Intervention Programs

The community resource centres, referred to as either centres or 'the project' in subsequent quotes, are part of the 1990s wave of publicly funded early intervention programs in Canada targeted to 'high-risk' children, families, or neighbourhoods. The intent is to address some of the needs of parents and children seen as 'at risk' for future problems due to low income or limited education (Peters and Russell 1996; Schorr 1988). A modest investment of public funds provides core services, but volunteer or unpaid donations of time and services are needed to mount the range of programs envisioned in such early intervention models. The aim of such programs is to prevent future behavioural problems in the 'at risk' children while promoting healthy development. Like other such initiatives, the centres in this study drew inspiration from the family resource centres and the head start prevention programs of the last two decades. Added to the theoretical mix are community ownership ideas from the antipoverty ventures of the 1960s, such as the American community action and the British community development organizations (Cowen 1982; Loney 1983; Marris and Rein 1972).

These types of early intervention programs do not, however, address the problematic conditions that spawn the risks families encounter when raising children: conditions such as inadequate housing and minimal childcare services, unemployment, racism, and sexism (Cruikshank 1994). According to funding guidelines for the study centres, child care, jobs, and housing initiatives were explicitly excluded from possible programs that could be developed (Ontario Ministry of Community and Social Services 1990). Instead, the centres developed support programs for families that remain free and accessible to all who live in the neighbourhoods. These include breakfast, breastfeeding, and food clubs; family visiting and play groups; school tutoring and after-school child care; antiracism and cultural workshops; summer recreation events and community festivals; and, importantly, life skills, mediation workshops, and democratic decision-making committees sponsored by the centres (Pancer and Cameron 1994; Peters and Russell 1996; Reitsma-Street and Arnold 1994).

These resource centres are operating, however, at a time when governments and service organizations are downsizing, and when employment opportunities and family incomes are decreasing. Indeed, many social rights of Canadian citizens are under siege, especially the right to claim public funding for help with raising children (Freiler and Cerny 1998). For instance, designs for a national child-care program have been aborted. Family allowances are no longer universal or indexed but are now targeted only to poor families working in the labour market. The illusion of full employment policies has been replaced with more restrictions on eligibility and funds for the unemployed. Entitlement to adequate elder care and safe housing is nowhere on the public agenda. This downsizing and restructuring are made to appear inevitable, a by-product of the efficiency required to compete in a global economy. The reward, supposedly, will be increased business profits, which in turn will create more jobs and cash for citizens. However, the political climate is such that other options are not explored (Baines, Evans, and Neysmith 1998; Boyd 1997; Brodie 1996). In Chapter 8 Carol Baines documents similar dynamics in the post-Second World War design of services for poor children and their mothers. Members in these resource centres are finding that they often do not have basic necessities to care for themselves or their communities, yet they feel they must and often want to make contributions to keep their centres running.

The centres, started in 1991, had been developed in the context of a five-year research demonstration project for young children in poor urban communities (Peters and Russell 1996). On 17 April 1997 the Ontario government announced that the community resource centres would not close as originally planned. Rather than closing, the seven urban and one First Nations centres would become part of base budgets in regional government offices responsible for social services. The 17 April press release from the premier's office stated:

> The success of this investment is self-help. The community's own parents are emerging as the leaders and caregivers for others who need support. More than 1,000 hours are volunteered to the projects by community members each month. . . . [Projects] reduce duplication of effort and increase efficiency by bringing local residents, representatives of local schools, agencies and volunteer organizations together to promote healthy child development. It demonstrates that by working together, a community can find resources and address problems that would not have been possible if one group acted alone.

The press release referred to hours of volunteer labour based on data collected quarterly in the evaluation of the demonstration project (Mione, Neysmith, and Reitsma-Street 1996; Ontario Ministry of Community and Social Services 1990; Peters and Russell 1996). Reference to the 1,000 volunteer hours per month helped the government to explain the reason for keeping the centres open. Primarily economic arguments justified the decision: efficient reduction of duplicate services, prudent use of public dollars, and solid financial investment in community building.

The centres developed by the demonstration project were pleased they were no longer short-term research demonstration sites. Members of the centres were pleased that everyone's hard work, especially their volunteer contributions, did not go unnoticed. Paid staff were relieved that their jobs would not end. The steering committees of the centres could finally begin to plan stable programs for the 1,000 children under ten years of age and their families who lived within each of the centre's boundaries.

Joy, however, was mingled with serious concerns. The funding is not substantial, approximately $500,000 per year per centre. Consequently, the centres cannot operate according to their visions without sustained and substantial volunteer contributions and a systematic search for other funds. The needs of the neighbourhoods have increased, not decreased, since the centres opened. The average incomes of adults in the neighbourhoods have not gone up since 1991. One-third of neighbourhood families are on social assistance; they struggle with the 21 per cent provincial cuts in this income begun in 1994. Adults worry about the increased surveillance of their behaviour due to tightened eligibility criteria in unemployment and welfare regulations. It also does not seem fair that children and families with similar needs living outside the centres' boundaries do not have any funding for their own community resource centres.

It is within this context that we explore the debates, nature, and tensions of community work. Data include transcripts of nine focus groups conducted late in 1996 and early 1997 with forty-six adult members of three centres, and the quarterly records on donated hours from 1994 to 1997.[2] The three centres were selected from the population of eight community resource centres to ensure a diversity in geography, cultures, and programs. The study centres were in cities with less than 100,000 people and were less than six hours' drive from Toronto. Two centres focused on programs for families of children ages 0 to four, while one worked primarily with children ages four to eight. Forty-six adults, 70 per cent of whom were parents of children under eighteen years of age, participated in the focus groups. Three of the focus groups were for women community members, three for men, and three for male and female mostly paid staff acting as organizational informants. The self-defined cultures of the focus group participants closely mirrored the variety of cultures served by the centres. Although White and English speaking are the dominant cultural characteristics in the neighbourhoods served by the centres, from one-quarter to one-third identified themselves as from another culture. Of the thirty-one women and fifteen men who took part in the focus groups, 44 per cent had household incomes of less than $20,000, 61 per cent did not have full-time employment, and 42 per cent did not have degrees or certificates. The education and income of the organizational informants were higher than the community volunteers. In a population survey of all the 125 volunteers involved with two of the centres completed in the fall of 1996, we found that over 80 per cent were women who lived in the neighbourhood served by the centre. Three-quarters did not have full-time paid work or postsecondary education.

We also bring to this chapter reflections from years of personal association with the funders, researchers, and community groups participating in the centres. It matters to us what happens in the centres. We are proud of the centres' accomplishments and energies, but our reflections are laced with trepidation. The contradictions embedded in community intervention programs were reflected in the uneasiness that permeated reactions to earlier draft articles and presentations we did on the volunteer labour that participants contributed to the centres. On the one hand, we puzzled over how to talk about the threats and spectres without betraying the achievements, pride, and loyalty the centres' members had for what they invested in their communities. Likewise, we recognized that without the support of public funds and the commitment of senior government bureaucrats, the centres would not exist. On the other hand, we could not avoid asking ourselves what the implications are of an unequal community-government partnership. What happens to people if one partner is less free than the other to negotiate the nature of community work? Despite these trepidations, our community and academic critics insisted that the examination had to continue. Community work in poor areas is too important to ignore. It fosters human agency within constraints (Connell 1987), rebellious daily attempts to create meaning, and 'small scale pockets of solidarity' despite poverty and racism (Apethker 1989; hooks 1993). It is hoped that talking about the debates and spectres in community work will aid in developing a clearer analysis of what is possible under restrictive social conditions.

The Debates on Community Work

What happens if one thinks of community work as a type of caring labour? Caring work is action that sustains the quality of people's lives in their daily, immediate world (Apethker 1989). The 'other-regarding character' is in the foreground of caring work, including the emotional acts of caring *about* other people and the physical tasks of caring *for* the needs of people (Leira 1994; Moore Milroy and Wismer 1994:72). In caring work, resources are marshalled not to make a profit or pursue individual achievements. Rather, the focus is to 'prendre soin'—to take good care of ourselves and each other in the never-ending, unfinished, complex search for dignified survival. Community work is 'other regarding' and attends to the life quality of those beyond family or friends in geographic, cultural, religious, or other types of localities that are bounded by a common link. The work includes the maintenance of relations and structures for keeping communities alive and well today, and the actions that are needed to build better places for the next generation (Lundström 1996; Lustiger-Thaler 1993; Moore Milroy and Wismer 1994; Naples 1991; Wharf and Clague 1997).

We and the focus group respondents reject equating community work with informal neighbourly services, or seeing it as only volunteer time for organizations or politicized civil action. All these activities may occur within community work (Baldock 1990; Collins 1991; Pearce 1993; Ross 1990; Sokolowski 1996) but as concepts, each is too limiting or problematic (Abrahams 1996; Lewis 1993; Rekart 1993). There was strong interest among participants in the resource centres to break down barriers and stereotypes about who gives what 'time or services-in-kind' and why.[3]

It's new, a new way of thinking about volunteering. . . . Mom started, now she is a home visitor. . . . [T]here isn't any stigma to receiving services and providing them at the same time. . . . [I]t really is blurred from one way to the other. It's a very kind of dynamic, flexible way that people participate.

Throughout the transcripts there was discomfort with words like volunteering, and incredible pride when people could *not* tell if someone was or was not a volunteer. There was resistance to dividing people neatly into separate categories of staff, neighbours, volunteers, and participants. It may be that the blurring of boundaries helps to break down the hierarchical and isolating relations that dominate the lives of those living in impoverished communities (Frazer and Lacey 1993:170). We propose that community work encompasses volunteering, neighbourliness, and civil action, but goes beyond these. It is more like a highly skilled 'craft' (Baldock and Ungerson 1991:138) that weaves together specific helpfulness and general regard for others in the world beyond one's immediate family. To capture this complexity we would prefer to refer to this work as community care work. However, this term has been associated with home-care services for so long that it could be misleading. As a consequence, we have decided to use the phrase 'community work' instead.

Like Moore Milroy and Wismer (1994) we see community work as part of a three-sphere model of work: (1) community work; (2) domestic work that includes mothering work, personal services to kin, and housework; and (3) 'traded' or market work in which people exchange their labour, time, and skills for wages. Caring work is performed in each of the three spheres of work, whether directly or indirectly with people. Sometimes the caring work is paid; often it is unpaid. The spheres are distinctive but interpenetrate and affect each other.

Negotiating the relations and tensions between the three spheres becomes a complex task. Conditions that affect negotiating caring work between the spheres of market and domestic are sketched in ethnographic studies by Hoschild (1989, 1997) and policy research by Knijn and Kremer (1997). In the following quote we see a woman trying to understand the apparently lower status that paid staff at the resource centres attribute to someone doing unpaid work compared to the status of the same person when she is paid for her contributions:

> I get a recognition certificate. I like a pat on the back. It is weird though. I was paid on one of those training programs, and then the staff said to me, good to have you on board. But I was on board for five years! I felt like my work before was not recognized; it was a slap in the face. What about all the work I used to do when I was not paid? I am on both sides.

Hirings and lay-offs, pay scales and pay equity policies, new programs and cutbacks were flash points for conflict in the resource centres. There was more conflict in one centre where wages and salaries were 'all set above market value', so there were fewer jobs to go around and more need for unpaid contributions. Those centres with flatter pay scales had less conflict between paid and unpaid workers, but did not escape the insolvable contradiction of too few good jobs and skimpy services in the neighbourhoods. One man spoke of both his pride and frustration with community work. During funding cutbacks to the resource centres, he felt that the contributions of paid staff were valued more highly than those of unpaid workers, and he resented the cuts in honorariums, child care, meals, and transportation for those making unpaid contributions: 'So, it's not a matter of wanting more money, we just want respect in the community from the people we work for. But every time something needs to be cut, it's us that they cut first.'

Similar delicate, tense intersphere negotiations are identified by Prentice and Ferguson in their examination of unpaid mothering and paid daycare work in Chapter 6. Likewise, Belinda Leach and Roxana Ng argue in chapters 10 and 11 that rural and immigrant women see their paid factory jobs as one aspect of 'caring for' their families. They negotiate training or new jobs in the context of their sense of caring responsibilities in both the domestic and market spheres of work.

Learning how people negotiate caring commitments in and among the three spheres of community, domestic, and market work is long overdue, but the argument we wish to make here is more basic. The remainder of this chapter explores the specific nature of community work in poor neighbourhoods. We found that the work was meaningful to participants, but involvement needed funds, time, skills, and vision to sustain it. We also found that community work in poor neighbourhoods is vulnerable. If you can't pay the rent or if you are not free to engage or disengage, community work suffers or it is restructured into something contradictory and problematic.

'Six Hours at the Laundromat': The Labour in Community Work

What does community work actually look like in poor urban neighbourhoods? Based on census data and boundaries, the average household income in the neighbourhoods served by our study centres was one-half the provincial average; also, three times as many parents had not completed high school compared to the provincial average. Despite the deprivation in income and education, we found that community work in these neighbourhoods is varied and needs a range of skills and lots of time. It is noteworthy that this work takes place in low-income, culturally mixed communities that are seldom seen by funders as hot spots for traditional volunteering (MacDonald 1996; Naples 1992, 1998).

What people said they did as community work for their centres can be described in four categories: service, relationship building, planning, and shadow activities. First, there is what might be called the 'grunt' direct service activities to meet daily needs. People reported that they play with the children and serve breakfast, cook in community kitchens, run errands, lug boxes, drive people to meetings, make presentations, write newsletters, work on bingo, organize festivals, and fundraise. A story captures the service aspect of community support work: 'Last night this young woman who was at the front desk spent six and a half hours at the laundromat for a woman whose four preschoolers all ended up with lice and she needed some help.'

Second, there is the relationship aspect to community work. Many spoke of the time required to talk, to visit, to listen even in the middle of the night, and to laugh. All the centres took care to *not* look like traditional agencies so that children, youth, and adults would feel free to drop in and visit. It was the effort put into relationship building that attracted people to the centres in the first place. Later they began to contribute a little, increasing their contributions over time: 'Unpaid time would be coming here to work on the agenda, discuss issues, and sometimes just coming to visit. You need people around you. If you need somebody to talk to, even if it has nothing to do with the project, somebody will still listen to you.'

The phrase 'I get to think today' captures the third aspect of community work, which takes up substantial hours of paid and unpaid time. Thinking, planning, and making political decisions are activities that Arnstein (1969) and others (e.g., Gutierrez 1991; Naples 1998) argue are associated with more advanced, complex forms of participation and empowerment in contrast to the less developed forms of consulting and advising. Important decisions affecting the projects are made during the planning aspect of community work: hiring, reviewing, and firing paid staff; starting new projects or supporting political action; monitoring budgets and signing cheques; organizing community meetings and electing representatives to the steering groups.

Of the unpaid hours counted in the quarterly statistics, 15 per cent were categorized as administration and research. In addition, from one-third to one-half of the recorded unpaid hours in the various program areas were categorized as committee work as opposed to direct service. At least one-half of the centres' steering committees are made up of community members who participate, unpaid, in the biweekly or monthly meetings. In brief, the planning aspect of community work, whether for services or political action, required many unpaid hours of work.

Behind direct service, relationship building, and planning is the fourth aspect of community work, what we call 'shadow work'. We doubt if any of the hours of shadow work were recorded in the quarterly statistics that were routinely collected by each resource centre. Nevertheless, shadow work is very evident in discussions, especially in the talk among women respondents.[4] Participants spoke of grandmothers who babysat children so that they could come to meetings. Typical is the example where a child 'is only able to participate because [another] parent picks them up when it is over. They will stop and visit, talk to people and get to know them.' In one centre a respondent said: 'The men who volunteer have home support and so are able to work in those hours when women can't, and they do more.' In another centre, the women declared that the unpaid time comes mostly from women: 'There were a lot of males volunteering their time and then when they found out that when the jobs come, they are not high-paid jobs, they sort of just gradually pulled out.' The gendered nature of shadow work needs particular emphasis in examinations of intersphere negotiations around community, domestic, and market work.

These four aspects of community work—service, relationship building, planning, and shadow work—do not emerge naturally from altruism, wisdom, neighbourliness, or discretionary time. Stable funds, substantial time, and a sustaining vision are needed. All respondents stated that it was necessary to have money to pay some staff to keep the work on track, and to provide material help for participants in the form of babysitting, transportation, and meals. Says one woman: 'having child care paid for is a big thing because people on welfare make nothing'.

Besides funds, time is needed to do community work: time of paid and unpaid people. In each centre there is a core of five to seven full-time positions paid by the project funders, and sometimes over twenty part-time positions are funded by seasonal contracts with private foundations or various government ministries. On average, the number of full-time positions are doubled each year if we transform the unpaid hours recorded in the 'time-in-kind' quarterly statistics into position equivalents.[5] If the hours contributed by students, low-wage trainees, and professional secondments are included, then the full-time positions in each centre are tripled annually. Yet these quarterly statistics are very conservative counts. They do not include the shadow work mentioned earlier or the evening visiting that builds the relationships so vital to community work or the hours of unpaid work put into activities associated with the centres as suggested in these words: 'It's a huge number of hours that go into planning and demonstration activities, into the coalition for social justice. . . . The Green Dollar Barter system has 200 members and the Good Food Box is volunteer driven. . . . Our members sit on the boards of other organizations.'

Finally, even if time and money are available, community work decreases unless there is a vision that fosters member relationships in which people are free to negotiate meaningful activities. When someone is treated as 'low scum' or excluded from important decisions like hiring and firing, then resentment festers. People leave with their feet, as indeed has happened at the centres. A long-time centre member sums up the vision needed: 'What they feel is important, and so is how you create an environment where they are going to feel empowered. They are going to feel more "autonome"; that they are feeding their souls. If you can't create that kind of environment, then forget it.'

In summary, the strongest theme in the data is the pride, even awe, that respondents have for what they created in their poor, battered communities. They spoke of the intentional processes used in the centres to connect people to one another for common purposes. Key components of the process for building a common vision include hiring many staff from the neighbourhoods, ensuring that important committees were made up of at least 50 per cent community residents, and using consensus decision making to guarantee that all voices were heard and opposition valued. 'People listen to us now', 'we're in charge of it', and 'we're doing something that not only needs to be done but is being done very well' are examples of comments heard frequently throughout the focus groups and our years of observations. Between 200 and 300 adults had become members of each centre by the fifth year of the project; many of these adults also used the services in the centres. One-third of these members gave back at least a few hours per month of unpaid time to the centres. The statistical record of unpaid hours indicate the steady contributions of time each quarter during the three study years from April 1994 to the end of March 1997.

By the third study year, however, changes in employment and welfare laws were making community work more difficult to negotiate freely. Moreover, the centres faced cessation of funds upon completion of the research demonstration project in 1997. People in the focus groups were very worried that their centres would disappear if no funds were found. All were adamant that depending on unpaid, volunteer hours to keep the centres open would not work. While writing the results of our study, the above-mentioned 17 April 1997 government decision to not close the eight demonstration community resources centres had been announced to everyone's relief, but no new ones were opened, despite the pressing needs of dozens of equally poor neighbourhoods. Respondents in this study felt badly about denying services to children and adults living outside the targeted neighbourhoods who had similar needs, but were without access to similar resource centres. Members also worried that new laws and restrictive regulations regarding, for example, welfare assistance, disability pensions, and unemployment insurance, along with increasing pressures for centre services, would make it difficult for the centres to keep their vision, becoming instead 'like another agency trying to impose on the neighbourhood'. It is to these worries that we now turn.

'Can't Pay the Rent':
Community Work as Hoax or Scary Dance

Throughout the development of the centres, people spoke of the stresses common to most caring work—juggling too many tasks and being treated as a 'glorified joe boy' cleaning up messes. Group disputes prompted by differences in personalities, language, boredom, and exclusion sometimes escalated into nasty conflicts. Difficulties like these are not uncommon to any group of people, especially if there is a history of being systematically excluded, marginalized, or ignored (Bishop 1994; hooks 1993). Poverty, racism, élitism, and sexism often leave one feeling that one is 'not part of running it as much as the other people', as one respondent summed up the worry.

Compounding these fears was the profound worry that the community work of the centres would become totally dependent on unpaid contributions. This dependency loomed just when community needs were increasing and other services were shrinking. People spoke of feeling overwhelmed, burned out, giving too much, being taken for granted, and wanting to say no. No government funds could be used by the centres for steady adequate child care, housing, and employment for parents in the neighbourhoods. Good jobs are rare in poor neighbourhoods, especially given the minimal education of one-third of the residents. Members who gave unpaid time often wanted to be hired for pay when there were jobs in the centres or elsewhere. Until the April 1997 announcement, it was expected that the demonstration project would end that year, and the centres would have to become 'self-sufficient'. Thus, even the few who had jobs as staff in the community resource centres worried about losing them.

Consider the following quote. In it a participant wonders if the funders of the original demonstration project had played a horrible hoax on the community. How could anyone expect community work to continue without funding? Pride, a vision, and untold unpaid contributions would never be enough:

> A community like this doesn't have a lot of money, but it has a lot of other wealth, like time and wisdom. And there is a fallacy to me in current thinking, that poor people can evolve into being self-sufficient. I question the premise of self-sufficiency; [I see it] as a rich people's hoax on poor people. A hoax. I come from an underdeveloped country, so I know that hoax well. There is no such thing as self-sufficiency. Everybody must be in the network to get the resources they need from each other. If not, what you have is exploitation.

People were poor when the centres first opened in 1991. Despite the benefits of and their contributions to the community resource centres, most people in the neighbourhoods experienced increased poverty over time. The impact of the 21 per cent cuts in welfare rates in Ontario in the fall of 1994 and reductions in services and entitlements reverberated throughout people's lives (Bezanson and Valentine 1998; Hamilton n.d.). Our respondents spoke of asthma and anaemia worsening after the cuts; homes lost; hours spent scrambling for any job; self-esteem shattered as 'people are afraid to talk because they are so poor'. After the 1994 cuts, the three study centres channelled more unpaid time into efforts to redistribute food, clothing, and medicines, and to making political and economic protests. But no matter how much one gives to the centre, and no matter how much the community resource centres try to do, says one woman, sometimes 'you can't pay rent. We can pool our money, but we can't necessarily buy milk, and milk is not provided at the food banks, nor eggs, meat, and cheese.'

The hoax is more than a worry. It felt very real to respondents and threatened community work. People wanted to disconnect themselves from the relationship building, shadow work, planning, and service activities of community work in the centres. The next quote speaks of the downward spiral that limits energy available to give to community work, no matter how valued it is. The shame of deepening poverty and the struggle to survive dry up one's desire to give 'positive regard to others' in the world beyond one's immediate family:

> People are just reeling from the shock. And you know, they're so busy trying to exist that, you know, that's where their energy was. It's just all your time is sucked up trying to make, make up for what's lost. . . . You just may not want to be around people or you know, you might be too ashamed if all of a sudden you're a lot poorer than what you thought you were.

The government's continued funding, the determination of centres to keep their vision, and the continued unpaid contributions of community members all helped to counter the threats implicit in the metaphor of a hoax, but there was another serious concern about the changing nature of the community work in the centres. For this concern we use the metaphor of a scary dance to capture the strong ambivalence between the desire and the fear of dancing with a partner, such as the government, who is so much stronger and can arbitrarily change the rules of the dance. In the focus groups and in our conversations with centre members during 1996 and 1997, people said they wanted to continue volunteering, yet they were very worried that their capacity to negotiate openly and freely their meaningful contributions to community work were threatened.

On one hand there was anxiety that volunteering freely was becoming too risky, threatening people's eligibility for pensions or insurance. Contributions to community work could turn into furtive giving with considerable risks and penalties, as suggested by one focus group participant:

> There are a lot of risks if they are on unemployment and they want to come and do some volunteer time. There is a risk, if they are found out, of being penalized. If you go on welfare there is a risk too. If you come here and get help from us in some way you are penalized on your cheque. [For example], babysitting: If I go over to somebody's house and say 'I have some free time why don't you go somewhere and I'll watch your kids for nothing?' If that is found out. . . .!

On the other hand, it was becoming more difficult to donate volunteer time freely, especially for the one-third of the population in the neighbourhoods served by the centre who are dependent on welfare. The work-for-welfare, or workfare policies piloted in 1996 and turned into the Ontario Works law in November 1997, will affect all who apply for welfare assistance (Ontario 1997). To remain eligible after four months on welfare, individuals and families on assistance must continue to look for paid work and 'volunteer' for short-term, six-month community placements at seventy hours per month or engage in work training schemes such as resume writing and job clubs. If they do not comply, they risk losing three months of benefits for the first 'non-compliance' and six months for the second offence. Furthermore, appeal procedures in the proposed new law were to be very restrictive, making it difficult to contest the increased surveillance and rigid eligibility procedures.

Our study of volunteering in the community resource centres ended before workfare laws were fully implemented and enforced, so their impact is not yet known. We did learn that the decision-making groups in each of the centres had refused to participate in the pilot workfare projects and had refused workfare placements. More of their energy went into joining protests organized by community and provincial social justice groups to fight the increased surveillance of those needing welfare and their decreased entitlements in the pilot projects and the proposed legislation (CUPE n.d.; Ontario Social Development Council 1996; Workfare Watch 1996). But centre members anticipated strong pressure from their own members dependent on welfare, and from their municipal and provincial funders, to accept workfare placements in the future. They worried about how people could continue to negotiate freely their community work when there were such high risks for non-compliance and extensive surveillance. How could the centres complete the extensive paperwork, monitor people, and report lapses as expected with these short-term volunteer community placements and still keep the new approach to volunteering so painstakingly developed in which volunteers were not in a separate class of people, and in which people could both use services and give freely of their time to plan and run the services? Despite the pride and pleasure associated with giving time to community work in the resource centres, there were strong contradictions and fears for the future.

Concluding Comments

MacDonald (1996:19) found that adults in a depressed local British economy willingly engaged in volunteer work or 'labours of love'. We too found adults with incomes of less than one-half the provincial average taking pride in belonging, in learning, and in doing worthwhile activities for the children and adults in their neighbourhoods.

This study of non-profit community resource centres in poor urban neighbourhoods clearly demonstrates that with the help of some stable funding and a vision, people will give thousands of unpaid hours to care about and for others in the communities beyond their homes. The funders of the centres decided not to close the centres as originally planned, in part due to the economic efficiency of community work. Community work goes beyond volunteering for organizations, neighbourliness, or political action. We found that the skilled craft of community work was made up of equal parts of specific services, relationship building, planning work, and shadow activities. All aspects were used to keep the centres open, with programs free, inviting, and accessible to families in poor neighbourhoods.

However, the study also reveals the fragility of community work, especially in poor communities. There are no short cuts. Many hours of paid and unpaid time are needed to create the processes that enable people to engage in community work. People with the fewest options about where they could live or what paid work they could do had the most appreciation of these processes. People stopped their community work quickly if they felt dismissed, devalued, or excluded.

Threats to stable funding increase the likelihood of exploitation. Without funding it is difficult to maintain the vision of negotiating meaningful activities and relationships. Non-profit organizations, like our community resource centres, are not confident that they can find the unpaid hours to pursue their vision and provide services. Staff worry about how to do this without exploiting volunteers or risking penalties. In addition, there are the pressures that come with cuts in welfare rates and government services, restrictions on eligibility, and continued high unemployment rates for minimally educated people. Living in such social conditions, how can people's desire to do community work be supported without exploiting those who do it?

People can be exploited because even with some funding and good processes that support negotiating meaningful activities, much community work is barely visible. The service, planning, and relationship building aspects of community work depend on the fourth aspect, the shadow work or 'informal care' (Rekart 1993:146) performed mostly by women as they cook, tend children, keep house, visit the sick, and sooth the emotions associated with group conflicts in the centres. Without this shadow work, men, women, and youth would not be able to lug boxes, supervise community gardens, go to meetings, and hire centre staff. People, mostly women, can be enticed by the vision of community work, but also become ensnared to do caring labour without any reciprocal benefits in terms of entitlements or income security (Abrahams 1996; Baldock and Ungerson 1991; Naples 1991, 1992; Oliker 1995; Rose 1993).

What happens to community work if more policing and surveillance are added to the daily stresses of living in poverty? MacDonald (1996:28) reported what he called 'involuntary volunteering' in his study of community volunteering initiatives in depressed areas of Britain. Most of the American research concentrates on examining whether the restructured welfare policies and workfare, learnfare, and job training experiments of the past fifteen years 'put welfare recipients to work', control government costs, and minimize the impact of severe poverty on young children (Besley and Coate 1992; Mead 1989; Tanner, Moore, and Hartman 1995). Although there is some recognition that the results of the most rigorous, longitudinal research are mixed and not necessarily cost effective, especially in areas with high unemployment, there is little attention in the American mainstream policy literature on how the caring work done by women in the community, domestic, and market spheres are affected by policies that increase surveillance and decrease the freedom to negotiate one's paid and unpaid labour (Brasher 1994; Gueron 1996; Oliker 1994). Most invisible and problematic is what happens to the perversion of what community work is all about, as Naples (1998) argues in her thirty-year review of the analysis of community participation in antipoverty initiatives.

Despite the pleasure and pride that members in our three study centres took in their voluntary community work, by fall 1996 there were deep concerns, concerns hinted at in previous Canadian research on welfare, about workfare types of reforms (e.g., Evans 1995; Reynolds 1995). To remain eligible for employment assistance, unemployed people in our study felt they had to hide the time they volunteered and were not out looking for a non-existent job. In order to continue receiving social assistance in the future, recipients worried they would have to prove they had given volunteer time that was recorded and monitored by an organization on contract to the municipal authorities. By early 1998, all municipalities in Ontario were obliged to enforce obligatory 'voluntary work' if people were to remain eligible for social assistance.[6] A 1999 interim analysis of Ontario Works (that province's new welfare law), based on focus groups and individual interviews with 230 people in ten cities, concluded that, despite the promises of the law and the hopes of people on welfare for jobs, training, and assistance, the outcomes were disappointing, discouraging, and disturbing (Workfare Watch Project 1999). The economic climate in Ontario had improved by 1998 for those with education and skills, but those who need assistance were living in increasingly desperate circumstances. The new law made life more difficult: subsistence was so low that it hurt health; assistance in training and support had not materialized; there were few community placements; and it was very difficult to find good jobs.

As for the law's impact on volunteering and community work, people reported that their experiences of negotiating 'participation agreements' regarding community placements, work search, and training were rushed, confusing, unhelpful, and totally unlike the mutual, participatory process promised by law. Few not-for-profit organizations were willing or able to create community volunteer placements. Municipalities used innovative but problematic ways to meet targets set by the provincial government, including placements in 'trash gangs' clothed in bright identifiable shirts; placements that filled paid positions; the waiver of monitoring requirements; and incentives like transit passes if people found their own placements. Only 4,400 placements had been created by the end of 1997, or 40 per cent of the target, according to the provincial auditor. As these placements by law must be short term (e.g., six months), they are not secure, and energy is needed to renegotiate them with new people. Under these conditions it is difficult to promote the stable development of volunteering and volunteers so necessary to community work. When discussing their experiences with the new law in the focus groups, people spoke of their desire to improve their skills and their frustration with the poor quality and stigmatizing nature of the placements. They felt driven and without choices. With few exceptions, they did not feel that the community placements helped them find paid work. They also spoke of their resentment that their previous volunteering was being changed into something different and coercive in order to retain their eligibility for welfare. Workfare was a key part of the government's plans to change welfare policy in Ontario, but the report also suggests that workfare is restructuring the nature of community work: 'This is creating serious dilemmas for non-profits and may have damaging long-term consequences for voluntarism. It pits welfare recipients, who are desperate to get any additional assistance they can, such as a transit pass, against agencies who are reluctant to participate' (Workfare Watch Project 1999:50).

It is imperative that we continue to look carefully at how increased surveillance and resource starvation restructure the caring for and about others that occurs in community work. How can autonomy, empowerment, the sense of belonging, and community cohesion increase when paid staff (or volunteers) are expected to categorize, separate, train, and monitor the free volunteers, the workfare volunteers, the involuntary trainees? What pockets of resistance will emerge? As we near the end of the twentieth century, inequality and injustices seem to be increasing rather than decreasing. One result is a greater demand on women's unpaid caring labour in the community, domestic, and market spheres (Cameron 1997; Evans and Wekerle 1997; Evers 1996; Hudson 1998; Lewis 1993; Rekart 1993). There are fewer resources to support processes that enable people to engage in meaningful activities on behalf of others in the world beyond that of their immediate family. We desperately need careful analysis of those sites of struggle that are resisting pressures to restructure community work in ways that deprive people in poor neighbourhoods of the freedom to negotiate freely the conditions under which they do caring labour.

Notes

Many thanks to those who gave us so many unpaid hours to count and debate the work of community development in this case-study of three community resource centres. Thanks to Joan Kuyek and Patricia Rogerson for teaching through action. We appreciate the practical and theoretical assistance of Angela Mione, Mechthild Maczewski, and our colleagues in the Women's Caring Network. Thanks to Ray Peters, Doug Angus, and Carol Russell for including the cost-benefit analysis in the evaluation. Funds from the University of Toronto, the University of Victoria, and a Social Sciences and Humanities Research Council Strategic Grants-Women and Change (816-94-003) made this study possible. The Ministry of Community and Social Services, the Ministry of Health, and the Ministry of Education in Ontario funded the resource centres and the evaluation research.

1   Marge has been closely associated with one centre since 1989 as a proposal developer, site researcher, and project consultant until the summer of 1997. In 1992 she was invited to become a member of the central Queen's University Research Coordination Unit, and has participated in yearly sessions with researchers of all the centres. Since moving to Victoria in 1997, she remains a 'friend' of the project. Sheila joined Marge in 1994 to study the services-in-kind data in the centres. We had access to the following unpublished documents on

the centres. A. Mione, S. Neysmith, and M. Reitsma-Street, '1995 Report on Services In-Kind for Seven Urban Better Beginnings, Better Futures Sites' (30 September 1995, ten pages); D. Angus, 'Better Beginnings, Better Futures Economic Analysis Update' (March 1995, thirty-two pages); J. Vanderwoerd, 'Report on the Involvement of Neighbourhood Participants in the Onward Willow-Better Beginnings, Better Futures Project' (18 January 1993, seventy-eight pages); J. Vanderwoerd, 'Management and Organization of the Onward Willow Better Beginnings Project: Principles, Processes, and Practice 1990–1995' (June 1996 111 pages); No date or author on the 'Kingston Resident Participation Report' (fifteen pages); J. Vanderwoerd and D. Blessing, 'Management and Organization of Better Beginnings for Kingston Children 1991–1995' (February 1997, seventy-three pages); Lamine Diallo 'Resident Participation in the Better Beginnings, Better Futures Project in Sudbury 1989 to 1992 (15 January 1993; fifty-eight pages); L. Diallo, 'Report on Management and Organization of Better Beginnings, Better Futures, Sudbury' (June 1996, forty-seven pages, plus appendices).

2 Research committees in each centre piloted the focus group questions and decided what criteria helped to distinguish the variety of time-in-kind contributions in their communities. There are more community than academic researchers in the research committees. Each participant signed consent forms, and could participate in a meal and use child care provided during focus groups. Transcripts of focus groups were sent to the research committees— with identifying information in code. Early versions of this chapter were presented to forty community members in one centre, and written drafts distributed for comment to the research committees in all study centres.

3 'Time-in-kind' and 'services-in-kind' are labels used in the resource centres to record both the unpaid hours of staff and community and the hours donated by service providers and those on low-wage training programs in quarterly statistics for funders and researchers.

4 Given the differences in the worlds and work of men and women, and given that often poor women feel freer to speak in the absence of men, we decided to conduct same-sex focus groups for community members in each of the centres. Organizational paid informants, both male and female, were interviewed together in a separate focus group.

5 Time-in-kind data were available on five centres from 1994 to 1997. The five full-time equivalent positions are based on taking the average of the total unpaid hours recorded as contributions of staff and community members per year, divided by fifty weeks, and then by thirty-five hours.

6 A small percentage of welfare recipients are able to go to school instead of doing volunteer work, but only for upgrading in literacy or high school. As of fall 1995, no person on welfare can go to college or university. Another small percentage of recipients are eligible for the twelve-month employment-support programs.

References

Abrahams, Naomi. 1996. 'Negotiating Power, Identity, Family and Community: Women's Community Participation'. *Gender and Society* 10, no. 6:768–96.

Aptheker, B. 1989. *Tapestries of Life: Women's Work, Women's Consciousness, and the Meaning of Daily Experience*. Amherst: University of Massachusetts Press.

Arnstein, S. 1969.'A Ladder of Citizen Participation'. *Journal of American Institute of Planners* 35, no. 4:216–22.

Baines, C., P. Evans, and S. Neysmith, eds. 1998. *Women's Caring*, rev. ed. Toronto: Oxford University Press.

Baldock, Cora Vellekoop. 1990. *Volunteers in Welfare*. Sydney: Allen & Unwin.

Baldock, John, and Clare Ungerson. 1991. '"What D'Ya Want If You Don' Want Money?": A Feminist Critique of "Paid Volunteering"'. In *Women's Issues in Social Policy*, edited by M. MacLean and D. Groves, 136–57. London: Routledge.

Besley, Timothy, and Stephen Coate. 1992. 'Workfare Versus Welfare: Incentive Arguments for Work Requirements in Poverty-Alleviation Programs'. *The American Economic Review* 82, no. 1:249–61.

Bezanson, Kate, and Fraser Valentine. 1998. *Act in Haste . . . The Style, Scope and Speed of Change in Ontario* (Speaking Out Project). Ottawa: Caledon Institute of Social Policy.

Bishop, A. *Becoming an Ally: Breaking the Cycle of Oppression*. Halifax: Fernwood.

Boyd, S.B. 1997. 'Challenging the Public/Private Divided: An Overview'. In *Challenging the Public/Private Divide: Feminism, Law, and Public Policy*, edited by S. Boyd, 3–36. Toronto: University of Toronto Press.

Brasher, C. Nielsen. 1994. 'Workfare in Ohio: Political and Socioeconomic Climate and Program Impact'. *Policy Studies Journal* 22, no. 3:514–27.

Brodie, Janine, ed. 1996. *Women and Canadian Public Policy*. Toronto: Harcourt.

Cameron, Andrew A.F. 1997. 'In Search of the Voluntary Sector: A Review Article'. *Journal of Social Policy* 26, no. 1:79–88.

Collins, Patricia Hill. 1991. *Black Feminist Thought: Knowledge, Consciousness and the Politics of Empowerment*. New York: Routledge.

Connell, R.W. 1987. *Gender and Power: Society, the Person and Sexual Politics*. Oxford: Polity Press.

Cowen, E.L., ed. 1982. 'Special Issue: Research in Primary Prevention in Mental Health'. *American Journal of Community Psychology* 10, no. 3:239–50.

Cruikshank, B. 1994. 'The Will to Empower: Technologies of Citizenship and the War on Poverty'. *Socialist Review* 23, no. 4:29–55.

CUPE (Canadian Union of Public Employees, Ontario Division). n.d. 'Tory Tall Tales: Or Why "Ontario Works" Won't Work'.

Evans, Patricia M. 1995. 'Linking Welfare to Jobs: Workfare, Canadian Style'. *Policy Options* (May):5–9.

_____, and G.R. Wekerle, eds. *Women and the Canadian Welfare State: Challenges and Change*. Toronto: University of Toronto Press.

Evers, Adalbert. 1996. 'Part of the Welfare Mix: The Third Sector as an Intermediate Area'. *Voluntas* 6, no. 2:159–82.

Frazer, Elizabeth, and Niccola Lacey. 1993. *The Politics of Community: A Feminist Critique of the Liberal-Communitarian Debate*. Toronto: University of Toronto Press.

Freiler, Christa, and J. Cerny. 1998. *Benefitting Canada's Children: Perspectives on Gender and Social Responsibility*. Ottawa: Status of Women Canada.

Gueron, Judith M. 1996. 'A Research Context for Welfare Reform'. *Journal of Policy Analysis and Management* 15, no. 4:547–61.

Gutierrez, Lorraine. 1991. 'Empowering Women of Color: A Feminist Model'. In *Feminist Social Work Practice in Clinical Settings*, edited by M. Bricker-Jenikins et al., 199–214. Newbury Park: Sage Publications.

Hamilton, Cheryl, ed. n.d. *Reality Cheque: Telling Our Stories of Life on Welfare in Ontario*. Toronto: Ontario Social Safety NetWork, Social Planning Council of Metro Toronto.

hooks, bell. 1993. *Sisters of the Yam: Black Women and Self-Recovery*. Montreal: Between the Lines.

Hoschild, Anne. 1997. *Time Bind*. New York: Metropolitan Books.

_____, with A. Machung. 1989. *The Second Shift: Working Parents and the Revolution at Home*. New York: Viking.

Hudson, Peter. 1998. 'Welfare Pluralism in the UK: Views from the Non-profit Sector'. *Canadian Review of Social Policy* 41:1–16.

Knijn, T., and M. Kremer. 1997. 'Gender and the Caring Dimension of Welfare States: Toward Inclusive Citizenship'. *Social Politics* (Fall):328–61.

Kyle, I. 1993. *Towards an Understanding of Best Practices in Family Resource Programs*. Ottawa: Canadian Association of Family Resource Programs.

Leira, Arnlaug. 1994. 'Concepts of Caring: Loving, Thinking, and Doing'. *Social Service Review* 68, no. 2:185–201.

Lewis, Jane. 1993. 'Developing the Mixed Economy of Care: Emerging Issues for Voluntary Organisations'. *Journal of Social Policy* 22, no. 2:173–92.

Loney, M. 1983. *Community Against Government: The British Columbia Development Project 1968–1978*. London: Heinemann Educational Books.

Lundström, Tommy. 1996. 'The State and Voluntary Social Work in Sweden'. *Voluntas* 7, no. 2:123–46.

Lustiger-Thaler, Henri. 'Social Citizenship and Urban Citizenship: The Composition of Local Practics'. *Canadian Journal of Urban Research* 2, no. 2:115–29.

MacDonald, Robert. 1996. 'Labours of Love: Voluntary Working in a Depressed Local Economy'. *Journal of Social Policy* 25, no. 1:19–38.

Marris, P., and M. Rein. 1972. *Dilemmas of Social Reform: Poverty and Community Action in the United States*, 2nd edn. London: Routledge and Kegan Paul.

Mead, Lawrence M. 1989. 'The Logic of Workfare: The Underclass and Work Policy'. *The Annals of the American Academy of Political and Social Science* 510:156–69.

Mione, Angela, Sheila Neysmith, and Marge Reitsma-Street. 1996. 'Better Beginnings, Better Futures: Urban Sites Services-in-Kind Revised Code Book'. Mimeo. Laurentian University and University of Toronto.

Moore Milroy, B., and S. Wismer. 1994. 'Communities, Work and Public/Private Sphere Models'. *Gender, Place and Culture* 1, no. 1:71–90.

Naples, Nancy A. 1991. 'Contradictions in the Gender Subtext of the War on Poverty: The Community, Work and Resistance from Low-Income Communities'. *Social Problems* 38, no. 3:316–32.

_____. 1992. 'Activist Mothering: Cross-generational Continuity in the Community Work of Women from Low-Income Urban Neighbourhoods'. *Gender and Society* 6, no. 3:441–63.

_____. 1998. 'From Maximum Feasible Participation to Disenfranchisement'. *Social Justice* 25, no. 10:47–66.

Oliker, Stacy J. 1994. 'Does Workfare Work? Evaluation Research and Workfare Reform'. *Social Problems* 41:195–213.

_____. 1995. 'The Proximate Contexts of Workfare and Work: A Framework for Studying Poor Women's Economic Choices'. *The Sociological Quarterly* 36, no. 2:251–72.

Ontario, 1st Session, 36th Legislature, 46 Elizabeth II. 1997. *Ontario Works Act*, Bill 142. Royal Assent, 28 November.

Ontario Ministry of Community and Social Services. 1990. *Better Beginnings, Better Futures: An Integrated Model of Primary Prevention of Emotional and Behavioural Problems*. Toronto: Queen's Printer.

Ontario Social Development Council. 1996. 'OSCD Board Resolution Opposing Workfare', 29 March. See shookner@web.apc.org, 7 June 1996.

Pancer, S.M., and G. Cameron. 1994. 'Resident Participation in the Better Beginnings, Better Futures Prevention Project: Part I—The Impacts of Involvement'. *Canadian Journal of Community Mental Health* 13, no. 2:197–211.

Pearce, Jone L. 1993. *The Organizational Behaviour of Unpaid Workers*. London: Routledge.

Peters, R.D., and C.C. Russell. 1996. 'Promoting Development and Preventing Disorder: The Better Beginnings, Better Futures Project'. In *Preventing Childhood Disorders, Substance Abuse and Delinquency*, edited by R.D. Peters and R.J. McMahon, 19–47. Thousand Oaks: Sage Publications.

Reitsma-Street, Marge, and Robert Arnold. 1994. 'Community-Based Action Research in a Multi-site Prevention Project: Challenges and Resolutions'. *Canadian Journal of Community Mental Health* 13, no. 2:229–40.

Rekart, Josephine, 1993. *Public Funds, Private Provision: The Role of the Voluntary Sector*. Vancouver: University of British Columbia Press.

Reynolds, Elisabeth B. 1995. 'Subsidized Employment Programs and Welfare Reform: The Quebec Experience'. In *Workfare: Does It Work?*, edited by I. Sayeed, 105–42. Montreal: Institute for Research on Public Policy.

Rose, Nancy E. 1993. 'Gender, Race, and the Welfare State: Government Work Programs from the 1930s to the Present'. *Feminist Studies* 19, no. 2:319–42.

Ross, David P. 1990. 'How Valuable Is Volunteering?' *Perception* 14, no. 4:17–18.

Schorr, E. 1988. *Within Our Reach: Breaking the Cycle of Disadvantage*. New York: Anchor Press.

Sokolowski, S. Wojeciech. 1996. 'Show Me the Way to the Next Worthy Deed: Towards a Microstructural Theory of Volunteering and Giving'. *Voluntas* 7, no. 3:259–78.

Tanner, Michael, Stephen Moore, and David Hartman. 1995. 'The Work Versus Welfare Trade-off: Analysis of the Total Level of Welfare Benefits by State'. Cato Policy Analysis, no. 240, September, Washington. See www.cato.org/pubs/pas/pa-240.html.

Wharf, Brian, and Michael Clague. 1997. 'Lessons and Legacies'. In *Community Organizing: Canadian Experiences*, edited by B. Wharf and M. Clague, 302–25. Toronto: Oxford University Press.

Workfare Watch. 1996. Quarterly newsletters and Internet bulletins, February 1996, Social Planning Council of Metropolitan Toronto. See www.welfarewatch.toronto.on.ca.

Workfare Watch Project. 1999. *Broken Promises: Welfare Reform in Ontario*. Toronto: Community Social Planning Council of Toronto. See also www.welfarewatch.toronto.on.ca/promises/paper.

Chapter 8

Restructuring Services for Children: Lessons from the Past

Carol T. Baines

News reports that highlight child poverty and children at risk evoke considerable sympathy from the Canadian public, but this has had little impact on improving the material conditions of children and their families. In Ontario during the last five years of the twentieth century, the Conservative government led by Premier Harris has been the architect of punitive and harsh policies that affect the lives of poor women and children most dramatically. Work for welfare (workfare) and reduction policies in welfare assistance rates have exposed more families and children to the risks that accompany living in poverty. State policies aimed at deficit reduction and an erosion of social services point to the impact that globalization and economic restructuring, discussed elsewhere in this volume, are having on social work as a profession—the agents who work most directly with poor families (Dominelli 1996). Nowhere is this more evident than in the field of child welfare.

The children and families served by our child welfare system have always been among the poorest in Canada. Yet the Child and Family Services Act in Ontario (1999) is not directed at providing supportive services to families but rather focuses its attention on identifying individual mothers who expose their children to emotional, physical, or sexual abuse and neglect. The act is also aimed at increasing the accountability of social workers and other professionals to identify and report incidents of abuse. For service providers, the professional protocol emerging is the Ontario risk assessment model, an instrument that attempts to standardize eligibility for service, the type of intervention and a safety plan.[1] The adoption of this model has dramatically increased the number of allegations of abuse and the number of children coming into care. In Ontario there has been a 20 per cent increase in the number of children in care—the highest it has been since the implementation of the 1984 Children and Family Services Act (Lindgren 1998). Similar increases are evident if we examine the increases in the number of reports of abuse and neglect from the UK, Australia, and North America. For example, in the US, child abuse reports have increased from

9,563 in 1967 to 2,936,000 in 1992 (Parton 1998:18). Although child physical and sexual abuse remains a critical problem, risk-assessment policies are directed at detecting risks of abuse without attending to other factors, such as poverty, inadequate housing, isolation of the mother, and school problems that are crucial to a child's development.

Risk-assessment protocols, like earlier forms of professional technology, fail to address the socio-economic and cultural-racial context in which the needs of children and families occur. While the state is reducing public expenditures and cutting services, children's aid societies are confronted with the task of equipping child welfare workers with the requisite knowledge and skills that will facilitate the identification of children at risk.[2] Social workers employed in child-welfare agencies will be expected to operate within a professional paradigm that includes the psychological, developmental, clinical, and medical knowledge that will allow them to make what they believe will be more scientific and defensible judgements of children. Ironically, the increased number of children in the care of children's aid societies adds to the cost of child-welfare services. Workers are directed away from providing support to families or assisting them in gaining supplementary resources to investigating parental inadequacies. Thus, social workers are inadvertently contributing to reframing the problems endemic in child welfare and to the solutions. Risk assessment has become a model of intervention that is highly bureaucratic, directed at accountability, intrusive, and time consuming for social workers. Hailed as an objective and scientific tool, it fails to address the risks that confront child-welfare workers who are forced to make judgements about parents that cannot always be predictable. Blending professional goals with state directives and bureaucratic procedures has been an ongoing reality for the human service professions. The resulting contradictions have been equally ongoing.

These dual obligations to a profession and to an organization and the conflicts that ensue are not new. During the 1950s, an affluent period in Canada when services for children expanded, the standard of living for Ontario's poor families did not keep pace with the rising prosperity of the overall population. Struthers has argued that during the 1950s and 1960s, the purpose of social work was the regulation of family life, particularly single mothers, who were encouraged to give up their children (Struthers 1994). Much of this monitoring occurred in social agencies in which women as social workers provided services to mother-led single families.

The relationship between women's paid and unpaid caring labour and the welfare of children has been central to the history of state/family responsibility debates. Women as volunteers, mothers, and low-paid workers, committed to what today we would call an ethic of care, initiated and developed services for children and families in the early twentieth century that cast the foundation for our contemporary child-welfare system. Bestowed with sanction and authority from the state, the so-called caring professions such as social work and nursing evolved within the context of their own professional aspirations and as partners in providing services for some of the poorest members of society (Hugman 1991). This relationship has been replete with contradictions for those in the professions and for the clients they serve. Gender, class, and bureaucratic hierarchies have been crucial dimensions in these tensions. Women as workers have been subjected to managerial control by their male counterparts, and women as clients have had their needs defined by others. Committed to values that encompass equal rights, compassion, and entitlements, but employed in organizations in which reductions in welfare costs and moralistic and punitive programs reflect the state's agenda, social workers are faced with the reality of being active players in implementing policies and programs that frequently reproduce rather than reduce their clients' difficulties.

An examination of the services and programs that have evolved over the course of the last century in periods of retrenchment and expansion highlights the chronic inadequacy of material resources available to poor families, which are typically mother-led families. What has changed over time is how professionals conceptualize the problems confronting poor families, the language and discourse used for describing them, and the interventions considered appropriate for addressing them. Thus, the recent adoption of risk-assessment protocols by child-welfare agencies dovetails with a changing conception of the causes of child abuse and neglect on the one hand, and a return to mother blaming and the individualization of social problems on the other.

Several chapters in this book discuss current renditions of the 'single-mother problem'. In this chapter I step back to an earlier era in an effort to uncover the processes through which social workers contribute to the social reproduction of a policy paradigm that repeatedly situates mothers as culpable if children are deemed 'at risk'. The analysis in this chapter comes out of my ongoing research into the history of social work practice. Specifically, this analysis traces how services developed to care for poor children after the Second World War resulted from a struggle between class interests as reflected in traditional charity/religious approaches to alleviating the effects of poverty, the secular claims to expert knowledge that characterized an emerging profession, and public administration that was part of the developing welfare state. The chapter examines the transitions experienced at the Earlscourt Children's Home from 1949–64 and the impact that restructuring at that time had on services for children and their care providers. The director of the organization, Dorothy Moore, a professional social worker, set in motion the transformation of Earlscourt from a resource for poor families who needed substitute care for their children to a centre that would meet the needs of a newly identified client group labelled 'emotionally disturbed children'. The Earlscourt Children's Home was one of several child-care institutions during this period that were confronted with the task of transforming itself into a specific purpose agency if it was to avoid the threat of closure.[3] This journey into the past echoes some of the current debate about services for poor families and their children and the dramatic increase in removal of children from their parental home. Some of the questions informing this study are: How do social workers wrestle with competing ideologies? What part do professionals play in implementing and transforming policies? How does this affect services for families and their children? And what part does gender play in the implementation and transformation of services?

Professionalism and the State

In Ontario the crusade to professionalize child-welfare services and the beginning of a broader and more public funding base proceeded rapidly in the post-Second World War period. State-supported institutions for children began to replace the small voluntary organizations that had operated within a moral framework of providing care and utilized the labour of lowly paid and unpaid women.[4] In 1948 the Toronto Welfare Council and the Child Welfare Branch of the Ontario government, concerned about the shortage of foster homes in the city, began to advocate residential care for children with special needs. Concerned about the rising costs of residential care, the Child Welfare Branch discouraged the use of institutions for children who were privately placed by their families. By insisting that professional social workers assess all requests for private placement, the state fostered the growth of social work as a profession while infringing on the rights of parents (frequently mothers) to determine what was best for their children. Not surprisingly, this was a period in which human service professionals— social workers, child-care workers, psychologists, and psychiatrists—began to assert their expertise and develop strongholds of professional power. Concomitantly, families (particularly mother-led families) were subjected to the power of professionals and the increased authority of the state. The caring professions began to acquire ideological as well as material power to define who is a client and who gets services, power that is often made invisible by the caring commitment and intimacy that characterizes the professional/client relationship (Hugman 1991).

Earlscourt began operation in 1913 as a daycare centre under Methodist auspices. From 1915 until 1948, under the leadership of a charismatic superintendent, Hattie Inkpen, and the financial and administrative support of the Wimodausis Club (a group of upper-middle-class women), it offered short- and long-term residential care for children from families who, for reasons such as poor health, lack of housing, or the death of a parent, were unable to provide care for their children. Most of the families were poor and the majority were single-mother-led families. Today, the transformed Earlscourt Child and Family Centre continues to offer supportive services to poor families, primarily mother-led, with children identified as 'aggressive'. The history of Earlscourt speaks to the way in which organizations have had to adapt to the pressures of limited state funding yet struggle to meet the needs of the families they serve.

Transforming Earlscourt's mandate was the challenge confronting Dorothy Moore when she was appointed superintendent in October 1948. Moore was an active member of the Canadian Association of Social Workers and had child-welfare experience with the Protestant Children's Home and St Faith's Lodge in Toronto. As a fledgling professional, Moore was committed to the postwar emphasis on casework as the crucial element in the practice of social work and initiated a policy change to admit emotionally disturbed children. From the board's perspective, the need to provide alternative care for poor children still existed and they preferred to retain this mission as long as it was financially viable. This conflict in mission reflects some of the tensions that emerged as a middle-class aspiring professional woman struggled to reinforce her views in an area traditionally controlled by upper-class men and women committed to a charity model of welfare.

Late in 1949, Earlscourt began to receive a per diem rate of five cents for each child under the Charitable Institutions Act.[5] The provision of these meagre grants also brought public accountability. Earlscourt would be inspected and would have to meet the standards and expectations of the child-welfare authorities. One of these expectations was that family casework be utilized to assess and ensure that no child who did not require special care was admitted. Poverty or the request for placement by a mother was not grounds for admission. Casework or case management, as it is known today, was gradually beginning to transform child-welfare work.

The intake policy that evolved at Earlscourt was an attempt to marry past policies with changing conceptions of what constituted professional social work practices and the mandates of the major child-welfare agencies, children's aid societies. At a board meeting in April 1949, the intake policy at Earlscourt was modified to include:

1. Children of normal intelligence between the ages of 4–10 from broken homes or homes where one parent is hospitalized and the other parent must work.

2. Children of normal intelligence between the ages of 4–10 who are unable to accept foster home placement, and who, in the opinion of the director, will benefit under our care.[6]

This policy enabled Earlscourt to continue with its original mandate to be a resource for poor families, but also admit the 'hard-to-place' child and thus access provincial funds. However, this change at the policy level did not resolve the tensions Moore was experiencing with the board of directors. The

Earlscourt board was made up of men and women who were highly committed and intimately involved in the running and management of the home, but who remained uncertain about the changes. However, both Moore and her board were also confronted with the external expectations of a professional community, outside agencies, and provincial jurisdiction. By the late 1940s, policies and practices of the US child-welfare community began to influence services in Ontario.

In 1949 the Child and Family Welfare Division of the Toronto Welfare Council, prompted by a shortfall in the Red Feather campaign, the major private fundraising resource, engaged the Community Chest and Council of New York to complete a major survey on individualized services for children and adults. With consultants from five American agencies, the survey examined issues such as adequacy, strengths, duplication, priorities, accountability, the relationship between private and publicly funded services, and the gaps in services for children.[7] The final report of this study, released in 1950, was a forecast of the types of changes that would occur at Earlscourt. According to the consultants, the policies of the twenty-eight agencies surveyed had not kept pace with professional philosophy or method. From the perspective of these American experts, none of the five sectarian-based institutions in Toronto that were providing residential care for a total of 225 children was considered capable of developing a program for residential treatment.

The above analysis assumes that treatment was the appropriate goal, thus rendering invisible the problems of poverty.[8] Although the report identified the major problems facing families in Toronto as housing, unemployment, and inadequate relief, the final recommendations emphasized the need to improve the quality of casework and other therapeutic services. The problems of children who required placement outside their family unit were increasingly viewed by policy makers as individual problems in interpersonal relationships. While foster care, which embodied family care was the optimum resource for children who were unable to live with their natural parents, it was recognized that some children needed group care in special institutions such as Earlscourt, and social workers possessed the expertise to make these judgements. The fact that foster care, which relied on the caring labour of foster mothers, was also cheaper than residential care was not part of the debate. Publications from this period stressed the need for residential treatment services for problem children, but were opposed to the institutionalization of normal children, reinforcing the idea that a home such as Earlscourt was no longer beneficial unless it could adapt to the emerging view.[9] Although organizations like Earlscourt served a similar function for poor families as private boarding schools did for upper-middle-class families, low-income mothers who needed and preferred residential care for their children were denied this option, setting the stage for a more intrusive relationship by social workers into the lives of poor families.

According to the above report by the US team of consultants, inadequate training and poor salaries remained major issues with which agencies needed to contend (Burns 1952). This report, which affirmed the importance of professional social work, was essentially the work of 'male experts' committed to efficiency, planning, the utilization of objective and scientific knowledge, and the establishment of professional turf. This period has been depicted as the triumph of psychology in dominating social work's knowledge base; however, the professional discourse was also a vehicle for the beginning of a more managerial and patriarchal approach to social services.

Professionalism and Child Care

The changes that occurred at Earlscourt from 1948 to 1964 show how children and families were diagnosed and the kinds of services that were implemented. In their study of the caring professions, Pamela Abbott and Claire Wallace make a case that professionals are powerful because they:

> . . . create both the object of their intervention—the neglectful mother, the wayward teenager, the bad patient—and at the same time make these the targets of their intervention. Intervention is designed to normalize, to make subjects conform to the defined norms. In this model people are seen as having or being problems and the experts as having solutions—the knowledge to solve the problem (Abbott and Wallace 1990:6).

Over the course of the 1950s, children who needed alternative care because their parents were unable to care for them or because the child-welfare system lacked foster home resources began to be defined as 'emotionally disturbed children'. While the children and families remained poor, their emotional needs and behaviour became the target for intervention.

The Canadian experience mirrored trends in both American and British social work. For instance, Younghusband's (1978) report on social work in Britain from 1950-75 stated that one in three children in care had behaviour problems and, interestingly, their problems intensified while in care. Not unlike the situations confronting workers today, the prevalent reasons for children requiring care were: illness of the mother (today this might be drug addiction), illegitimacy, unemployment, poor housing, poverty, death, desertion, divorce, separation, and abandonment (Younghusband 1978:45–7). Although poverty and the life circumstances of children remained the critical factor in their identification as children in need, the response of caregivers began to be organized around the child's behaviour. Casework, with its knowledge base drawn from psychology, became the preferred intervention and the central focus of social work education. The language and terminology in this discourse embody the power of the social worker's expertise and the client's powerlessness.

An analysis of the records of the children who were admitted to Earlscourt during this period indicate that the agency was succeeding in its efforts to adopt a more 'professional' approach to the assessment of the children. Forty-six per cent of the children were six years of age or under when they were admitted. There was a fairly equal representation of boys and girls (ninety-three boys and ninety-nine girls). More than half of the children were wards of children's aid societies. The remaining ninety-two children were recorded as being placed by their parents. In fact, most of this latter group came from single-mother families beset with housing and financial difficulties. While it is likely that the children who were wards came from similarly fragmented family situations, there is little information on the families of these children. In over half the cases the records revealed only basic information and the reason for admission was 'behaviour'. Moore's descriptions of the children reflected the belief that the primary causes of 'emotionally disturbed children' were inadequate relationships within the family.

While the records suggest some differences between the children who were wards and those who were privately placed, the differences were marginal. In only a few instances were children described as 'normal or well-adjusted'. The behaviours identified in the records included pilfering, lying, truancy, and fighting. At the opposite extreme, there were unusually shy, timid, and withdrawn children. Others were assessed as disturbed with uncontrollable tempers and, occasionally, psychotic tendencies. Mixed in with this population were children who might be developmentally disabled, of mixed race, and/or with unusual physical difficulties. Many of the children were described as having 'habit disorders' such as soiling, enuresis, masturbation, and precocious sexual behaviour. Interestingly, in interviews I had with both Jessie Watters and Lois Gordon, who were leading consultants for the Children's Aid Society during this period, both recalled that children with severe disturbances were not placed at Earlscourt.[10]

An emphasis on the psychological development of children coupled with mother blaming was common in the case records of this period. For example, in her observations of Morris, a four-year-old boy from a single-mother family who was admitted in 1949 and remained at Earlscourt for six and one-half years, Moore recorded this note:

Morris was an effeminate little boy, very beautiful and his behaviour was good. During placement he remained more fem. [feminine] than masculine probably due to mo's [mother] hatred of men. Mo. curled and waved M's hair & at one time put coloured nail polish on him. When I discussed this with her she stopped. M. was a very nervous boy & did badly at school due to nervousness rather than lack of intelligence. He seemed to want to be boyish & played games hard but could not take knocks and cried bitterly very easily. He went home for weekends & always came back a much younger boy. His mo. babied him a great deal.[11]

Another example was Gerald, aged five, admitted in 1955 and discharged in 1963. His mother was unmarried, a recent immigrant who worked as a domestic. This case captures some of the urban realities of Toronto as postwar immigration began to complicate and challenge traditional ideas of child care and family life. Despite the social, personal, cultural, and economic pressures faced by this young woman, the assessment of Gerald pinpoints his mother's limitations:

July/55. Mrs. S. had brought mo. [mother] over from Germany on a guaranteed employment basis. Mo. continued to work for Mrs. S. throughout the placement. Mo. told in initial interview that her husband was dead but later confided she was unmarried. She had great guilt feelings about this. Throughout placement mo. was most cooperative, friendly and appreciative. She was high-strung, neurotic, tense and babied Gerald. She was completely under her employer's control and feared her criticism. Therefore, Gerald was kept in the bedroom on weekends. Talked in a whisper & seemed completely subjugated. Gerald was a very thin, pale little boy, quiet & scared when first admitted. He had to learn to play with other children but was never whole hearted & robust in his play until his last 2 years with us. He then began to assert himself but I felt his play was never really normal. He was just an average pupil. At camp Gerald was a different boy & thoroughly enjoyed the activities. (Eight weeks away from mother). Mother arranged to take Gerald to live with her after camp in Aug/63. I tried to arrange fo. ho. [foster home] placement but mo. would not consent.[12]

While this case record indicates how the mother's caregiving was clearly hampered by a coercive employer, low wages, and lack of kin support, the emphasis, in keeping with the prevailing knowledge during this historical period, was placed on her limitations as a mother and the belief that unmarried mothers were, by definition, unfit mothers.[13] Blaming unmarried mothers was reflected in both practice and policy. Social workers involved in advocating for the original Mothers' Allowance programs were instrumental in denying assistance to both deserted women and unmarried women (Struthers 1994:160). It was not until 1956 that unmarried mothers in Ontario were eligible for Mothers' Allowance. The knowledge base of professional practice, rooted in an understanding of the importance of the mother-child relationship and highlighted in Bowlby's scathing and widely read 1951 report on the detrimental effects of maternal deprivation contributed to mother-blaming (Bowlby 1951). The 1950s was an era that romanticized the nuclear family and, not surprisingly, most social workers believed that foster families provided the best alternative for children. What is surprising is that, despite the strong messages that mothers received about what was in their children's best interests, some clients resisted professional advice and made their own plans for their children. Clients were not simply targets for intervention; they often assumed agency to obtain the resources they needed for themselves and for their children.

Professionals and Volunteers

Changes in the delivery of programs for children were also evident in the administrative practices of the organization. The adoption of a professional child-welfare service demanded a professional board, a point made by the Child Welfare Survey in 1950. This report also identified the undesirability of maintaining boards of directors that were primarily all men or all women. Although this recommendation was directed at groups such as Big Sisters and Humewood House in Toronto, which were governed by women, it had implications for Earlscourt and the role of the Wimodausis Club. Early social service organizations in Toronto had depended on a strong community of supporters for their financial and human resources. Boards of these preprofessional organizations were united by shared social, personal, and often religious goals. In contrast, the ideal standard emerging for boards of agencies in the 1950s was that they should be diverse, efficient, and objective, modelled on the same goals as professionalism.

The drive to develop a professional board coincided with changing expectations of women volunteers in the 1950s. A hands-on involvement with the Earlscourt home, coupled with the large sums raised by the original Wimodausis Club, were a challenge for the second generation of Wimodausis members. Lacking the support of domestic servants, which many of the earlier club members enjoyed, these women volunteers struggled with balancing their commitment to Earlscourt and the needs of their own families.[14] As Noreen Hull, an active member of the club and the board observed, 'we needed to work like dogs' to provide Earlscourt with the resources essential for its survival.[15]

While the Wimodausis women struggled to understand their changing role, Moore tried to explain and educate the board on the needs of 'emotionally disturbed children' and the developing social work community. Despite these efforts, the board remained ambivalent about Earlscourt's changing mandate and wanted to retain some of the personal and direct contact with children they had experienced in its preprofessional charity phase. In contrast, Moore, like other social workers during this period, wanted to direct Earlscourt away from its missionary ideology and vision of moral reform, but she had difficulty convincing the board that a professional program was in Earlscourt's interest. Clearly, middle-class professionals and upper-middle-class benefactors were operating from different ideological positions. Both of these groups, at Earlscourt and elsewhere, failed to recognize clients' rights to participate in the identification of the programs that might meet their needs. Ironically, reduced government funding of programs for children today leads organizations such as

Earlscourt to seek once again upper-class corporate donors and board members.

Despite these tensions, Moore's main area of support remained the Wimodausis Club whose members initiated a number of strategies to help them understand the transition to professional care. The club instituted a welfare committee, which became the main link between the home, its director, and the community.[16] Members of this committee assumed responsibility for attending and participating in outside conferences on children and seeking advice from other professional workers.[17] Earlscourt was slowly changing, and in 1953 received positive endorsement from the provincial child-welfare branch, as evident in the following report:

> The Board of Earlscourt is to be commended in their choice of Director. Miss Dorothy Moore has brought to this Institution a wealth of experience, a sensitivity and understanding of the needs of children and the knowledge of the best way to meet these needs. To her belongs the credit of choosing efficient staff also skilled in understanding the troubled children in their care.[18]

Acknowledging the work of the board, it went on to state that: 'This institution, which has been one of the pioneers in the modern group living concept would not exist today had it not been for a board possessing vision, wisdom and a courageous spirit'.[19]

Still, members of the Wimodausis Club were not comfortable with the changes. The gap between the goals of Moore and the board became obvious in the major survey of children's services undertaken by the Social Planning Council of Toronto in 1958. Although the board had built new facilities that provided Earlscourt with an attractive, homelike, and warm physical environment for the children, the Social Planning Council's report pinpointed the fact that a close working relationship did not exist between Moore and the board. In the survey, Moore had expressed concern that:

> The board does not understand the nature and purpose of Earlscourt. The director works without the support of or advice from the board. . . . [T]his relationship of board and director is the biggest deterrent to the institution's program. . . . The board's view was that children are cared for because they are needy and prefer to think of social workers as missionary-like people . . . dedicated to a life of service with minimum remuneration.[20]

Moore was acknowledging some of the tensions facing women in the caring professions. The board expected her to be dedicated, but criticized her in the Social Planning Council report for not providing the leadership needed to develop a unified child-care policy. That a middle-class, single woman such as Moore, who was trying to assert her own independence and expertise, was uncomfortable in sharing her power with a group of married, upper-class volunteers is not surprising. Viewing the director's thinking and practices as in advance of the board, the report nonetheless acknowledged that the children at Earlscourt received good care and that the staff, although untrained, 'gave love, understanding and patience as a means of helping children'. Even more laudatory was their comment on the high calibre of the casework services, which were considered 'more orderly and effectively accomplished than in any of the other institutions in the survey'.[21] However, the professional experts criticized Moore for what they perceived to be an overly involved relationship with the children. A 'professional' program for treating emotionally disturbed children needed to be based on objectivity, and the caring work of the women staff members essential for children's well-being was seen as less important. Earlscourt's administrative and organizational structure needed to be strengthened to include professional training of staff, the adoption of intake and personnel practices essential for a professional treatment centre, and a more diversified board.[22] These administrative changes marked the beginning of a more bureaucratic approach to services that would affect clients as well as professionals. Report writing, keeping of statistics, and accountability to a superior began to dominate social service agencies, a crucial issue for social workers today as accountability, computerized record keeping, and court work limit the time workers can spend in supporting families.

Professionalism, as it unfolded, moved the Wimodausis members away from direct work in the home. For some volunteers, such as Noreen Hull and Adele Coutts, direct involvement with the home was a critical part of their work at Earlscourt and they viewed it as their task to educate the other members. Hull viewed the transition from a direct service volunteer to fundraising as a progression, but her ambivalence also surfaced as she missed the hands-on work. Raising money was not as satisfying as having direct involvement with the daily activities of the home. Moore, like other social workers in this era, resisted utilizing volunteers in work with the children, but was also reluctant to seek help from the Wimodausis Club in administrative or secretarial work. Even when Moore was faced with extreme staffing pressures, she continued to maintain that 'there was little that individual volunteers could contribute and they lack the experience to relate to and work with disturbed children'.[23]

Dorothy Becker has made the argument that the introduction of casework treatment fostered the exit of the 'Lady Bountiful', as the latter was considered incapable of having direct relationships with clients (Becker 1964). Although the Wimodausis Club and Moore shared a commitment to children, Moore identified with an ideology of expertise that needed to distance itself from the caring labour of the preprofessional and the upper-middle-class volunteer (Ehrenreich 1986:121). Moore did not seem to recognize that a network of women, like the Wimodausis Club, could provide the type of support she needed. Although some of the Wimodausis members formed a positive relationship with Moore—and Moore had initially viewed the club members as a great help to her—she did not establish a collegial relationship.[24] Hull, a faithful member of the Wimodausis, recalled that members had loved 'Hattie' [the former superintendent] and considered her their friend, whereas Miss Moore, as she was called, was 'more businesslike, a professional' and 'seemed to demand respect'.[25] Coutts provided this view of the difference: 'Hattie was just a mother, untrained and uneducated, while Moore recognized the need for a professional program with government support and trained staff.'[26] Moore envisioned a different sort of partnership with the Wimodausis, one that emphasized a more hierarchical relationship between the professional and the volunteer.[27] Ferguson (1984) has argued that women in administrative positions often need to downplay their 'caring' to prove themselves as competent and compete in a male world of management.

Tensions between the professional goals of Moore and the board also emerged around staffing. Child-care work, then as now, was admired but not highly valued. Women worked long hours for low wages, and it was difficult for Moore to convince the board that additional staff was necessary. Although the Wimodausis members supported Moore's efforts to improve the personnel situation, the changes at Earlscourt had lessened the influence and power of club members. In 1954 Moore and her five staff members were caring for thirty-four children, half of whom were from the children's aid societies. While Moore 'acknowledged that the board had come a long way in understanding the needs of children', she was not successful in convincing the board that more staff was essential. Moore continued to assume responsibility for all the casework, as well as all the administrative and secretarial work.[28]

The burden on Moore was evident. She found it difficult to keep ongoing case records and discharge reports and assessments, a problem that continues to plague child-welfare workers today who are besieged with paper and computer work. Moore simply felt too pressured to attend to these aspects of professional practice.[29] Gradually, the board began to consider the need for additional social work personnel, and approved the following recommendations in November 1961:

> That we add to our regular staff a person who would be useful in the operation of the Home and would also run the camp—this person to be a caseworker with social worker training and who is acceptable to our Board and Miss Moore and the Children's Aid Society and that to relieve the director, the day to day administration of the camp probably requires a man to supervise it as well as the above-mentioned requirement of a social worker or other camp director.[30]

The patriarchal bias of the board is evident in this decision; advocating a more professional and complex camp program demanded the presence of a man. The fact that both the camp and the home had been run efficiently for more than forty years almost entirely by women escaped their notice.

By 1962, Earlscourt was moving to a more formal commitment to care for emotionally disturbed children. This was accelerated by the appointment to the board of Dr Angus Hood, a psychiatrist and the founder of the Hincks Treatment Centre for emotionally disturbed children, situated in Toronto.[31] Hood articulated to the board the problems of the children residing at Earlscourt:

> It must be recognized, however, that the children who are placed in Earlscourt Home are there because they have been unable to form mutually satisfying relationships with parents, foster parents and in most instances with other children. In some, this will be because of poor control over their feelings and impulses with resultant aggressive, provocative and even antisocial behaviour. In others, this child will be withdrawn, over-controlled, living more in a world of his own and unable to communicate meaningfully with other people. It is hoped that a child in the setting of the Home will begin to develop a trust in himself and those around him in a way which will permit him to enter satisfying relationships with other people.[32]

Absent from this psychological diagnosis is any recognition of the socio-economic conditions that shape the lives of children and their families. Although some members of the Wimodausis Club continued to believe that Earlscourt was still a resource for poor children, male members of the board in particular seemed more comfortable accepting the advice of Hood, an expert in his field. Late in 1962, Paul Argles was hired as assistant director and caseworker.[33] Although the personnel committee had been the responsibility of Wimodausis members, the male members of the board and Dr Hood were instrumental in the hiring of Argles.[34]

Argles, in his first summer as camp director, reviewed the multiple functions that were the responsibility of the camp director. In his view, the importance of developing a therapeutic milieu for children conflicted with the extensive administrative tasks expected of the camp director. By distinguishing between the administrative and treatment responsibilities, Argles was able to persuade the board to secure secretarial help. One of the first things that the Wimodausis Club purchased for Argles was a dictating machine for case recording, necessitating the employment of a secretary. In contrast, Moore had received only occasional secretarial support.

The power struggles that pitted expertise, class, and patriarchal claims against each other led to a renegotiation of privilege among the players. The results became evident in January 1963 when the board asked Hood to 'make a study of the relation of the Home to the community and Child

Welfare service'. Moore questioned the need for such a study; she was of the view that Earlscourt was well known within the community.[35] The board, with Hood's advice, saw the study as a means of formalizing their mandate to serve emotionally disturbed children. Moore retired the following year.

So What Happens to Women and Children?

The move to professionalize child care had different impacts on the three groups of women involved in this process: the director, the volunteers, and the clients. Moore was confronted with the contradictions of trying to integrate a professional/managerial role with traditional child-care services that had relied on charity and the lowly paid and unpaid work of women. As a professional, Moore was expected to be formal, knowledgeable, objective, and businesslike—and it was this side she exhibited to the Wimodausis members. In contrast, as a housemother and colleague, she was remembered as warm, caring, and responsive to the needs of children. In order to gain professional recognition, she needed to understate the caring nature of child-care work. Indeed, she was criticized for being too emotionally involved with the children. It was also apparent that although she was in an administrative position, her commitment to service and practice undermined her position as the superintendent.

The second generation of Wimodausis women also experienced difficulties in combining their private and public lives. In an era that emphasized Canadian women as 'the heart of the home', juggling volunteer responsibilities with their own child-care responsibilities proved to be onerous (Prentice 1988:308). They were upper-middle-class women committed to volunteer work, but limited in their resources and less sure of the knowledge and skills they brought to a professional board. Thus, professionalizing child care posed difficulties not only for Moore but for the Wimodausis women who had contributed countless volunteer hours to Earlscourt. As the agency restructured its program under a discourse of professionalism, the work of the Wimodausis women was limited to fundraising and some of their commitment was lost. Maintaining a community of support continues to be a challenge for children's agencies. As public funding is withdrawn, corporate donors are being solicited to sit on boards alongside lawyers, accountants, and psychiatrists. Access to such expertise is essential for managing contemporary social services, but how volunteers are utilized within professional child care remains ambiguous. This dilemma is also discussed in chapters 6 and 7.

If the story of Earlscourt is seen primarily as one of professionalizing child-welfare services, it is easy to overlook how the workings of gender and class reinforced differences among groups of women. Moore did not have a strong network of support. The idea that professionals should be independent may have prevented Moore from utilizing the support that a women's group like the Wimodausis could offer. The members of the Wimodausis Club admired Moore for her dedication, but were ambivalent about her orientation and maintained a formal relationship with her.[36] As mothers themselves, the Wimodausis members believed that providing a caring environment was crucial for children and were critical of Moore's treatment philosophy. In contrast, Moore may well have believed she needed to distance herself from these upper-middle-class volunteers whose experiences were very different from her own and the clients served at Earlscourt. Class and rigid expectations about the caring responsibilities of women undoubtedly contributed to the divisions that emerged. Indeed, Charlotte Whitton, when she was executive secretary of the Canadian Welfare Council and one of Canada's most prominent social workers, was extremely critical of volunteers and married women who worked whether they were sister social workers or clients (Struthers 1987).

The move to professionalize child care during the postwar period was dominated by the American experience, reflecting the broader influence of US culture in Canada. This professional model was imbued with patriarchy, a hierarchical relationship with volunteers, and a medical approach in the treatment of children. As a designated 'professional', Moore was treated circumspectly by the board of directors whose understanding of a professional was 'a competent, well-organized and businesslike man'. This view must have taken a toll on Moore, who lived on a daily basis the contradiction of supporting a professional model that necessitated a lot of unpaid and unseen work. Much of the time and energy she spent with the children was not categorized as treatment, that is, as professional work. The professional model also necessitated recording and administrative procedures. By the end of her tenure at Earlscourt, male governance was evident both in terms of the agency's leadership and its service model—her successor was a young man and the board of directors was dominated by men such as Dr Hood. The irony could not have been lost on Moore that the presence of male actors necessitated the employment of clerical and administrative staff to do the work previously undertaken by volunteers or assumed to be part and parcel of being a female director.

For the children and mothers in this study, one can draw some tentative impressions. By adopting policies that disallowed private placements without an investigation by a social worker, the state prevented poor families (usually mothers) from negotiating their own arrangements for their children. The fact that residential care rather than foster care was a service preferred by working-class families was not acknowledged.[37] Professionals adopted the ideology of the expert and the voices of mothers and their material conditions were unheard and invisible. When the state did cast a wider net in the form of providing financial assistance to poor women, it did so only if women stayed at home to care for their children, even if they might have preferred or benefited from employment in the labour market.

Thus, the lives of poor women and children were regulated by idealizing 'family care'. This model also effectively controlled the costs of the more expensive residential model of care. Services were regulated by professionals and families could access such services only if their children were classified as 'hard to place or serve' or, in today's parlance, deemed 'at risk'.

In moving towards professional child care, the context for viewing families was dramatically altered. Assessments of families at Earlscourt were centred on the mother-child relationship, although it seems apparent that many children would not have come into care if more resources were available to their families, particularly their mothers, an observation also made in the Younghusband report. Linda Gordon (1992:274) has pointed out how mothering became more difficult as natural kin-support networks broke down with dramatic changes in industrial organizations. It is somewhat ironic that women in fields such as nursing, teaching, and social work found paid work only by rejecting the role of wife/mother, yet were cast as experts on child welfare for working-class mothers.[38] The contradictions continue today as women who are caring professionals are part of the regulatory mechanisms that reproduce conditions of scarcity even as they monitor the use of services by poor women. Many women and children who have utilized child-welfare services are now excluded unless they are defined as 'at risk'. The effects of poverty may be recognized as a contributing factor, but it is seen as outside of the professional mandates of child-service providers.

The optimism that characterized social work in the postwar period has not been realized. At the end of the twentieth century, social work and child welfare are again under attack. Recent child deaths and inquests have accelerated an approach to child welfare that is blaming and punitive to mothers, individualizes the problem, and places the social worker as an investigator of risk and a case manager. Indeed, investigation of child abuse has become the major concern of child-welfare workers. With an increased number of children in short- and long-term care, service providers are confronted with the problems endemic to the separation of children from their birth parents. Providing supportive services that are sensitive to the diversity of child-welfare clients has become increasingly difficult as the social worker is forced to attend to the requirements of risk assessment (Wall and Woolverton 1990).

Poor children in the 1950s were defined as 'emotionally disturbed', and during this period social workers and child-care experts utilized what they thought were scientific interventions modelled on psychiatry. Social workers focused on the psychological well-being of children and paid less attention to their life circumstances. Today, social work in child welfare is shaped by the professional discourse of a risk-assessment model purported to be rational and scientific, which renders invisible the diminishing resources available to meet the needs of poor women and children. Social workers are asked to work in situations in which it is not easy to identify the best interests of children and have few resources available to address children's needs

(Dominelli 1996:168). The danger, as Parton (1998) has argued, is that the practice of social work in child welfare is becoming managerial and mechanistic as workers are pressured to focus on 'high-risk' clients and the rationing of resources. The model also implies that families and children can be controlled and that their behaviour can be predicted. Social workers need only turn to their own history to challenge a discourse that promotes increased control of families and diminishing care and resources as beneficial to the profession or to the poor women and children they serve.

Notes

1 For an excellent discussion of risk assessment as it is unfolding in the United Kingdom and North America, see Parton (1998):5–27.
2 The Ontario children's aid societies, representatives of the Ministry of Community and Social Services, and deans and directors of Ontario schools of social work began meeting in 1998 with the goal of developing training programs for risk assessment for students in schools of social work.
3 Minutes, Wimodausis Club Meeting, March 1948, ECH Archives.
4 Chambers (1986) has argued that a coalition of men and women shaped the beginning of social work in the US, but professionalism was rooted in Western, White patriarchy, which set the stage for the subordination of women in social work. Chambers goes on to point out that the breakdown of this coalition in the 1930s was influenced by women's inability to understand that, in adopting professionalism, they were adopting a male perspective and abandoning a strategy that had been extremely successful—the creation of a strong female community of support. James Struthers, a Canadian historian, has advanced a similar argument in which he identified the paradox for women social workers. They were stereotyped as nurturers and emotional beings, confined to caring for others despite their determined support for a male professional ethos. See Struthers (1987).
5 See *Final Report of Community Chest and Council of New York*. The director of the survey was Mr William D. Schmidt, and the Children's Institutional Specialist was Mr Fred A. Schmacher. SC40 Box 9, City of Toronto Archives.
6 Minutes, Earlscourt Children's Home board meeting, 11 April 1949, ECH Archives.
7 Ibid.
8 Final Report, *Survey on Individualized Services For Children and Adults*, Toronto Welfare Council. The other institutions included in the study were the Carmelite Orphanage, Sacred Heart Orphanage, the Salvation Army Children's Home, and the Working Boy's Home. SC40 Box 9, City of Toronto Archives.
9 For a discussion of the role of institutions, see Burns (1952:31–4).
10 Personal interview, Jessie Watters, 14 September 1988 and Lois Gordon, 13 June 1988.

11 Case #54.
12 Case #732.
13 For a discussion of this, see Chorow and Contratto (1992).
14 Personal interview, Noreen Hull, 19 November 1986. Hull identified the balancing that is required for volunteer work—sometimes involving sacrifice to one's work and at other times to one's family.
15 Personal interview, Adele Coutts, 19 November 1986.
16 Minutes, Earlscourt Children's Home board meeting, 16 October 1950, ECH Archives.
17 Minutes, Wimodausis Club meeting, December 1948, ECH Archives.
18 Letter from E. Gertrude Campbell, field supervisor, to Mr Robert Fulford, president, Earlscourt Children's Home, 12 May 1953, ECH Archives.
19 Ibid., 5.
20 Findings of 1959 Study of Children's Institutions, Child Welfare League of America SC40, Box 2, City of Toronto Archives.
21 Ibid.
22 Ibid.
23 Minutes, Earlscourt Children's Home board meeting, 22 April 1960.
24 See Children's Services Division, Earlscourt Children's Home, 1946–59, letter from M.J. Newton to B. Beaumont, 29 June 1949, RG 29 Temp, Box 5, Province of Ontario Archives.
25 Personal interview, Noreen Hull, 19 November 1986.
26 Personal interview, Adele Coutts, 19 November 1986.
27 For a discussion of the changing relationship between volunteers and professionals, see Lubove (1965).
28 Report from Social Planning Council, visit to Earlscourt, 18 March 1954, SC 40, Box 46, File 8, City of Toronto Archives.
29 Minutes, Earlscourt Children's Home board meeting, March 1961, ECH Archives.
30 Minutes, Earlscourt Children's Home board meeting, *Report of Committee Appointed to Study the Earlscourt Camp*, 28 November 1961, ECH Archives.
31 Mr Lloyd Richardson of the Children's Aid Society had recommended that Earlscourt include a psychiatrist on the board. Hood joined the board on 5 March 1962. Minutes, Earlscourt Children's Home board meeting, 5 March 1962, ECH Archives.
32 Minutes, Earlscourt Children's Home board meeting, report to board from Dr Angus Hood, 19 November 1962, ECH Archives.
33 Minutes, Earlscourt Children's Home board meeting, 14 December 1962, ECH Archives.
34 See Minutes, Earlscourt Children's Home board meeting, 14 December 1962, for notice of the appointment of Argles, ECH Archives.
35 Minutes, Earlscourt Children's Home board meeting, 21 January 1963, ECH Archives.
36 Personal interview, Sally Phibbs, 20 November 1986.

37 See Younghusband (1978):66. This British study demonstrated that more children were returned to their own homes from residential care than foster care.
38 See Giles (1995) for an elaboration of this argument.

References

Abbott, Pamela, and Claire Wallace, eds. 1990. *The Sociology of the Caring Professions*. London: The Falmer Press.

Becker, Dorothy. 1964. 'Exit Lady Bountiful: The Volunteer and the Professional Social Worker'. *Social Service Review* 38:57–72.

Bowlby, John. 1951. *Maternal Care and Child Health*. Geneva: World Health Organization.

Burns, K. Phyllis. 1952. 'Institutional Resources in Canada for Dependent Children'. *Canadian Welfare* XXVIII, no. 5(1 November):31–4.

Chambers, Clarke. 1986. 'Women in the Creation to the Profession of Social Work'. *Social Service Review* (March):1–33.

Chorow, Nancy, and Susan Contratto. 1992. 'The Fantasy of the Perfect Mother'. In *Rethinking the Family*, edited by Barrie Thorne and Marilyn Yalom, 191–214. Boston: Northeastern University Press.

Dominelli, Lena. 1996. 'Deprofessionalizing Social Work: Anti-oppressive Practice, Competencies and Postmodernism'. *British Journal of Social Work* 26:153–75.

Ehrenreich, John. 1986. *The Altruistic Imagination: A History of Social Work and Social Policy in the United States*. Ithaca: Cornell University Press.

Ferguson, Evelyn. 1984. *The Feminist Case Against Bureaucracy*. Philadelphia: Temple University Press.

Giles, Judy. 1995. *Women, Identity and Private Life in Britain 1900–50*. London: Macmillan.

Gordon, Linda. 1992. 'Family Violence, Feminism and Social Control'. In *Rethinking the Family*, edited by Barrie Thorne and Marilyn Yalom, 262–86. Boston: Northeastern University Press.

Hugman, Richard. 1991. *Power in Caring Professions*. London: MacMillan.

Lubove, Roy. 1965. *The Professional Altruist: The Emergence of Social Work as a Career, 1880–1930*. Cambridge: Harvard University Press.

Parton, Nigel. 1998. 'Risk, Advanced Liberalism and Child Welfare: The Need to Rediscover Uncertainty and Ambiguity'. *British Journal of Social Work* 28:5–27.

Prentice, Alison, et al. 1988. *Canadian Women: A History*. Toronto: Harcourt Brace.

Struthers, James. 1987. '"Lord Give Us Men": Women and Social Work in English Canada, 1918–1953'. In *The Benevolent State: The Growth of Welfare in Canada*, edited by A. Moscovitch and J. Albert, 126–43. Toronto: Garamond Press.

_____. 1994. *The Limits of Affluence: Welfare in Ontario, 1920–1970*. Toronto: University of Toronto Press.

Toronto Welfare Council. 1950. *Survey on Individualized Services for Children and Adults*, Final Report. Toronto: Toronto Welfare Council.

Wall, M.S., and M. Woolverton. 1990. 'Risk Assessment: The Emperor's New Clothes'. *Child Welfare* 69:483–511.

Younghusband, Eileen. 1978. *Social Work in Britain: 1950–1975, a Follow-up Study*, vol. 1. London: George Allen & Unwin.

Part 3

Disappearing Jobs
Reappearing as Invisible Work

Chapter 9

Knowledge, Gendered Subjectivity, and the Restructuring of Health Care: The Case of the Disappearing Nurse

Marie Campbell

Introduction

Contributors to this book have examined the specific conditions under which women's caring labour in the home and community becomes intensified at the end of the twentieth century in Canada. Public sector caregiving is being collapsed back into 'the family' or 'the community'. New initiatives to cut social spending mean that professionally prepared and paid carers are finding their jobs changing, even disappearing. This chapter focuses on professional nurses and argues that they and their work are being eliminated, both actually and virtually. Labour force changes are actually claiming nurses' jobs as hospitals are restructured. Although the loss of nursing jobs has not been well researched, Baumann et al. (1996) and Sibbald (1997) in Canada and Shindul-Rothschild et al. (1996) in the US recognize this phenomenon as part of major shifts in the organization and management of health care. Head nurses, as a category, have largely been done away with in Canadian hospitals. Since the mid-1990s there has been a trend to replace professional 'bedside' nurses with less highly educated workers, and full-time nurses with 'casuals'. This chapter analyses some frontline accounts of registered nurses (downsizing survivors) working in hospitals in British Columbia and shows how the organizational grounds of nursing are shifting under their feet. In analysing these nurses' adaptive and intelligent actions, one can see how their efforts are implicated in the restructuring of health care.

Besides actual labour force changes, there are virtual disappearances in nursing as well. In some restructured sites where preplanned protocols are followed, what nurses do to accomplish safe and effective care disappears from sight. Nurses, as knowing subjects of their own actions, including the constitution of gender, are being disregarded, their contributions unrecognized. Official disregard of nursing may reflect the inflated regard for biomedical knowledge and technology that seems prevalent in the late twentieth century, or it may be related to lingering patriarchal views of women's work. Nurses are part of a very complex history of gender relations in health care, as McPherson (1996) and Reverby (1987) suggest. In this chapter, I explore a contemporary form of gender in restructured nursing settings, taking up Smith's (1987) interest in the traditional gender regime. It is in that notion of women's work that one can see nurses mediating the concrete particulars for the managers and professionals who have superior positions in an abstract division of health care labour. Smith (1990:19) points out that the more successful women are at doing this mediation of the local to the extralocal, the less men have to be engaged with and thus conscious of the local world of everyday/every night experiences. Registered nurses, it seems, have been so successful in this invisible mediation that the work process through which it gets accomplished is being, or is in danger of actually being, cancelled. The current restructuring of caring work imposes the 'superior' world of rationality, objectivity, and impersonality into the experientially diverse world of nursing as if the former accounts for and supersedes the latter. Looking closely in this analysis at what nurses say about doing their work exposes important attributes that are submerged and suppressed as accountable features of the registered nurse and her work. This chapter addresses how and to what end these disappearances are happening.

Looking to the literature for answers is not sufficient as much of it is written from the standpoint of those who manage care. Much of the literature on hospital restructuring is prescriptive, not analytic, taking the potential benefits of various reforms and reorganizations for granted. There are critical perspectives on this topic, of course. For instance, Jackson (1996:577) points out that re-engineering has made millionaires out of its gurus by scaring managers into thinking that their own survival depends upon learning and implementing re-engineering. Leverment et al. (1997) researched health professionals' responses to a re-engineering program in a British National Health Services Trust hospital and found that the promised empowerment of staff was not borne out; rather, they saw the potential for both winners and losers in restructuring. A Canadian study points out that in the multiplicity of strategies employed under various names in health care restructuring, it is difficult for researchers to identify similarities, let alone compare their impacts (Baumann et al. 1996). Beyond the confusion of multiple strategies, the management standpoint embedded in much of the restructuring research makes productivity gains more interesting to researchers than nurses and nursing. In one such instance, Freeman and Cameron (1993:12) disregard the individuals involved and talk instead about downsizing as a 'strategy that affects the size of a firm's workforce' to accomplish the sought-after increases in productivity and efficiency. At the same time, organization theory is paying new attention to the efforts of individuals and to their creativity and commitment to produce efficiently and effectively (Gerlach 1996). Gergen (1996), a postmodernist organization theorist, helps to clarify this apparent contradiction by pointing out that modern organizations and theory, too, ignore, but at their peril, the inevitable social collaboration on which a firm's machine-like rationality depends. This is the direction my analysis takes. It explicates and validates the importance of nurses' social collaboration in the organization's efficiency.

I am not attempting to analyse the particular restructuring strategies that frame the reformed environment for nurses' work (and in which I claim they may 'disappear'). Rather, this analysis looks at what the nurses who survive downsizing are doing as they conduct their caregiving within these reforming institutions. 'Disappearances' as such cannot be studied by observational methods, of course. What can be seen and brought to light is work that is systematically overlooked. By refocusing attention on nurses at work, I analyse what it means to health care and its efficient organization when it takes nurses and their work for granted. In the course of this exploration, I show the nurse as a knowing subject acting on the basis of knowledge that is not gender-neutral. I am making a case for the existence and necessity of nurses' intelligent action—the product of a knowing subject. This knowledge and action make possible the efficiency of the contemporary hospital, even the restructured one.

Restructuring Nursing Labour/Actual Disappearances

Nursing care came under new kinds of pressure in the health care reform that swept across Canada in the 1990s. Lomas (1997:818), in surveying the provincial restructuring of health care governance, found that devolution (or decentralization) of authority to regions had been principally expected to be a local support for spending cuts as 'more aggressive governance of the system' was put in place. But the logic of more aggressive governance in the health care system(s) comes from a management discourse applied across national boundaries to restructure public health, education, and welfare provision by governments of all political stripes (Jackson 1993:54). Critics argue that through managerial reforms, the social sector in Canada is being tied ever more securely to the market and to private wealth creation, all legitimated by pervasive appeals about the need to respond to global competitiveness. Competitiveness is a relatively new concept in the Canadian public sector, adding impetus to a growing clamour for more efficiency. Indeed, Canadian health care managers are looking for new ways, often learned from the American health industry, to gain a competitive edge in the increasingly market- or quasi market-oriented health care system.

It seems that the delivery of patient services offers one new (or yet to be fully exploited) site for such activities. To restructure the delivery of patient services and inject it with more of the vigour of the market means organizing caregivers to do their work differently. Traditional practices and relations within and between professions are being challenged and revamped.

For individual caregivers such as the nurses quoted in this chapter, competition may mean being expected to alter their work practices in response to concern about waiting lists or tertiary level bed costs; it may mean adopting new approaches to therapeutic regimens for hospital out-patients, and hurrying in-patients out of hospital beds.[1]

As Canadian hospitals implement these strategies, one outcome that is already seen in the US is that registered nurses (RNs) are being replaced and/or supplemented by less highly educated nursing staff, such as licensed practical nurses (LPNs) and even unregulated health care workers (Baumann et al. 1996). American proponents claim that a multiskilled team brings greater precision to the division and coordination of nursing labour and facilitates the elimination of costly, non-value-added functions. This direction in cost-effectiveness is having a decidedly mixed reception in Canada. Many worry that RNs cannot be replaced without undermining the effectiveness of the health care in which RNs now play such a major part. Nursing leaders are beginning to worry about the destruction of nursing, both the organized profession and the practice, as we know it today (Sibbald 1997). Multi-skilling has the potential to split the unionized nursing labour force into bitterly opposed factions as RNs and LPNs struggle over the remaining jobs. Buried within such conflicts are the class and race differences (Callista 1993; Das Gupta 1996) within nursing that remain largely ignored by both professional associations and unions. Yet beside the conflicts that the initiatives have spawned among differently situated groups of nurses, their concerned leaders are seeing that long-standing differences can be put aside to make a united response to this element of reform (RNAO 1997a and 1997b). Nursing's positioning within health care reform has a contradictory edge. While the organized profession supports, indeed implements, reform, many nurses worry that the hospital restructuring part of reform challenges the traditional caring role that RNs have claimed as theirs.[2]

I have argued elsewhere that among other policy changes Canadian nursing has undertaken, the profession has been continually changing its traditional practices to accommodate an increasingly managed approach to health care. Over the last few decades, the introduction and use of a variety of management technologies in nursing settings have required nurses to incorporate more and more managerial accountability into their work (Campbell 1988, 1992, 1998). To some extent, this has just happened rather than being the result of a definite policy choice by nurses. Nurses, as managers themselves or as management consultants, are situated in positions from which they devise and implement strategies, and supervise and train caregivers, to work in ways that are congruent with care that, under current public policy, must be managed for efficiency. Nurses understand such responsibilities as expressing professionalism.

For instance, beginning with patient classification in the 1970s and 1980s, nurses have grown accustomed to thinking about their work in such managerial terms as direct or indirect care. A scarcity of time orientation was programmed into nurses' thinking about caring, through their involvement in classifying patients in units of time needed for care. Patient classification made it possible for hospital managements to value differentially different aspects of nurses' work and to exercise some influence over how paid nursing time was to be occupied. Once the work was 'captured' abstractly (as classifications, units, and levels of care), hospitals could reconfigure the financial allocation to nursing labour and thus, by creating scarcity, require nurses to pick up the pace of their work. Beginning in the 1970s, less generous staffing decisions made nurses themselves alter their nursing practice, reducing their caring labour to accommodate the tighter time frames. This has resulted indirectly in substantial changes in nursing care over the past twenty years, so it must be noted that the content of traditional nursing practice is not static but fluctuates in response to a variety of internal and external conditions. At the present time, managerial technologies are targeting nursing practice more directly than patient classification did, putting individual caregivers' decisions about their practice more securely within the managerial sphere of influence. 'Clinical pathways',[3] for instance, is one current form of planning that some hospitals have implemented to streamline treatment, including nursing care, and to expedite patients' movements through costly hospital stays.[4] Expediting a patient's movement by having staff adhere to a plan such as a clinical pathway means that the nurse caring for the patient will eliminate all but essential care in order to meet the plan's targets. Not doing so could result in a variance that requires explanation, a form of text-mediated enforcement of the protocol in nurses' practice. The literature is now using the term 'non-value added' to refer to those activities that nurses would be expected to drop to meet targets.[5] Managers attempting to achieve their organization's new efficiency and effectiveness goals are looking for ways to identify and reduce nurses' non-value-added work in order to reduce the number of nurses needed to care for patients.[6] Labour adjustment accords in BC have moderated the most drastic effects of bed closures and restructuring, yet here, as across the country, many nurses have lost their full-time jobs.[7]

As already noted, there are wide variations across hospitals in what particular cost-cutting measures are used. Some achieve cost reductions by reducing the skill level of the nurse labour force, in other words, substituting other staff for RNs. In order to substitute an objectively managed process for a professional nurse's on-the-spot knowledge and action, nursing must be understood as a set of discrete, or potentially discrete, tasks. Schweikhart and Smith-Daniels (1996) propose a methodology for reorganizing nursing and redeploying nurses in a manner that reduces non-value-added work. These US management experts see nursing as two classes of care work that 'are linked through an iterative process by which a plan for a patient's care is developed and then executed by the appropriate staff members' (Schweikhart and Smith-Daniels 1996:23). Their interest is in plans that will support nursing in skill-mixed teams that include what in Canada would be called unregulated health care workers. They categorize nursing work as being either *care production* or *care management* tasks, although they note that there may be some overlaps between the two. Care production, they say 'represents the hands-on execution of each patient's care plan' that 'tends to be highly-structured, task-oriented and repetitive' such as 'assisting patients with activities for daily living, monitoring of vital signs, administering IVs, medications, and treatments and giving patient and family education' (Schweikhart and Smith-Daniels 1996:23). 'Care management is concerned with planning and coordinating care delivery activities . . . and is typically characterized by relatively high levels of decision-making, autonomy and accountability' (Schweikhart and Smith-Daniels 1996:23). This work 'directly includes communication and coordination among clinicians and other care providers and indirectly helps advance the clinical expertise of staff and the knowledge base of the organization' (Schweikhart and Smith-Daniels 1996:23).

This conceptualization of what nurses do, like the earlier classification of patients by care requirements, is a necessary precursor to innovations in nurses' work organization that is designed to make nursing more objectively manageable, more cost efficient, etc. I have cited US experts, but this kind of thinking is the basis for similar work that appears under various names in Canadian nursing. The two nursing interviews that I draw from later challenge this rather narrow and technocratic view of nursing that, as I argue, eliminates the nurse as subject of her knowledgeable and intelligent actions.

Virtual Disappearances in Nurses' Everyday Work

Even if RNs keep their jobs (downsizing survivors, they are called by Baumann et al. 1996), a re-engineered nursing job requires different things from a nurse. The re-engineered and restructured nursing work that I describe earlier appears to replace the nurse's authority with a plan or protocol, undermining the credibility of her professional knowledge. Yet health care still relies paradoxically on nursing professionalism and its incorporation into the gender regime. This is another contradiction at the heart of redesigned and restructured nursing jobs. There is, however, an implicit critique of nursing in much of the writing on restructuring of health care, for instance, in Schweikhart and Smith-Daniels (1996). Restructuring is expected to improve not just nursing efficiency but patient satisfaction, too. For some time, health care critics from inside and outside nursing have worried that caring as the central concern of nursing is actually on the decline. The profession is addressing this problem as an educational matter. The behaviourist curriculum and the medical model thinking that it programmed into registered nurses' practice is being dismantled in favour of a more care-centred curriculum (Bevis and Watson 1989). Nursing theories of caring (Leininger 1980; Watson 1988), drawn from phenomenological and feminist literature (e.g., Colliere 1980; Noddings 1984), elaborate a philosophy to replace behaviourism and the medical model as the basic tenets in nurses' education and work. For example, in the University of Victoria's undergraduate nursing curriculum, caring is defined as 'a moral imperative to act ethically and justly and is the motivating power underlying all nursing realities and possibilities' (Hills et al. 1995).

While caring is a complex and perhaps indefinable notion, nurses see themselves as responsible for mediating health care interventions into the life-world and control of the person who is receiving services. The University of Victoria nursing curriculum adds:

> Human care requires high regard and reverence for a person and human life. . . . There is a high value on the subjective life-world of the person experiencing health-illness-healing conditions . . . on helping the person gain more self knowledge, self control and readiness for self healing, regardless of the *external condition* (P.1–18; emphasis added).

Here I draw explicit attention to the external conditions of nurses' work. Between the strongly held values of caring expressed in curriculum statements and the possibility of acting under difficult conditions lies the socially organized context of nursing action. Nursing leaders and the profession's ruling bodies understand that nursing happens in a milieu not of their own making, but generally hold the view that nurses' practice is constrained by medical dominance, intricately combined with various manifestations of occupational hierarchy and gender (but see Amos 1996 for an analysis of the social organization of gender in the nursing profession). Feminists have long noted nurses' subordination to the medical or administrative professions, and often identify nurses' lack of autonomy over their work as gender-based oppression. It is less well understood how the hard-nosed business objectives in today's health care exemplify some of the external conditions that influence how nurses care for their patients. The efficiency of their caring work has not been analysed in relation to their performance of gender, a topic that my analysis addresses.

To help frame the topic of this analysis as virtual disappearances, I turn to some studies that differentiate managerial conceptions of work from the actual everyday activities (Jackson 1994). Jackson challenges the idea that work can be properly understood and represented objectively by 'going and looking', as if (nursing) work were naturally occurring phenomena, locatable empirically as tasks. Recognizing that there is a knowing subject at the centre of action in any work process is vitally important for those who would understand caring as work, as Graham (1983) and others recommend. Nurses, for instance, have always claimed that much of what they do is invisible, unrecognized, and undervalued (e.g., Wolf 1989). Following Jackson's thinking would mean that an adequate description of work must take account of the knowing subject.

Yet on the other hand, the removal of the subject in the conceptualization of work plays an important part in the exercise of (management) control. The separation of knowing from acting, with tasks constructed as stable objects, is the hallmark of management practice (Braverman 1974). Jackson draws attention to how the subject is eliminated in the method of control that relies on the objectification of work and performance of tasks. She says:

> . . . 'performance' becomes a form of action from which the 'knowing subject' has been removed for all practical purposes. It is a moment of abstraction, a separation of subject and object, a rupture in the internal continuity of knowledge and action. It is precisely this separation that provides for the possibility of external definition and control—it creates a position of authority outside the [worker] from which [his/her] activities may be defined, measured, evaluated for someone else's purposes (Jackson 1994:344).

Work organized as tasks without a subject creates a disjuncture between knowing and doing in the new health workplace, which is organized to maximize efficiency and effectiveness. I have been describing how the new workplace reconceptualizes and redefines nursing work from the standpoint of those who need to reorganize and control it. When work appears to emerge 'spontaneously out of organizational design' (Jackson 1994:342), it is being theorized *from a management standpoint* and for the purposes of those who need to know it in this form. (When nursing appears as accountable tasks that relate to a clinical pathway, the purpose of this reconceptualization will be to influence a balance sheet that may be either financial or a tally of patients waiting for surgery.)

The distinction between the nurse's and someone else's purposes addresses the unsatisfactory relationship of care planning to caregiving in nurses' work. When managerial technologies—not individual nurses—plan the work, the hospital's need to reduce expenditures on non-value-added work appears to be accommodated. In managerial texts, the nurse as active subject is lost sight of in the shift of authority that takes place when nursing decisions are preplanned and reassigned away from her, but there is a wild card in this otherwise tidy organizational process. In actual health care workplaces, unexpected things happen that continually require reliably intelligent intervention by nurses. No plan can be counted on exclusively because, as Jackson observed, no plan ever 'gets it right'. The eliminated nurse is constantly being expected to hold nursing workplaces together, but she has to do so behind the scenes in an unrecognized way.[8] This is what I call the virtually disappeared nurse.

A previous analysis of plans as inadequate guides to nursing action (Campbell and Jackson 1992) draws on Lucy Suchman's (1987) brilliant research on problems faced by computer programmers as they tried to capture clerical work as a set of procedural steps. Suchman (1987:50) argues that clerical work (and I would add nursing work as well) can only be understood as 'situated action' in which '[e]very course of action depends in essential ways upon its material and social circumstances. Rather than attempting to abstract action away from its circumstances and represent it as a rational plan, the approach is to study how people use their circumstances to achieve intelligent action'.

In the following stories, nurses achieve intelligent action on behalf of their patients, physicians, and their hospital employers. They do this in complementary ways within the reformed and restructured health care systems in which they are working. Their contribution is fitted into the interstices of new organizational strategies, plans, etc., that either ignore any need for such involvement by nurses or, more troubling, seem to rule out its necessity and even its possibility. My empirically based analysis shows that the efficiency that the managerial strategies 'organize' depend in unrecognized ways on the work that nurses contribute (outside those strategies).

Intelligent Action

Two stories, reconstructed from interviews with several registered nurses working in different hospitals in British Columbia in 1996–7, provide the data that bring to light the contribution of nurses to the reformed and/or restructured organization.[9] Noreen (a pseudonym) works in the out-patient department of a community hospital in a small town. Betty (also a pseudonym) works on a surgical unit in a regional district hospital in a small city. Each nurse talks about her work and illustrates both its taken-for-granted nature and how it is 'intelligent action'. The details have had to be carefully teased out, by questions that the interviewer asked, to fill in the missing pieces as each nurse originally told it. Missing from the original account is how the new organizational strategies and technologies alter the nurse's control over the work. Missing as well, until sought out, are the knowledge resources that the nurse uses, resources that underpin her competence and her value to the organization. The stories show nurses conceptualizing how to take action and the effects of the actions taken. Some actions appear that would otherwise remain invisible, unremarkable, and unrecognized within the organization. Gender emerges as a major theme in this unrecognized work of which registered nurses are expert practitioners.

Noreen is certified specifically to administer both in-patient and out-patient chemotherapy treatments in her small community hospital. Recently, and in line with provincial policy to treat people at home or close to home where possible, the provincial cancer agencies have been discharging patients back to their local communities where they are under the supervision of local general practitioners for their prescribed courses of postsurgery chemotherapy. Noreen tells a story of her (routine) efforts to conduct her work properly and professionally. Her story reveals much about her knowledgeable involvement in making the treatments safe and comfortable for the patient and efficient and effective for the hospital, the physician, and the patient. In Noreen's hospital, the work organization offers her considerable leeway to take personal responsibility for changes in her work process that would improve its efficiency. She explains:

> ... like my chemo program—when you find that things don't work, communication doesn't work, you come up with a system that does work. We have just developed a system to communicate with the general practitioners and the (cancer) agency, a new form that the patient takes down to the doctor, because many of the local doctors aren't familiar with the side effects [of chemotherapy].

When Noreen says '*we* have just developed', she actually means, '*I* originated it'. Hers is a modest presentation of the 'facts' of the matter. In interviewing her together with another RN, I heard accounts of how both of them were reviewing and revising the documentation in the specialty areas of the hospital that are undergoing rapid changes towards ambulatory care, short-stay admissions, and so on. The documentation that had worked effectively before these changes occurred had become outmoded, slowing down the connections between departments and individuals whose smooth collaboration was required to make patient care efficient and effective. These two staff nurses discussed their work on the documentation as 'just doing their jobs', but, of course, this goes beyond the ordinary work that RNs are expected to do and that they are accountable for.

It is instructive to scrutinize a little more closely how this nurse does her job. Is Noreen doing 'care management', as Schweickhart and Smith-Daniels (1996) saw it, when she creates a new reporting form? She is obviously working through an evolving relationship between the hospital, the doctor, and the patient, one that has troublesome effects on her own day-to-day nursing work. Her dilemma is that the standards set by the cancer agency, as well as her own standards as a nurse, are not being met. Noreen is concerned that local physicians are not reviewing their patients' progress properly and are thus not making appropriate alterations to the chemotherapy regimen that she is expected to administer in the hospital's Emergency Department. Noreen knows what blood work should be done routinely, and she knows how to read the lab reports and how to revise the chemotherapy dosages accordingly. This is a medically approved 'transfer of function' for an apparently narrow range of actions that would seem to increase the nurse's scope of practice and thus her control over her work. It becomes apparent that to maintain adequate control requires extra work. When Noreen finds herself faced with the problem of physicians' mismanagement of their responsibility, she recognizes the dangerous implications for ill people. She elaborates:

> The physicians did not assume responsibility for local care of the patient that the cancer agency had discharged into the community. They either didn't have the knowledge to assume the care or somehow they thought that somebody miraculously was doing it for them. . . . Instead of being reviewed prior to each chemotherapy session [as per standard], it's conceivable that the patient would go through nine cycles of chemo and have seen the doctor only twice. That's dangerous.

Noreen is caring for her patients, helping them avoid setbacks and unnecessarily debilitating outcomes. She recognizes that it is up to her to take charge of this situation. (Later in this chapter I comment on her suggestion that physicians expect someone 'miraculously' to take responsibility for their patients.) After these troubles in her communication with physicians, she drafted a policy to authorize the nurse (i.e., herself) to act on the basis of her knowledge, as long as she advised the physician immediately. She developed a communication form to accompany the patient between the hospital and the doctor's office, to make the treatment process explicit and accountable. In a re-engineering context, this might be conceptualized as a costly integration of care management and care production and be treated as an opportunity to split the work and redeploy it to team members prepared differently. But I want to insist that an approach that looks promising on paper may need to be rethought, given local conditions. The point is that actually doing the work both tells the nurse what the problem is and how to manage it. Here we see the value to the organization of an appropriate, efficient, on-the-spot response to a dynamic treatment environment made by a knowledgeable staff member. Like nurses everywhere, Noreen works within the constraints of professional propriety: 'So, as the initiating nurse, I want [the local physicians] to check [and] watch, these are the side effects. . . . But it's done in such a way [that] it's discreet.'

She realized that she must take care not to upset physicians' feelings by revealing that she recognizes that they may not be familiar with the side effects of chemotherapy. Fortunately, in this hospital, Noreen has some organizational resources to help her with this problem. Her hospital supports nurses in using their initiative and they have developed a 'shared governance' process for bringing nurses' ideas forward for approval and action by other colleagues.[10] Because Noreen's situation requires the cooperation of all the local general practitioners, the nurses' group (the hospital's Nursing Practice Council) took charge of the problem and forwarded

Noreen's proposed solution to the hospital's medical committee who accepted it on behalf of all physicians.

This story speaks to the routine attention that an RN gives to patient safety during medical treatments. Interestingly, it makes visible a line patrolled conscientiously by nurses between their own and physicians' use of knowledge. Noreen was able to make legitimate use of knowledge that came from outside nurses' normal sphere. In many nursing settings, nurses are not encouraged to know something that belongs within the sphere of scientific medicine controlled by physicians when, for instance, that would result in a nurse challenging the administration of drugs based on her own interpretation of a patient's lab reports or symptoms. *Nevertheless, RNs routinely watch for danger to patients caused by physicians' lack of attention, knowledge, or judgement and are accountable for such observations.* Owing to these politically charged knowledge conditions under which they routinely work, nurses take on the extra responsibility of circumventing dangers to patients while being subordinate to physicians.

One might assume that nurses and doctors would be of one mind where patient safety and comfort or efficiency in use of hospital staff time and other costly resources were concerned. In a related story, Noreen shows this is not necessarily the case. There are conflicts in how orders for blood transfusions come in from doctors' offices to the Emergency Department. She describes nurses' work to improve the efficiency and effectiveness of the referral procedure. Blood analysis must precede a transfusion. The nurses in the Emergency Department are aware that the preliminary *stat* blood work can overload the hospital laboratory's modest capacity. Delays from snarled systems may mean that a transfusion may take as long as nine hours, tying up an Emergency Department bed for that period and unnecessarily tiring an already weak patient. Before any systematic solution can be implemented (and Noreen and her colleagues were working on a solution), it is the nurse's job to get the doctor to realize that he is creating a problem and to cooperate in solving it. This is itself a dilemma of some magnitude.

In describing this problem, the nurses suggested that I, having been a nurse myself, should be able to understand their situation without them having to put it into words. Noreen said 'You're a nurse, aren't you?' when I asked her what held her back from putting her idea into action immediately. She meant that the problem she was facing was commonplace and taken for granted by nurses as the way things are between doctors and nurses. The implication was that it didn't need to be talked about but simply worked around. When I encouraged her to explain, she said: 'Doctors' immediate concern is to get the patient out of their office. They don't worry about the way things unfold at the hospital. That's for the nurse to solve.' Similar to the earlier comment about doctors' expectations for a 'miraculous' intervention, this is a problem not only in caring for patients but in diplomacy. Nurses' routine work includes the use of tact in managing relations with physicians to bridge gaps in the systems that, if left unattended, would be costly for everyone.

This is a performance of gender relations in which nurses enact their subordination to physicians. Noreen recognizes the professional boundary between her knowledge and the doctor's knowledge. Her professional responsibility requires her to act in an area outside that boundary. As a nurse, she knows how to do this. It requires attention, tact, and diplomacy to get the doctor to realize that 'he's creating a problem'. That this is central to a nurse doing her job is a gender issue. Nurses perform gender when they play the expected role and maintain their subordination to physicians. Nurses' mediation of gaps in the system is one example of what I referred to earlier as the traditional gender regime. Gaps arise from various pressures, including changes in health care policy. When routine interagency practices are altered, ripples are felt all along the system and adaptations must be made. It is unlikely that many of the ripples or their effects can be planned for and eliminated entirely. Change in systems is an almost daily occurrence as health care administrators look for new ways of organizing more effectively. Noreen's story points out how important it is to have knowledgeable nursing practitioners involved who interpret their responsibilities broadly, as RNs do, because they are accountable to physicians, to their hospital, to the patients, to nursing authorities, as well as to their own practice standards.

In this case, Noreen's actions addressed concerns for all of these participants in the health care system. Had she not been watching for gaps in the treatment regimen, her patients would have suffered. If she had not understood the organizational meaning of the laboratory work processes and how its relation to the chain of events ended up tiring out the patient, a solution might have never been found. If she were not attentive to the gender subtext of all her interactions with physicians, she might create major upheavals in the system, perhaps undermining her own career in the process. In some ways, Noreen tells about a common set of problems that have seemingly obvious and unremarkable solutions. A nurse is simply going about her work, facing commonplace challenges and working through them, yet much of the work discussed here is not in a job description. It might not be seen as value-added, nor indeed as caring. How Noreen works owes its particularities to her location in a small hospital where relations among participants in the health care system are more or less open and negotiable. In more complex organizations, where systems are more sophisticated and abstract, nurses' experiential and theoretical knowledge may be even more crucial to the identification and bridging of gaps and breaks in service provision. Several kinds of knowledge—professional/technical, organizational, social/gender-related, abstract and experiential—make it possible for RNs to consolidate the everyday world of the hospital unit and the therapeutic regimen with the patient as a person. This knowledge is taken for granted and, as I discuss more fully later in the chapter, it is also a gendered contribution by registered nurses to the health care system.

The second story I analyse comes from an RN working in the in-patient surgery unit of a larger hospital where 'same-day admits' (a reorganized admission process) expedites the movement of patients through preadmission work-up, surgery, postsurgical recovery, and eventual discharge. A new protocol called a clinical pathway organizes the care for patients to facilitate their timely release from the hospital. Betty, the RN who tells the story, peruses a new postsurgical patient's chart towards the beginning of the afternoon shift. Betty discovers that this elderly woman, who has just had a total knee replacement, has diabetes that is controlled by oral hypoglycaemic medication. Betty notes from the medical record that a previous operating room date had had to be cancelled because the patient's diabetes was 'out of control'. On further review of the chart, she discovers that there are no orders relating to her diabetic condition and she sees this as a problem.

Based on what she recognizes from this set of circumstances, Betty takes the following actions. She checks the chart for readings of the patient's blood sugar, knowing that for a patient with this condition, and particularly in view of its recent instability, blood tests would need to be done several times a day. She finds no account of a blood sugar reading preoperatively, nor in the operating room, nor in the postanaesthesia room, nor in the several hours since she has returned to the surgical nursing unit. Betty then talks to the patient and finds out that she has been doing her own blood sugar tests four times a day at home. Betty said, 'I didn't necessarily have to phone the doctor, but . . . I knew that what was best for the patient was that she should be on sliding scale [insulin] in order to see her through. So, I started the procedure, which I knew was going to be lengthy [to get the necessary orders].' Asked to explain what she was thinking when she made this nursing judgement, Betty replied:

I didn't want her to be too hyperglycaemic. She might start suffering from the signs and symptoms of hyperglycaemia. This patient's sugar is just going to go up over night because she's getting the sugar in her IV. Also, she's going to be stressed physically from the surgery. Normally, she wouldn't have any caloric intake all night. The next day who's to know if she'll be in any condition to eat? In fact, she's not going to be eating a full breakfast in the morning for sure. So [rather than] her diabetic pills in the morning because she won't be able to eat . . . she needs an order for sliding scale insulin overnight and into the next day until she can eat. She really needs just a wee bit of insulin. If her blood sugar goes too high, she's going to feel rotten. I mean, I was pretty sure that this lady was going to be fine, but there is this condition that non-insulin diabetics can get. They can get really dehydrated and go into shock. The sugar in the blood gets really high and pulls all of the fluid out of the cells; then they pee it all out and can get really ill. . . . I needed to be safe and know she was going to be feeling okay.

What happened next is an instance of a commonplace knowledge negotiation between doctors and nurses that nurses find frustrating. Betty phoned the orthopaedic surgeon who was on call; she reported (to the interviewer) that this was 'hopeless because he didn't know anything about diabetes'. He wanted her to call the orthopaedic surgeon who did the surgery, but Betty mused:

> . . . since *he* was the physician who wrote the post-op orders (missing the diabetes), I questioned how well he knew the patient; anyway, I called him and he didn't want to write anything. After some discussion, he did seem to think she needed a sliding scale insulin order. I agreed. He wanted me to suggest what to write, which is par for the course with these guys who depend on nurses to write their orders for them, but I refused. I was mad by this time. I think that I could have easily given her a low dose of sliding scale insulin.

When the surgeon didn't know how to write the orders, he recommended that Betty call the patient's general practitioner, a process that extended the time she had spent getting orders to about a half hour.

Two general points need to be made about this story that Betty claims was an unremarkable incident in her everyday nursing practice. First, Betty's interventions on behalf of this patient and her medical treatment seem fortunate, although it would be a mistake to see them as simply fortuitous. RNs recognize that their professional responsibility extends to knowing the patient holistically, as opposed to simply following orders or conducting tasks and procedures. This thinking component of caring is put at risk in the re-engineered nursing labour process, which breaks up patient care into task components related to skill levels.[11] The new focus on efficiency, embedded in the clinical pathway, appears to make redundant (and identify as inefficient) nurses' professional interest in knowing the patient. Pre-established plans related to the category of treatment determine the sequence of nursing actions, and they are the same for everybody. Because reading the patient's medical history on the chart is a time-consuming activity (not on the task list), nurses are likely to skip it in order to maintain the clinical pathway schedule. This approach to nursing disorganizes nurses' efforts to combine the responsibility and capacity to intervene knowledgeably.

Second, Betty's account of her interactions with the physicians involved in this case provides another glimpse into the maintenance of wasteful professional boundaries in the hospital workplace and how gender is constituted in these negotiations. Each participant expertly plays the expected part to maintain the boundaries of his or her 'place' in the power relations of their professions and the work setting. Nobody seems to notice that this is inefficient. In a setting reorganized for more efficient delivery of care, it seems peculiar that this inefficient practice is not questioned.

Knowledge, Gender, and Efficiency

Nurses are expected 'miraculously' to articulate professional, managerial, and therapeutic tasks in the always shifting, everyday routine of patient care in hospitals. Not just physicians, but the whole structure of health care relies on nurses to accomplish this expert feat professionally and seamlessly. Nurses are very good at acquiring and applying the requisite knowledge, often without noticing that it is a skilled intelligent practice (and not a miracle at all). More to the point, this professionally expert intelligent action never appears in any organizational accounting of nurses' work. Therefore, it can be discounted organizationally and treated as 'miraculous'. If other health care workers replace registered nurses, the knowledge that RNs contribute to health care in hospitals will be lost. It is particularly important, therefore, at this time of restructuring to recognize that RNs' work is not accurately portrayed by the information collected about it. When that minimal account of nurses' work is programmed into protocols, nurses are held to a distorted version of what they must do—provide safe care. Nor is it a solution to put more and more effort into getting better and fuller technical descriptions of what nurses do, using standard language.[12] More standard information may help health care managers 'guarantee' efficiency by creating text-based systems for health care workers to follow. Such research and development undertakings are costly and their guarantees ephemeral. Rational and information-based systems are not the answers in themselves for efficient and effective practice. Any protocol must be implemented knowledgeably in the always variable world of health care. As shown here, making a protocol work takes intelligent action performed in real time by knowledgeable people.

In everyday life, nurses' work is done by actual individuals in real time; that is, by knowing subjects who are products of their social environment responding to local conditions. When the work is understood from the nurses' standpoint, their professional judgement, experience, skill, and practical knowledge become apparent. Betty's intervention regarding her patient's diabetes (fortunate, but not fortuitous, I called it) showed a nurse acting outside the planned steps of the clinical pathway. It was not unusual nursing behaviour. It is not accidental that a nurse is interested in her patient's medical history. But there are actual effects on nursing of a work organization that in one day admits people for surgery and rushes them through several hospital units and different people's care to a ward where the strongest priority after surgery is to get patients discharged. One outcome is that nurses do not have time routinely to read their patients' medical histories. Doing so might, I suppose, be characterized as non-value-added work. From Betty's story it is also possible to see that strategies holding a team of workers to a particular performance of tasks that are targeted to time-lines may achieve certain efficiencies in terms of discharges, but do so at some risk to the patient. Betty's knowledgeable behaviour was lucky for this patient. As a story about disappearances, it draws attention to organizational conditions that support, or in this case detract from, the possibility of nurses taking such intelligent action. Only some nurses will see their responsibility as going beyond the organizationally required protocol. Currently it is these more experienced nurses who maintain the viability of efficiency strategies when they recognize the limitations of the defined protocols or efficiency-oriented expectations. As this generation of nurses retires, the next may more actively believe in protocols and not know how to perceive gaps or how to bridge them. The risk to patients will grow.

Both stories illustrate how traditional interprofessional relations in hospitals are gendered in ways that are costly. My analysis highlights experiences and interactions that are all too common, yet still not acknowledged. Because gender is not being noticed, it can't be 'targeted' in efficiency campaigns, even though the new reformed health governance structures have as one of their goals, according to Lomas (1997:818), 'that preservation of private domains is expected to give way to public objectives'. How might gender relations be put more directly on the table for discussion as nurses struggle with changing requirements and heightened expectations for efficiency? First, gender has to be acknowledged as part of the actual practices of individuals and thus as something that can be changed. That is, health care is not essentially and irreversibly gendered just because its occupational roles are stereotypically filled by men in the case of doctors or by women in the case of nurses.[13] To begin to alter the gender practices that hinder the work, more needs to be known about them. How nurses like Noreen work around taken-for-granted difficulties with physicians, not by confronting those difficulties head on but discreetly, is a topic for critical analysis that might help nurses rethink 'best practices'. Nurses can begin to query how they are kept (and keep themselves) within the bounds of traditional professional behaviour. What are the expected consequences that prevent nurses like Noreen and Betty from acknowledging the inefficiencies that this traditional (gendered) relation creates? Would a nurse who challenged the preservation of physicians' private domains find any support from her peers, from nursing management, or from the broader governance structure? It may be useful in this regard to note that the strategy of 'shared governance' (mentioned in Noreen's story) involves nurses in decision making in new ways. Its proponents claim that it increases nurses' confidence and organizational ability and heightens nurses' profile in interprofessional settings.[14] But the shared governance process that Noreen described carefully preserved the hierarchical relation between physicians and nurses, even though the work itself was becoming more interprofessionally collaborative.

The stories discussed in this chapter show people 'performing' gender. This argument about gendered relations is substantially different from one that blames physicians, or men in general, for what happens between physicians and nurses. Men and women learn how to act 'properly' according to sex-related social norms that are generated and supported institutionally. This brings a contradictory dynamic into nurses' work. Sexism has meant that nurses have been expected to accept a low value on their work and high expectations on their altruism because both are 'natural' to women. Hospitals, physicians, and the health care system have benefited from sexism in the past. Gender, as discussed in this chapter, is emerging as a slightly different and more contradictory phenomenon that nurses co-construct. Here it can be seen that gender relations continue to hold health care together and make efficiencies 'work', but beyond that, gender relations are a significant drag on nurses' efforts. As seen operating here, gender relations appear to be a poorly understood cost, not just to nurses but to the whole organization. Costly pretences of not knowing about medical treatments, etc., may keep those nurses who are less confident than Noreen and Betty from taking actions that may be beneficial to their patients, especially when time is scarce and the organization seems to value efficiency over everything else. Nurses and health care agencies might benefit from paying more attention to how RNs and physicians enact gender relations expertly. But that would mean that organizational leaders would have to accept that a health care worker's subjectivity is important to efficiency and give up trying to rule out all but targeted and managed action. That would call into question the health labour force strategies that rely on discrete task definition. It would mean recognizing the key role that professional nurses play in health care. I have attempted here to illustrate why, in the interest of the best use of staff intelligence and energy, nurses' knowledge and mediating efforts need to be recognized and valued rather than submerged and ignored. Reversing this disappearance could liberate nurses' energy and creativity and boost the effectiveness and efficiency of their caring work.

An important message about health care restructuring emerges from this analysis. The nurses quoted here were talking about everyday events in their work lives, not unique or unusual occurrences. These stories, as explicated here, show a side of restructuring that is not often seen or understood. The prevalent belief about organizational restructuring is that experts, given systematic information, can make better decisions than local health care staff. Thus, the thinking goes, organizational systems must replace local discretion to obtain acceptable levels of efficiency and effectiveness. Recognizing the relation between organizational systems and the everyday, as this analysis does, allows rediscovery of women's work and the attendant gender regime that operates invisibly to hold things together. But restructuring is changing local health care settings. As professional nurses are replaced either actually or virtually, their situated knowledge can no longer be counted on to repair the gaps that appear. This is a feature of health care restructuring that could be very, very costly.

Notes

1 Competitiveness in BC hospitals is spurred by extra funding available to hospitals that can reorganize 'delivery systems' to reduce waiting lists for high-profile surgeries, such as knee and hip replacements (Minister of Health's press release, 3 November 1997). Because waiting for health care is a politically charged issue, governments and health care agencies respond to waiting lists with special attention to 'efficiency'.

2 Baumann et al. (1996) make an analysis that reflects the ambivalence that many nurses, especially those in leadership positions within the profession, feel about hospital restructuring. They see the contradictions for nurses in restructured hospitals, and they also understand nursing's embeddedness in a public policy framework that prioritizes fiscal restraint.

3 Baumann et al. (1996:11) mentioned clinical pathways and patient care protocols as among the leading cost-reduction strategies reported from a study of 103 North American health care executives.

4 Janet Rankin's forthcoming Ph.D. research on nursing management includes analysis of how nurses work with clinical pathways technology, and I appreciate her explaining it to me.

5 Schweikhart and Smith-Daniels (1996) offer some context re non-value-added services: 'Many early adaptors of patient care redesign were hospitals . . . follow[ing] a delivery paradigm that is often called *patient-focused care*. . . . Drawing from world-class manufacturing principles, the patient-focused care model proposes elimination of structural inefficiencies and streamlining of operations. . . . Organizations redesigning their patient care delivery operations are formulating new work processes. . . . Those undertaking patient care restructuring initiatives expect improved performance in a number of areas . . . [through] (1) eliminat[ing] "nonvalue added" activities, (2) deliver[ing] "value-added" services to patients and physicians. . . .' (Schweikhart and Smith-Daniels 1996:21–2, emphasis in original).

6 The picture about lay-offs is blurry both because researchers haven't collected this information and because downsizing may take place not through lay-offs but by curtailing new full-time hirings. An August 1997 Nursing Employment Cross-Country Check-up, published by the Canadian Nurses Association, speaks of a recovery from previous poor labour market conditions for RNs. Yet in referring to the number of RNs on employment insurance benefits in 1996, the point is made that the figure (3,930 Canadian RNs), while lower than in the previous three years, does not reflect those who have left nursing, given up looking for work, or who have not yet found a first job in nursing.

7　A Labour Accord signed by BC health care unions in 1993 and renewed in 1996 required agencies to find alternative employment for laid-off staff, and thus reduced unemployment of nurses in BC during that period.

8　Ellen Balka (1997) offers a useful analysis of this as a systematic feature of women's work.

9　One account came from interviews I conducted in the course of another project; for the second account, I am grateful to Janet Rankin, who told me a story she uncovered in her own fieldwork; she assisted me in reinterviewing the nurse involved to make explicit her taken-for-granted knowledge.

10　Shared governance is a programmatic approach to nurses' shared decision making about nursing and its administration in hospitals. See Porter-O'Grady and Finnigan (1984) or Allen, Calkin, and Peterson (1988).

11　See Leira (1994) for a discussion of how thinking (skilled interpreting and integration of various kinds of knowledge) is central to a human service professional's caregiving.

12　In contrast, for instance, to beliefs expressed by Clarke (1998). It is my view that the production and centralization of nursing data bases is the prerequisite for development of exactly the kinds of protocols that I am criticizing here and that restrict nurses' professional discretion in the interest of cost savings. While being efficient is unquestionably necessary, I would want nurses to maintain control over their capacity to nurse intelligently.

13　The increasing number of women in medicine creates a more complex picture that needs more study before anything definitive can be said about female doctor-female nurse relations. The same is true of men in nursing, although their numbers are still relatively small.

14　Colleen Black, executive director of Mount Saint Mary Hospital, when describing her experiences of using shared governance techniques, gave several instances where RNs gained new respect from physician colleagues as the nurses demonstrated their knowledge (interview, April 1996).

References

Allen, D., J. Calkin, and M. Peterson. 1988. 'Making Shared Governance Work: A Conceptual Model'. *Journal of Nursing Administration* 18, no. 1:37–43.

Amos, Wendy. 1996. 'Charting a Course: An Exploration of the Construction of Nursing Practice'. Master of Nursing thesis, University of Victoria.

Balka, Ellen. 1997. 'Sometimes Texts Speaker Louder Than Users: Locating Invisible Work Through Textual Analysis'. In *Women, Work and Computerization: Spinning a Web from Past to Future*, edited by A.F. Grundy, D. Kohler, V. Oechtering, and U. Peteres, 163–76. New York: Springer-Verlag.

Baumann, Andrea, Linda O'Brien-Pallas, Raisa Deber, Gail Donner, Dyanne Semogas, and Barbara Silverman. 1996. 'Downsizing in the Hospital System: A Restructuring Process'. *Healthcare Management Forum* 9, no. 4:5–13.

Bevis, E., and J. Watson. 1989. *Toward a Caring Curriculum: A New Pedagogy for Nursing.* New York: National League for Nursing.

Braverman, Harry. 1979. *Labor and Monopoly Capitalism.* New York: Monthly Review Press.

Callista, Agnes. 1993. 'Women of "Exceptional Merit": Immigration of Caribbean Nurses to Canada'. *Canadian Journal of Women and the Law* 6, no. 1:85–102.

Campbell, Marie. 1988. 'Management as "Ruling": A Class Phenomenon in Nursing'. *Studies in Political Economy* 27:29–51.

———. 1992. 'Nurses' Professionalism in Canada: A Labour Process Analysis'. *The International Journal of Health Services* 22, no. 4:751–65.

———. 1998. 'Institutional Ethnography and Experience as Data'. *Qualitative Sociology* 21, no. 1:55–73.

———, and Nancy Jackson. 1992. 'Learning to Nurse: Plans, Accounts and Action'. *Qualitative Health Research* 2, no. 4:475–96.

Clarke, H. 1998. 'Invisible Nursing Made Visible'. *Nursing BC* (May-June):10–12.

Colliere, M. 1980. 'Invisible Care and Invisible Women as Health Care Providers'. *International Journal of Nursing Studies* 23, no. 2:95–112.

Das Gupta, Tania. 1996. 'Anti-Black Racism in Nursing in Ontario'. *Studies in Political Economy* 51:97–116.

Freeman, S.J., and K.S. Cameron. 1993. 'Organizational Downsizing: A Convergence and Reorientation Framework'. *Organization Science* 4, no. 1:10–29.

Gergen, Kenneth. 1996. 'Organization Theory in the Postmodern Era'. In *Rethinking Organization: New Directions in Organization Theory and Analysis*, edited by Michael Reed and Michael Hughes, 207–25. London: Sage Publications.

Gerlach, Neil. 1996. 'The Business Restructuring Genre: Some Questions for Critical Organization Analysis'. In *Organization: The Interdisciplinary Journal of Organization, Theory and Society* 3, no. 3:425–38.

Graham, Hilary. 1983. 'Caring: A Labour of Love'. In *A Labour of Love*, edited by J. Finch and D. Groves, 13–30. London: Routledge and Kegan Paul.

Hills, Marcia, E. Lindsey, M. Chisamore, J. Bassett-Smith, K. Abbott, and J. Fournier-Chalmers. 1995. 'University-College Collaboration: Rethinking Curriculum Development in Nursing Education'. *Journal of Nursing Education* 33:220–5.

Jackson, Bradley. 1996. 'Re-engineering the Sense of Self: The Manager and the Management Guru'. *Journal of Management Studies* 33, no. 5:571–90.

Jackson, Nancy. 1993. 'If Competence Is the Answer, What Is the Question?', *Australia and New Zealand Journal of Vocational Education Research* 1, no. 1:46–59.

_____. 1994. 'Rethinking Vocational Learning: The Case of Clerical Skills'. In *Critical Issues in Sociology of Education*, edited by L. Erwin and D. MacLennan, 341–51. Toronto: Copp Clark Pitman.

Leininger, M. 1980. 'Caring: A Central Focus of Nursing and Health Services'. *Nursing and Health Care* 1, no. 3:135–43.

Leira, A. 1994. 'Concepts of Caring: Loving, Thinking, and Doing'. *Social Service Review* (June):185–201.

Leverment, Y., P. Ackers, and D. Preston. 1997. 'Professionals in the New NHS: A Case Study of Business Process Reengineering'. Presented at the British Academy of Management annual conference, London, September.

Lindsey, Elizabeth. 1995. *Collaborative Curriculum Guide*, developed by the Partners of the Collaborative Nursing Program in British Columbia: Camosun College, Douglas College, Kwantlan University College, Langara Collelge, Malaspina University College, North Island College, Okanagan University College, Selkirk College, University College of the Cariboo, and University of Victoria.

Lomas, Jonathan. 1997. 'Devolving Authority for Health Care in Canada's Provinces: 4: Emerging Issues and Prospects'. *Canadian Medical Association Journal* 156, no. 3:371–7.

McPherson, Kathryn. 1996. *Bedside Matters: The Transformation of Canadian Nursing, 1900–1990*. Toronto: Oxford University Press.

Noddings, N. 1984. *Caring: A Feminine Approach to Ethics and Moral Education*. Berkeley: University of California Press.

Porter-O'Grady, T., and S. Finnigan. 1984. *Shared Governance for Nurses*. Rockville: Aspen.

Reverby, Susan. 1987. *Ordered to Care: The Dilemma of American Nursing 1850–1945*. Cambridge: Cambridge University Press.

RNAO (Registered Nurses Association of Ontario). 1997a. 'Open Letter to Ontario Citizens from the RNAO'. *RN* (January-February):6–7.

_____. 1997b. 'RNAO News: RNAO and ONA Speak Out on the Value of RNs'. *RN* (March–April):22.

Schweikhart, Sharon, and Vicki Smith-Daniels. 1996. 'Reengineering the Work of Caregivers: Role Redefinition, Team Structures, and Organizational Redesign'. *Hospital and Health Services Administration* 41, no. 1:19–36.

Shindul-Rothschild, Judith, Diane Berry, and Ellen Long-Middleton. 1996. 'Where Have All the Nurses Gone? Final Results of Our Patient Care Survey'. *American Journal of Nursing* 96, no. 11:25–44.

Sibbald, Barbara. 1997. 'Delegating Away Patient Safety'. *The Canadian Nurse* (February):22–6.

Smith, Dorothy. 1987. *The Everyday World as Problematic*. Toronto: University of Toronto Press.

_____. 1990. *Texts Facts and Femininity: Exploring the Relations of Ruling*. London: Routledge and Kegan Paul.

Suchman, Lucy. 1987. *Plans and Situated Action*. Cambridge: Cambridge University Press.

Watson, Jean. 1988. *Nursing: Human Science and Human Care: A Theory of Nursing*. New York: National League for Nursing.

_____. 1989. 'Transformative Thinking and a Caring Curriculum'. In *Toward a Caring Curriculum: A New Pedagogy for Nursing*, edited by E. Bevis and J. Watson, 37–50. New York: National League for Nursing.

Wolf, Zane Robinson. 1989. 'Uncovering the Hidden Work of Nursing'. *Nursing and Health Care* 10, no. 8:463–7.

Chapter 10

Transforming Rural Livelihoods: Gender, Work, and Restructuring in Three Ontario Communities

Belinda Leach

In November 1993, following months of speculation about the future of the company she worked for, and in particular its manufacturing plant in the community where she lived, Karen White, along with her husband and co-workers, was told that the plant would close in May of the following year. Walking home from work that day she made a detour and dropped in to K-Brand, the other major factory in the town, which had been there a few months making sports clothing, such as baseball hats, and there she picked up two application for employment forms. She described her husband's reaction when she handed him one of them: 'I'm not working at K-Brand' he said. And that was the end of the discussion. Karen quit her industrial job which would terminate anyway 5 months later, and took what she was offered at K-Brand at minimum wage. As she put it, 'I knew at least I'd still be able to get home at lunch time for Jason and Alex'. Six months later she was laid off from K-Brand, was unemployed for a couple of months, then found a part-time job in a local nursing home. Her husband took the lay-off in May, and was unemployed for 8 months until he found an industrial job about 60 km away from home.

—Field notes

This chapter draws on a qualitative study of the work lives of men and women who have been laid off from manufacturing jobs in rural communities in Wellington County, Ontario.[1] The findings of this study operate as a point of departure for thinking about how restructuring processes operate, are apprehended, and articulated within a gendered local culture. In the communities we have studied, men and women were employed alongside each other in factory work. When their workplaces closed, men and women workers faced the problem of finding new work on different terms. In this chapter I argue that at the moment of redundancy, factors came into play that directly affected women's strategies and options for new employment.

Women not only confronted the new economy but dealt with gendered work expectations shaped in the rural cultural context.

The chapter then explores the way in which women's involvement in a rural labour process is bound to rural ideology, which incorporates powerful ideas about paid and unpaid work, as well as to the experience of restructuring. The caring labour expected of women, in both paid and unpaid forms, becomes significant when they explore new job possibilities. As all forms of women's work are restructured, the relations of caring are restructured as well. In the following case-study, the attention women had to pay to their caring responsibilities led them into less economically secure forms of work and increased their economic dependence upon men.

A crucial argument here is that restructuring processes do not simply have local effects but are themselves shaped by rural ideologies and practices in multiple and complex ways. For example, cultural and ideological forces that shape gender relations and gender identity in the rural context also underpin the ways in which the rural emerges as an arena of consumption and as a locus of new service sector jobs as part of the overall dynamic of restructuring towards a service economy.

Restructuring in Rural Communities

Since the 1970s Canadian workers have faced massive numbers of plant shutdowns. The Economic Council of Canada (1990:15) concluded that plant closures signal permanent structural changes in the economy and are not simply signs of temporary conditions that will change with an upturn in the business cycle. Although there is considerable debate over what this means in terms of the jobs available to people in a restructured economy, it is clear that the service sector shows most vitality, accounting for almost 90 per cent of job growth in Canada since 1967 (Economic Council of Canada 1990:4–5; see also Betcherman and Lowe 1997). As well, there is a proliferation of so-called 'non-standard' forms of work. Part-time work grew through the 1980s from about 4 per cent of total employment to 15 per cent; and other kinds of non-standard work (such as short-term jobs, self-employment, and home-based work) also increased substantially and continue to grow. Correspondingly, long-term unemployment rates continue to increase, even in times of economic 'recovery' (Gera 1991:99).

The downsizing and loss of rural manufacturing facilities has been largely responsible for the loss in rural community employment, retail trade, declining property values, and increased strain on community service capacity. As Janet Fitchen (1991) has argued in her work on rural upstate New York, some rural communities are even more dependent upon manufacturing activity than major metropolitan areas such as New York City. Similarly, the labour force in some Canadian rural communities with a manufacturing base has been more concentrated in goods-producing industries than the urban labour force, at least since 1971 (Bollman 1992:Chapter 1). The long-term decline in manufacturing, coupled with the continuation of the farm crisis, poses particular problems for rural communities. Like workers facing restructuring outside rural areas, people in Fitchen's study were faced with accepting lower-paying, non-standard contingent work, with a decline in the quality of work on the job and a disproportionate impact on older workers and those with less education. Unlike non-rural workers, however, these people often had to commute farther to new jobs. Fitchen argues that the loss of factories in rural communities has had an even more pervasive and deeper impact than has the decline in farms (Fitchen 1991:70).

While both manufacturing and agricultural jobs are in decline in rural areas, the service sector shows growth. Yet 1991 census data for Canadian rural communities indicate that employment rates in producer services are only a third to a half of that in other regions (Canada 1995:20), and it is producer services that tend to provide many of the high-wage, high-skill jobs in the service sector. An assessment of the prospects for service sector employment in American rural areas found a predominance of lower-paid jobs in food stores, car dealerships, gas stations, utility services, estate agents and insurance offices, government services, building material supply companies, agricultural services, transportation, and private household services (Miller and Bluestone 1988). Overall, Miller and Bluestone (1988) have concluded that the growth in the service economy tends to bring lower-wage jobs to rural areas, while growth in higher-paid service employment tends to be concentrated in urban areas. As well, the historical dependence of rural areas on high levels of public expenditure in infrastructure (for example, on relatively small hospitals and schools) makes them particularly vulnerable to the downsizing of the state. Although this kind of restructuring is happening apace and with much controversy, social scientists are only just beginning to explore it.

Our research with workers facing the aftermath of plant closures in North Wellington County, Ontario, a mainly rural county about 120 km northwest of Toronto, has indicated a relatively higher incidence of service sector part-time work at a lower wage, accompanied by deteriorating work conditions and a disturbing proportion of older workers facing long-term unemployment (Leach and Winson 1995). However, my focus in this chapter is on a more detailed examination of the gendered nature of the restructuring of rural labour processes. For while superficially it would appear that men and women leaving similar jobs face common conditions in the labour market, I argue that in fact the experience of restructuring for men and for women is quite different.

Sarah Whatmore argues that despite the growth of European research interest in rural women in the 1980s, new work is needed that takes account of the contours of emerging rural economies, with serious attention to the rural context as a whole, recognizing the complex interactions and dependency between rural primary and secondary production, reproduction and consumption (Whatmore 1994:39). She argues that 'These global realignments . . . build on and, in turn, reshape rural gender relations' (Whatmore 1994:40). She goes on to point out that one of the major theoretical challenges facing research on gender is to recognize the 'highly differentiated nature of women's experiences of rural restructuring as these are associated with particular social and environmental contexts'. As she says: 'Women's access to, and control over, the rural labour process is likely to revolve around . . . the double burden of combining so-called "productive" work with domestic labour responsibilities . . .' (Whatmore 1994:47). In other words, women's caring labour at home will directly influence their capacity for taking on paid work outside the home.

The rich empirical studies emerging from feminist scholarship during the past couple of decades have shown how women are frequently segregated in particular occupations, such as clerical and caring work, and in particular types of work, for example, part-time and home-based. The specificity of women's experiences of the labour process historically are attributable at least in part (Beechey 1987) to their past and continuing responsibility for domestic labour—in other words, the unpaid kinds of caring labour—resulting in a different structural relationship to capitalism from that of men. One of the interesting features of our study is that men and women worked alongside each other, earned similar (though not exactly the same) wages for similar kinds of work and belonged to the same unions. While I am not arguing that men's and women's experiences of the labour process were the same, a key point is that the availability of jobs for women, which were comparable to men's and close to home for both, allowed them to meet on the shop floor on more equal terms. I am arguing that the degree of divergence that women experienced compared to men in trying to find a job after lay-off, and in the jobs they eventually found, was disproportionate to the degree of difference in their job situations before lay-off.

It is also worth noting that the women in the study were not women working off the farm to diversify the farm household income, as are many of the rural women mentioned in the literature. These were workers whose experience of work had been primarily non-agricultural as a result of the combined processes of the historical proletarianization of rural populations, as well as the more recent crisis in Canadian farming. It has been many generations since a majority of rural people in Ontario were directly connected to a farm. This is significant because the family farm is able to absorb surplus labour, at least in the short term, for example, if a farm wife is laid off from an off-farm job. In contrast, long-time proletarianized rural residents have no such cushion to absorb the impact of economic change.

There is now increasing evidence that, in much the same way that labour processes are gendered, economic restructuring too affects women workers in ways that are quite specific. For example, women are less likely than men to find full-time jobs in the new economy (Armstrong 1996). Moreover part-time, short-term, and home-based jobs that are created as part of corporate flexibility strategies often appear rather insidiously to fulfil women's needs for flexible work options as they perform domestic labour. In fact, as I have argued from my work with industrial homeworkers, these kinds of work represent a particular gendering of restructuring that may lead to new forms of gender inequality (Jenson 1996; Leach 1993, 1996). As well, state cutbacks to social programs—such as cuts in child-care services, assistance to the elderly, or early release from hospital—effects of which are documented in other chapters in this volume, place increased pressure on the domestic workload, in other words, on women. This occurs when other effects of restructuring—major ones like the loss of a household breadwinner's wage, or more everyday kinds like stagnant or declining real wages—make additional income even more essential (Redclift and Whatmore 1990:193). When Canadian rural post offices, which had provided decent employment for women as rural postmasters, were about to be privatized, one analyst wrote that 'job loss, decreased wages, capricious job security and lost employee benefits will exacerbate the existing economic instability that most rural women live' (Popaleni 1989:138). Work such as this suggests that while feminist scholarship has shown the considerable variation in women's experience of paid and unpaid work in terms of race, class, and family status, it is also necessary to focus on the particular experience of work, lay-off, and re-employment embedded in the rural context.

Taking a rural focus is in itself, however, problematic. There has been considerable debate in the rural sociology literature about what in fact constitutes 'the rural'. While it is not fruitful to revisit this debate here, it is important to make a number of points concerning the notion of rurality. There are some key features that distinguish a rural environment from an urban one. These features are not in dispute and are germane to the argument here. These include fewer opportunities for employment and lower population densities that create problems of distance and affect many areas of life, especially access to jobs, transportation, and child care (McKinley Wright 1995:218). While it could be argued that the material findings here are not specific to rural populations, the above factors are important in exacerbating the problems that result from restructuring. However, the changes taking place contribute in a number of ways to an overall process of urbanization, where people everywhere are tied in to serving the urban market economy, and though integrated into the market in different ways, women in both rural and urban settings experience increasing commonality in their lives.[2]

Beyond this the notion of rurality as an ideological construct is more complex. Yet while it may be troublesome as an analytical category, it remains a key signifier to people themselves. People who live in rural areas, even when they are close to a city, define themselves in relation to, and as distinct from, urban people, drawing upon conceptions of rurality developed historically in specific localities. Mark Shucksmith (1994) has argued that the idea of rural is actually a contested domain within rural communities themselves. In his research the definition of rural (as demonstrated by appropriate rural practices) was hotly disputed by groups with very different interests living in and around the same community. He argues that ultimately those best represented by local municipal officials won the day, and policy decisions were made in favour of their interests. In our own work we have seen how local municipal councillors publicly reacted to a newspaper report on our version of events and their outcomes, refuting our findings and questioning our methods, and denying the conclusions, which, they felt, reflected negatively on their community and its capacity to deal with restructuring (Leach and Winson 1999). The local press too involved itself, questioning the right of the workers involved to contribute to the discourse, asking 'Are unidentified workers who have just been fired from their job, the ones best qualified to say what happened and its effects on the community?' (Mount Forest *Olds* April/May 1996:3). Taken together these reactions politically marginalize working people and diminish the significance of what working-class people have to say. At the same time they reinforce the dominance of those interests represented in municipal structures and the press.

Plant Closings in Wellington County

In our study men and women worked for two major employers in three communities in North Wellington County. This is a rural region comprising eleven municipalities with a total population in 1991 of 25,835. The local economy of the region is rooted in agriculture, and one of the firms, Canada Packers, had operated in the villages of Harriston and Elora since late in the last century, processing locally produced milk into a variety of dairy products. Both these plants had unionized early. In 1990 Canada Packers was acquired by the British food-processing giant, Hillsdown Holdings PLC, which restructured the company, concentrating on high-profit areas such as value-added food products and joint-venture operations with American agribusiness. These actions appear to have been intended to take advantage of the continental market opened up by the Free Trade Agreement with the United States. During the two-year restructuring period, Hillsdown sold off entire divisions and closed down twenty plants, including Harriston and Elora, in January 1991 (Winson 1993).

The other firm closure we examined was Westinghouse, which opened a custom-built facility in the town of Mount Forest in 1981, building electrical products for government, public utilities, and industry. This appears to have followed a 'greenfield' strategy, aimed at moving some operations away from the unionized plant in the heavily industrialized and unionized

Table 10.1: Pre- and Postlay-off Wages by Plant (Canadian $)

	CP Harriston		CP Elora		Westinghouse, Mount Forest	
	Men	Women	Men	Women	Men	Women
Prelay-off (n = 68)	$11.77	$11.07	$12.00	$10.93	$14.90	$12.98
1994 (n = 68)	$11.03	$9.18	$8.75	$7.90	$16.50	$8.29
1996 (n = 34)	$12.39	$8.62	$14.00	$11.19	$12.90	$10.22

city of Hamilton, but a few workers relocated from Hamilton and the workforce was soon certified. During the real estate boom of the late 1980s, Westinghouse senior management made a foray into speculative real estate and other high-risk investments. The collapse of the North American real estate markets in 1990 as the recession took hold forced the company to write off $2.7 billion in assets and begin a massive restructuring program to cover bad loans (Baker, Dobrzynski, and Schroder 1992). This meant selling off whole corporate divisions and laying off several thousands of employees. In 1993 it was announced that the Mount Forest facility would close, and lay-offs were staggered over more than a year until July 1994.

For our study we interviewed laid-off plant workers in 1994 and obtained information on sixty-eight workers, which included fourteen couples working in the same firm. In the autumn of 1996 we went back to thirty-four of these people to find out what changes had taken place in their work lives. The following data indicates some of the changes that took place for these men and women between being employed in a steady job at either Canada Packers or Westinghouse to their personal situation in September and October of 1996.

Table 10.1 gives a sense of the differences between men's and women's full-time wages. These are not very far apart; the widest gap, about $2 an hour, was between men and women at Westinghouse in Mount Forest due to the different job classifications into which men and women were hired. Other differences between men and women included seniority, which has some impact on wages. For example, of thirty-four workers with more than ten years' seniority at Canada Packers in Harriston, only eight were women.

Since for most people the plants were close to home, the juggling of domestic labour and the industrial labour process was less of an issue than it is in many work situations. This is not to say that conflict over this and inequality of responsibility in these areas were absent. As in most places, women remained primarily responsible for domestic tasks, which was clear from our interviews with them. But the ability to walk to work and 'pop back home' at lunchtime, to pick up a few groceries, drive a child to a dental appointment, or visit an aging relative in the community made balancing work and family considerably easier for women and also enabled men to play a useful part in these activities.

This situation changed almost overnight as men and women workers laid off from similar industrial jobs found their re-employment trajectories markedly different. Some men and a few women were able to find comparable industrial jobs, but only if they were willing to commute considerable distances from home to small and medium-sized urban centres 50 or 60 km away. One couple who commuted together to Toronto missed the social activities they used to engage in after work. While many men travelled long distances to work, the women who commuted to industrial jobs were those without young children living at home. Most of the women were more likely to be working closer to home so they could be available for school-age or preschool children. One woman in Mount Forest with five children at home had been unable to find work since her lay-off and she attributed her continued unemployment to her unwillingness to travel very far. The work that could be found locally was in more precarious, competitive industries, in informal work, or in part-time employment in the service sector. These factors reduced both women's wages and their access to the benefits for which they had been eligible in their old jobs.

When we contacted people in 1996, we found that their hourly wages had changed perhaps less dramatically than we might have expected. However, the change in annual income between the year in which they were last employed by Canada Packers or Westinghouse and 1995 is quite dramatic for most workers, both men and women. Prelay-off average annual income was $31,000 for six men at Westinghouse and $24,000 for seven at Canada Packers. By 1995 five of the Westinghouse men had experienced a decrease in wages, reducing their average annual income to $25,000. Three Canada Packers men had considerable loss of income in 1995 when their earnings averaged $14,600.

For the women the situation was even more bleak. All except two of the twenty-five women experienced a decrease in their average annual wages, down from $29,000 at Westinghouse to $18,000, and from $23,000 to $12,000 at Canada Packers. These figures represent a loss of 38 per cent and 48 per cent respectively.

The difference between changes in hourly rates and annual income is attributable to the number of workers now employed in part-time jobs. By 1996, up to five years after lay-off for the Canada Packers workers, 78 per cent of the women were in part-time work, compared to 25 per cent of the men. This does not, of course, account financially for the loss in benefits.

From the difference in average hourly rate for part-time work compared to full-time work, it is clear that the average wage of men dropped significantly when they accepted part-time work. By 1996, the difference between

Table 10.2: Full- and Part-time Employment by Gender, 1994 and 1996

| | Men | | | |
	1994 (14)		1996 (12)	
	Full-time	Part-time	Full-time	Part-time
Total numbers	12	2	9	3
	(85%)	(15%)	(75%)	(25%)
Average hourly wage	$12.20	$8.85	$13.54	$10.85

| | Women | | | |
	1994 (26)		1996 (18)	
	Full-time	Part-time	Full-time	Part-time
Total numbers	12	14	4	14
	(46%)	(54%)	(22%)	(78%)
Average hourly wage	$8.11	$8.82	$11.00	$7.05

average full-time and part-time wages for women had widened. This seems to be attributable to a polarization between those (few) women who were willing to seek full-time jobs at some distance from their communities of residence, and those compelled (through their domestic responsibilities) to accept part-time jobs locally, where part-time wages dropped between 1994 and 1996. Our findings raise questions concerning the popular argument that women prefer 'flexible' forms of work. Certainly, for some, part-time work gave them more time with their children, yet a closer look at the women who felt this way reveals two significant factors. First, the part-time work they tended to be involved in was what we might call 'very part-time', i.e., approximately fifteen hours per week. Second, all of these women had husbands with well-paid, relatively secure full-time jobs. One woman who had worked in part-time jobs as a single parent for ten years described how the second income of her new husband made life manageable and comfortable. Another woman who had suffered serious health problems following her lay-off eventually divorced her husband and now has part-time jobs in two different communities. She told us, 'Life was a lot simpler and more organized when I worked at Canada Packers. Everything seemed to be thrown into chaos when I lost that job.'

Part-time jobs were often the only work that older women could find. One sixty-year-old woman was working at three different part-time jobs and would have liked to quit one of them (a job working as a nurses' aide in a nursing home) because she found it extremely stressful as workers fought for the limited hours available. However, her husband, who was laid off at the same time that she lost her job, had been working at a gas station since then. Although he had just found a better job, she still needed to keep her three jobs, and neither of them could entertain the possibility of retirement for several years.

Women with part-time jobs without benefits and whose husbands had decent full-time jobs were able to rely on the health benefits associated with their husbands' jobs. This was another factor involved in the decision that men should seek work further afield since they were more likely to find jobs with benefits in the larger labour markets of Guelph, Kitchener–Waterloo, and Toronto. Women working at jobs in new local factories frequently found no job security. Rather, they faced a cycle of lay-off (sometimes only weeks after being hired), unemployment, a new job or possibly recall to the old one, then lay-off again. This was due to the instability of new companies operating in the competitive sector. Since in many workplaces benefits only come into effect after a probationary period of three months, these families needed the advantages that came from working in more stable industries, but these were usually at a distance.

Full-time jobs for women were found in only one of the three communities, indicating that the nature of the local labour market shapes postlay-off opportunities in important ways. In Harriston a majority of women found part-time jobs, and half of these had more than one. In Mount Forest, however, three-quarters of the women found full-time jobs in 1994, most of them at K-Brand, where Karen sought work. Even in 1996, by which time part-time work predominated in the other communities, in Mount Forest there was a more even division between full- and part-time work. The trade-off for the valuable asset of working full-time close to home, however, was a dramatic loss of income. The prelay-off hourly wage for women at Westinghouse was $12.98, while those who moved to K-Brand averaged $6.90. These findings are remarkably similar to Fitchen's for rural New York State. She notes:

> Even where a factory closing was followed by an opening by another manufacturing firm, laid off workers who found new factory jobs suffered a substantial cut in pay not only because they were starting over, shorn of the seniority and raises they'd earned over the years and with little bargaining power in the employer's market, but also because the entire pay scale in the new manufacturing firms may be significantly lower than in the old firms (Fitchen 1991:70).

Many of the women lamented the loss of income that came with lay-off and less well-paid replacement jobs. They usually talked about this in terms of the family activities they could no longer contemplate, such as taking vacations and moving out of rental accommodation into their own home. They also missed being able to help adult children and their families financially when they needed it. One woman, who had recently found a job after years of unemployment, said how happy she was 'to have my own money again and my own bank account'.

A few people indicated to us that they had turned to informal self-employment, such as catering, dog breeding, and small engine repairs, but this usually happened after several unsuccessful attempts to rejoin the labour force and seemed in these cases to be an option of last resort. Overall, though, there is a significant shift in women's jobs away from the manufacturing sector and towards work in service industries. This shift echoes the broader shift in the economy and signals a crucial dynamic of restructuring.

It seems that rather than simply concluding that restructuring leads to a worsening in women's position *vis-à-vis* men, the divergence between men's and most women's postlay-off experiences of work needs further investigation and explanation. I argue that these differences are bound up in men's and women's respective relationships to caring labour, which are themselves shaped by particular ideologies and beliefs concerning appropriate gender roles.

Women's Work and Rural Culture

Recent studies examining restructuring and rural women in Britain and the United States indicate that women's employment options are tightly bound up with the particular cultural forms taken by gender relations in household and community in rural areas. Thus, we need to look at the ways in which gender and power relations are configured in the rural household and communities under study. Rather than seeing restructuring as a one-way street whereby social processes are determined by economic ones, it is necessary to consider how existing and dynamic gender and power configurations affect the experience of restructuring. In other words, the processes of social and economic change shape each other. This is particularly important because it permits agency and the possibility of resisting certain kinds of constructions of restructuring.

In writing about restructuring in small Iowa towns, Nancy Naples argues that 'traditional notions of rural community life' are used to try to make sense of the changing economic and social context, and to make a case against some of the changes people face (Naples 1994:114). Similarly, Jo Little, in examining women's employment in three English rural communities, argues that while household livelihood strategies vary according to the employment opportunities available for women, they also depend on their consistency with the ideologies and value systems of rural communities (Little 1993:14). She shows that 'the impact of restructuring is not only reflected in gender divisions, but is also determined by them' (Little 1993:22).

Deborah Fink (1992) has argued that, for the rural United States, agrarian ideology continues to influence ideas and behaviour profoundly in rural areas. Thus, the model for female behaviour is the farm wife, whose primary work is in the home, supporting her husband and raising her children to continue the farming tradition. Based on her extensive survey of the literature on women in rural areas of both industrialized and less-developed countries, Carolyn Sachs has extended this ideology beyond the United States. She says 'gender relations in rural areas continue to be steeped in vestiges of patriarchal relations in farm households' (Sachs 1996:140). Agrarian ideology stresses a traditional gender division of labour and a two-parent, heterosexual family as the natural household form and idealizes and romanticizes women's role.

In the British literature a number of writers have argued that a strictly hierarchical local power structure evolved between landowner and agricultural labourer in rural communities that deliberately excluded women. This then combined with a set of moral values that reasserted men's sexual control over women to reinforce women's position in the home and the belief that they are responsible for the organization and maintenance of the household (Davidoff et al. 1976). Following up on this work, others have argued that the historical stability of rural communities is attributable to the conservative nature of village life, and that both are central to gender relations in rural areas (McDowell and Massey 1984).

There is little literature dealing with gender ideology in the rural Ontario context and what does exist documents farm families, not those holding non-farm jobs. However, since rural life has been organized historically around agriculture and agriculture-related manufacturing and services, it seems reasonable to expect the existence of a local variant of agrarian ideology based on ideas emanating from the agricultural history of the region. On the basis of the findings of these studies, we would then expect both men and women to hold fairly conservative views about gender roles. A study by and of Ontario farm women published in 1983 stated: 'Though she may work hand in hand with her husband all morning, she can still be sure that she will be the one to put lunch on the table when they get to the house' (Ireland 1983:38). A slightly later study describes the response of farm men to their wives' increased off-farm work and political activities as 'bewilderment' (Daley 1985). In a rare study focusing on the political views of women in rural Ontario, Louise Carbert (1995) found that while farm wives' views have been modified to some extent by their exposure to feminism, they exhibit conservatism both politically and with regard to gender roles. Yet there is increasing documentation of women's engagement with strong and effective rural women's organizations, fighting for recognition of women's work, clarification of their legal status, and improved rural services (MacKenzie 1995; Shortall 1994).

In certain respects the factory work that the women in this study engaged in, like some of the rural women's organizations, shatters the stereotype of rural women as it redraws the distinction between public and private. It is clear from some of the preceding comments that women did benefit from the power that came from having money of their own. It is notable that in contrast to the men, women were keen to tell us how much they had loved their old factory jobs. Their agency is apparent in the way they set about finding new jobs and obtaining them fairly quickly. Ironically, women's willingness to take work of almost any kind (as long as it was close to home) made it easier for men to wait until they found better jobs. Like Karen in the opening vignette, while women got on with making a living locally, men could seek out jobs comparable to their old ones at a more leisurely pace and in more distant labour markets.

Although these women may have avoided living the stereotype while they held industrial jobs, old ideas remained strong in the culture in which they lived and came into play constraining their choices after lay-off. The dynamic of restructuring that shifts jobs from manufacturing to service also plays upon gendered, class, and urban/rural inequities, which are then used (though in different ways) by the social actors involved—women, their husbands, employers, and policy makers.

Some of the strongly held local cultural ideas are reflected in the continued popularity of rural village fairs, where the emphasis is on growing, cooking and preserving skills, animal husbandry, and technical skills associated with farm work (such as tractor pulls). These lend support to an enduring ideo-logy that privileges and romanticizes rural life and customs, and a prevailing set of gender roles and relations.

The popularity of rural village fairs, farmers' markets, and 'country crafts' gives a clue to understanding the trajectory of women's work lives after rural restructuring. Rural ideology, tied to a set of images and assumptions about rural spaces, is also important in shaping the use of rural areas. Little and Austin (1996) show how ideas about the 'rural idyll' in England, which invoke a nostalgia for the past and an escape from the modern, have shaped uses of rural areas. These include the exodus of urban populations to the country in search a 'simpler' rural life, which affects the kinds of employment opportunities women are likely to find there. This is one kind of changing use of rural areas, many of which demonstrate rural communi-ties' shift from production to theatres of consumption, with an associated service sector (see Marsden 1992). This shift will be more pronounced in those rural areas within striking distance of significant population centres, and those more remote ones that have particular environments and experi-ences to offer. In Wellington County urban dwellers are enticed to move to the 'estate-sized' housing lots bordering villages, to retire to cottages in idyllic communities, or move to long-term care facilities complete with breathtaking views. Urbanites are encouraged to visit and enjoy rural tourist attractions from summer theatre to berry picking, craft studios to restaurants featuring country-style cooking.

If we look more closely at these emerging attractions, we can see that rural communities are increasingly dependent on the consumption of their rural amenities for their continued survival. In addition, these attractions influence the restructured rural labour market in important ways, resulting in the kinds of service sector jobs that the displaced women industrial workers in our study take. Like Karen working at the seniors' home in my opening vignette, working-class women are servicing the middle class's consumption of rurality while their husbands cling to the vestiges of work in industrial production. At the same time, the jobs that are being created reinforce a conservative division of labour, picking up on gender-linked tasks such as nursing, food service, and handicrafts.

Conclusion

From a wide-ranging series of case-studies, Carolyn Sachs concludes that restructuring relies heavily on rural women's labour (Sachs 1996). For this particular case, and as is clear from Karen's example, it seems possible to go further and argue that rural women are actually at the leading edge of the restructuring shift of emphasis from production to consumption. The shift from manufacturing jobs to service provision of care re-emphasizes the caring kinds of work traditionally associated with women, the perception of caring as involving essentially female qualities, and the association of men with manufacturing work. There are also resonances here with the notion of deprofessionalization in the caring professions discussed in other chapters. The women here are picking up the emerging unskilled caring jobs that result from the restructuring of professional caring work.

This divergence in men's and women's work trajectories has negative implications for women. The overall changes in men's and women's incomes indicate that women are likely to face (again, for some) a situation in which they are economically dependent upon men, an idea that is supported by the woman who described her life as much easier since she remarried and now had some access to a male wage. This, of course, is dependent upon the individual man's job security, which is not always certain, but it raises serious concerns, for example, for women in abusive relationships. The imbalance between men and women has further economic consequences as women with insecure part-time jobs lose pension, employment insurance, and benefit rights (Baldwin and Twigg 1991:121).

The caring responsibilities are a constant burden for women that influence their other decisions, notably their choices concerning livelihoods. Women's flexibility in paid and unpaid work—their willingness to take on whatever is available and to construct a means of making a livelihood and caring for others in a patchwork fashion—is a key factor here. This flexibility is chosen by women because of their caring responsibilities at the same time that new, 'flexible' forms of work are increasingly the only ones available. This simultaneously contributes to their economic vulnerability, to the devaluing of all forms of women's work, and paradoxically to the survival of the household and the family. While life seems to continue as usual, in fact new forms of inequality built upon old ideas are being produced and reproduced.

Yet the important point here, as Nanneke Redclift and Sarah Whatmore (1990:191) stress, is that livelihood and reproductive strategies together contribute to the overall processes of social stratification, not simply to a series of impacts. A focus on just the outcomes of restructuring reinforces the idea that change is generated from outside, and makes it difficult to see the ways in which economic processes are embedded in social and cultural contexts, and how the two are mutually constituting. This kind of analysis enables us to see how women resist certain forms of restructuring, possibly using the family, as bell hooks (1984:133–4) has suggested for Black American women, by using local cultural ideas and practices to insist on the primacy of caring relationships within the family over the pursuit of a masculine job model. Attention to these issues begins to provide the basis for a more nuanced understanding of the transformation of rural livelihoods, and of gendered restructuring processes more generally.

Notes

1 This study was carried out with Tony Winson and was funded through the Tricouncil AgroEcosystem Health Project.
2 I am grateful to Marie Campbell for pointing this out.

References

Armstrong, Patricia. 1996. 'The Feminization of the Labour Force: Harmonizing Down in a Global Economy'. In *Rethinking Restructuring: Gender and Change in Canada*, edited by I. Bakker, 29–54. Toronto: University of Toronto Press.

Baker, S., J.D. Dobrzynski, and M. Schroder. 1992. 'Westinghouse: More Pain Ahead'. *Business Week* (7 December):32–4.

Baldwin, S., and J. Twigg. 1991. 'Women and Community Care: Reflections on a Debate'. In *Women's Issues in Social Policy*, edited by M. Maclean and D. Groves, 117–35. London: Routledge.

Beechey, V. 1987. *Unequal Work*. London: Verso.

Betcherman, G., and G.S. Lowe. 1997. *The Future of Work in Canada: A Synthesis Report*. Ottawa: Canadian Policy Research Networks Inc.

Bollman, Ray, ed. 1992. *Rural and Small Town Canada*. Toronto: Thompson Educational Publishing.

Canada. 1995. *Rural Canada: A Profile*. Ottawa: Supply and Services.

Carbert, L. 1995. *Agrarian Feminism*. Toronto: University of Toronto Press.

Daley, N. 1985. 'Male Response to Change in Farm-Wives' Sex Role in Rural Ontario'. Rural Sociological Society Association Paper.

Davidoff, L., J. L'Esperance, and H. Newby. 1976. 'Landscape with Figures: Home and Community in English Society'. In *The Rights and Wrongs of Women*, edited by A. Oakley and J. Mitchell, 139–75. Harmondsworth: Penguin.

Economic Council of Canada. 1990. *Good Jobs, Bad Jobs*. Ottawa: Economic Council of Canada.

Fink, D. 1992. *Agrarian Women: Wives and Mothers in Rural Nebraska 1880–1940*. Chapel Hill: University of North Carolina Press.

Fitchen, Janet. 1991. *Endangered Spaces, Enduring Places: Change, Identity and Survival in Rural America*. Boulder: Westview.

Gera, S. 1991. *Canadian Unemployment—Lessons from the 80s and Challenges for the 90s: A Compendium*. Ottawa: Economic Council of Canada.

hooks, b. 1984. *Feminist Theory: From Margin to Centre*. Boston: South End Press.

Ireland, P. 1983. *The Farmer Takes a Wife*. Chesley: Concerned Farm Women.

Jenson, Jane. 1996. 'Part-time Employment and Women: A Range of Strategies'. In *Rethinking Restructuring: Gender and Change in Canada*, edited by I. Bakker, 92–108. Toronto: University of Toronto Press.

Leach, Belinda. 1993. 'Flexible Work, Precarious Future: Some Lessons from the Canadian Clothing Industry'. *Canadian Review of Sociology and Anthropology* 30, no. 1:64–82.

_____. 1996. 'Behind Closed Doors: Homework Policy and Lost Possibilities for Change'. In *Rethinking Restructuring: Gender and Change in Canada*, edited by I. Bakker, 203–16. Toronto: University of Toronto Press.

_____, and Anthony Winson. 1995. 'Bringing "Globalization" Down to Earth: Restructuring and Labour in Rural Communities'. *Canadian Review of Sociology and Anthropology* 32, no. 3:341–64.

_____, and Anthony Winson. 1999. 'Rural Retreat: The Social Impact of Restructuring in Three Ontario Communities'. In *Restructuring Societies*, edited by David B. Knight and Alun E. Joseph, 83–104. Ottawa: Carleton University Press.

Little, Jo. 1994. 'Gender Relations and the Rural Labour Process'. In *Gender and Rurality*, edited by T. Marsden, P. Lowe, and S. Whatmore, 335–42. London: David Fulton.

_____, and P. Austin. 1996. 'Women and the Rural Idyll'. *Journal of Rural Studies* 12, no. 2:101–11.

McDowell, D., and D. Massey. 1984. 'A Woman's Place?' In *Geography Matters!*, edited by D. Massey and J. Allen, 128–47. Cambridge: Cambridge University Press.

MacKenzie, Fiona. 1995. 'Is Where I Stand Where I Sit? The Ontario Farm Women's Network Politics and Difference' . *Journal of Rural Studies* 10, no. 2:101–15.

McKinley Wright, M. 1995. '"I Never Did Any Fieldwork, But I Sure Milked an Awful Lot of Cows!" Using Rural Women's Experience to Reconceptualize Modes of Work'. *Gender and Society* 9, no. 2:216–35.

Marsden, T. 1992. 'Exploring a Rural Sociology for the Fordist Transition: Incorporating Social Relations into Economic Restructuring'. *Sociologia Ruralis* 32, no. 2/3:209–30.

Miller, J ., and H. Bluestone. 1988. 'Prospects for Service Sector Employment Growth in Non-Metro America'. *Review of Regional Studies* 18 (Winter):28–41.

Mount Forest Olds. April/May 1996.

Naples, Nancy. 1994. 'Contradictions in Agrarian Ideology: Restructuring Gender, Race, Ethnicity and Class'. *Rural Sociology* 59, no. 1:110–35.

Popaleni, K. 1989. 'Shouldering the Burden for Canada Post: Privatization's Impact on Rural Women'. *Resources for Feminist Research* 17, no. 3:136–8.

Redclift, Nanneke, and Sarah Whatmore. 1990. 'Household Consumption and Livelihood: Ideologies and Issues in Rural Research'. In *Rural Restructuring: Global Processes and Their Responses*, edited by T. Marsden, P. Lowe, and S. Whatmore, 82–197. London: David Fulton.

Sachs, Carolyn. 1996. *Gendered Fields: Women, Agriculture and Environment.* Boulder: Westview.

Shortall, Sally. 1994. 'Farm Women's Groups: Community, Feminist or Social Movements?' *Canadian Review of Sociology and Anthropology* 28, no. 1:279–91.

Shucksmith, M. 1994. 'Conceptualizing Post-Industrial Rurality'. In *Towards Sustainable Rural Communities*, edited by J. Bryden, 125–32. Guelph: University of Guelph, School of Rural Planning and Development.

Whatmore, S. 1994. 'The Achievements and Challenges of European Rural Gender Studies'. In *Rural Gender Studies in Europe*, edited by L. van der Plas and M. Fonte, 39–49. Assen: Van Corcum.

Chapter 11

Restructuring Gender, Race, and Class Relations: The Case of Garment Workers and Labour Adjustment[1]

Roxana Ng

Introduction

From 1991 to 1994, based on my research on and work with immigrant women, I was appointed the chairperson of a labour adjustment committee on the garment and textile sector in Toronto because many garment workers were immigrant women. The core members of this committee were representatives from the two unions in the sector, community groups, and the two levels of government.[2] Meanwhile, I was also an academic resource person in a research project on changes in the garment sector conducted by the garment union.[3] In my capacity as chair of the labour adjustment committee and as an academic resource person, I assisted the union in assessing the operation of two labour adjustment committees in this sector (Ng 1994). In this process, I saw first-hand the detrimental effects that changes in the garment industry had on the union and on the livelihood of garment workers.

In this chapter I reflect upon my experiences during this period in an attempt to understand the transformation of the garment sector and the labour adjustment process instituted by two levels of government, a process that was ostensibly mobilized to redeploy human resources in light of technological and economic changes. What I saw were the differential effects of technological changes and globalization on different segments of the working population, in this case garment workers, many of whom were immigrant women from Asia (India, Vietnam, Hong Kong, and China).[4] These changes led to the restructuring of the industry *and* the workforce itself, altering the conditions of work and workers' ability to organize themselves. The state, operationally defined as the multiplicity of bureaucracies, policies, programs, and actors that coordinate and administer the work of ruling (see Ng 1996), is a key player in mediating the restructuring of the workforce to bring it in line with the requirement of capital mobility and accumulation while ameliorating some of the detrimental effects of capital mobility transnationally. This is an aspect of globalization that does not appear in official accounts of the phenomenon.

In this chapter I argue that people's experiences of work restructuring and globalization is *always* differentiated on the basis of gender, race, ability, and so forth. This, I argue, *is* the process of class formation in late capitalism. By examining the situation of the garment industry and garment workers in Toronto, we gain an understanding of some of the mechanisms at work in globalization. I will show that the strategies used by the government and those who have control over the garment industry to facilitate the restructuring of this industry have led to the re-colonization of 'Third World' women in the 'First World'.[5] I will also show that different levels of the government have different priorities and objectives in dealing with restructuring. The situation of garment workers gives us glimpses into the differential ways in which 'the state', with its multiplicity of departments, policies, and programs, operates in globalization.

This chapter does not deal with the conceptualization of caring or caring labour directly, which is discussed in Chapter 1 and other chapters. In exploring the restructuring of garment workers' paid employment, however, we see the embeddedness of gender relations in everyday life. Similar to Belinda Leach's analysis of rural women and men in industrial displacement in this volume, we see how women's decision making about their paid work is organized around family and household responsibilities—a thoroughly gendered process, *even though* the mainstream discourse in restructuring frequently neglects to examine the gendered aspect of this phenomenon. Indeed, this collection shows the dependence of paid labour *upon* caring labour. My study, as well as others in this volume, shows how restructuring affects *all* dimensions of women's lives, not just their paid work. Indeed, the reality of garment workers in a restructured economy ruptures our notion of the private and public spheres as separate. It raises questions about how we conceptualize the relations between 'development' and 'underdevelopment', and between the 'First World' and 'Third World' in a world that is becoming more and more integrated economically.

I will begin with a brief sketch of changes in the garment industry in Canada, specifically in metropolitan Toronto, in the past fifteen to twenty years. I will then describe and analyse my experience of labour adjustment in terms of garment workers, and the role of the state in managing and facilitating labour market relations. I will discuss how I work with the concepts of 'gender', 'race', and 'class' to show their embeddedness in people's everyday experience. I will end with a discussion of the theoretical and political implications of my analysis.

Changes in the Garment Sector in Toronto[6]

The city of Toronto has been a major centre of garment production in Canada since industrialization. As an industry that makes use of what are assumed to be women's skills, the garment trade has always been an employer of female immigrant workers, at first from Europe and later from Asia. According to Statistics Canada data in 1986, 94 per cent of sewing machine operators were born outside of Canada, as were 83 per cent of pattern makers and cutters, and 83 per cent of the employees in various textile industry occupations (reported in *The Toronto Star*, 21 September 1992, A1). Whereas women constituted just 29 per cent of the workforce in manufacturing, 80 per cent of them were in the garment industry (Borowy and Johnson 1995). Thus, the garment and textile sector was and continues to be a major employer of immigrant labour.

Historically, homeworking and sweatshop operations were an integral part of the garment trade. With the formation of the International Ladies Garment Workers' Union (ILGWU), at first in the US and later in Canada, garment workers became the few unionized female workers who enjoyed decent wages and employee benefits. Unlike some other sectors with heavy concentrations of female immigrant workers, garment workers were protected by labour standard legislation and rights to collective bargaining. Since the 1980s, however, all this has changed. In the last fifteen to twenty years, Toronto witnessed the closing of many garment factories and massive worker lay-offs. Employment dropped from 95,800 in 1988 to an estimated 62,800 in 1992, corresponding with the signing of the Free Trade Agreement between Canada and the US. Between 1985 and 1992, the ILGWU membership dropped by 60 per cent, bringing the unionization rate from a high of 80 per cent to below 20 per cent (Borowy et al. 1993)

From the point of view of economists and policy makers, the garment industry in Canada is a 'sunset' industry because without heavy tariff and trade protection, it has little chance of survival from global competition (Borowy et al. 1993). For instance, the opening up of labour markets in the so-called 'Third World', especially the industrialization of the Asian Pacific Rim countries and the establishment of free trade zones there, has given manufacturers access to much cheaper sources of garment production.

Concomitantly, control of the industry has shifted from manufacturers to large transnational retail chains such as the Hudson's Bay Co. (which owns Zellers, Simpson's, Robinson's & Fields, and Kmart). Retailers' strategy, to keep up with global competition, is to deliver the most fashionable clothes to the market quickly. This is made possible, among other things, by technological innovations such as electronic data interchange to control the production process. This kind of computerized technology enables retailers to keep better records of their stock and to maintain lower inventories. Sales of garments on the rack in retail stores can be communicated to production plants almost instantaneously anywhere in the world. This cuts down on mass production, storage, and other overhead costs. Retailers also demand quicker turnaround time for production, and want suppliers to provide garments on consignment and/or at last year's price. Improved distribution and transportation systems deliver garments more quickly to stores, even from faraway places. Trade agreements, such as the North American Free Trade Agreement (NAFTA), make it possible for retailers to order garments from Mexico, for example, a practice that undermines both manufacturers and workers in Toronto.

Manufacturers in Toronto responded to their loss of control and technological changes in the following ways:

• Retire and get out of the business altogether. Since garment production is a relatively old industry in Toronto, many manufacturers have been in the business since the postwar period and are close to retirement age anyway.
• Produce offshore, either by setting up factories in cheaper locations such as Mexico and Asian countries, or by contracting production to factories established in these areas. (This is also a strategy used by retailers to keep production costs low, thereby undermining local manufacturers.)
• Become subcontractors to retailers by becoming jobbers. This is done by reducing the production plant, for example, retaining a few cutters but laying off sewing machines operators, or by using homeworkers on a piece-rate basis (Leach 1993). This last strategy is especially pertinent to the situation of immigrant women workers in Canada, which I'll discuss later.

The following story, recorded in Johnson and Johnson's classic, *The Seam Allowance*, describes this transition well:

Seven years ago, James Morris owned a clothing factory in Toronto. The enormous increase in imported clothing affected his business and he began losing money. He laid off all but one of his 45 workers—a skilled cutter—and started over again, this time without the factory. He began to take bundles of ready-cut cloth to the women who used to sew for him in the factory. They sewed up the dresses and returned them to him for finishing and pressing. Today, Morris runs a highly successful, moderately-sized dress manufacturing business. Says Morris: 'Home work is the only way to go in Canada . . . I won't replace homeworkers for a long time. I don't want another factory.'

Morris' workplace now employs only ten workers, who do the cutting, samples, finishing, pressing and office work. He also uses three contractors who have their own factories and/or homeworkers. Morris does not concern himself with the employment condition of the women who make up his dresses; he cares only that the finished product is made to his exacting specifications and delivered to him in the time agreed. James Morris finds that the homework system meets his needs (Johnson and Johnson 1982:19).

The effects of these changes are downsizing of industrial plants and factory closures in Toronto and elsewhere in Canada. They in turn have led to massive lay-offs and displacement of garment workers, many of whom are women from Asian countries such as Hong Kong, Vietnam, and India.

One important thing to note here is that the ethnicity and gender of garment workers have changed over the years. In the period immediately after the war, many garment workers were immigrant men from Europe. As they acquired skills and seniority and moved up the production hierarchy (e.g., by becoming cutters, who are considered more skilled than sewing machine operators), women replaced them as sewing machine operators at the bottom of the garment production hierarchy. It is noteworthy, although not surprising, that in employing immigrant women as sewing machine operators, the skills they have acquired in domestic settings (such as mending and sewing) are transferred to the industrial context. Nevertheless, employers regard these workers as unskilled or semiskilled (*vis-à-vis* cutters, who are seen as skilled). Furthermore, in the restructuring of the garment industry, it is the sewing machine operators (namely women) who were displaced. This does not mean that they have lost their jobs entirely. It means that they are now sewing garments as homeworkers, earning their wages on a piece-rate basis. They work in isolation without the benefits hitherto provided through unionization and through their employers.

The paradox is that women sometimes see this as a viable alternative and say that they 'prefer' working at home. Influencing this 'preference' is the fact that women are still primarily responsible for family and child-care responsibilities. As other studies in this volume document, when industries and governments downsize, women's options are organized around and constrained by their caring responsibilities *vis-à-vis* other family members such as spouses, children, and elderly relatives. Frequently, homeworking, especially as social services are cut back, is a way for women to manage their dual role as wage earner and caregiver. The gendered organization of the household, in turn, dovetails with employers' perceptions and use of women as flexible and dispensable workers.[7]

Moreover, in the process of doing home-based work, the labour of children and that of other household members is exploited because the distinction between the public place of wage work and the private sphere of the family is blurred. For all intents and purposes, a worker's domicile *is* also a production site. The following story collected by Laura Johnson illustrates poignantly how homeworking becomes a family enterprise that involves the labour of other family members:

> Angela Lo sews at home. She has two young children, aged three and five. She is married to a restaurant cook. The Lo family lives in a small two-bedroom apartment in a highrise, but they have hopes of moving into a house of their own.
>
> There is no extra room in their apartment, so Angela sews in a closet that she and her husband have adapted for the purpose. She works under an overhead lamp. Her sewing produces a high level of fabric dust and lint in the small, enclosed space.

The dresses Angela Lo sews require a lot of fine detail, and fabric patterns must be matched perfectly. It usually takes her between 45 minutes and an hour to complete a dress. At the rate of $2 to $2.50 for each garment, she is able to earn up to $150 in a good week.

Some months there is lots of work, enough to keep her busy six or even seven days a week, for as much as eight to ten hours of sewing a day. In other months, usually in mid-winter, there is no work. Last year, Angela Lo earned a total of $4,000.

Angela's husband uses the family car to do all of the pick-up and delivery of bundles of garments to and from a factory. Although it would be cheaper to go by public transportation, the bundles are heavy and bulky and one person would not be able to carry them. Besides, the round trip is about ten miles (Johnson and Johnson 1982:17–18).

In summary, the restructuring of the garment industry in Toronto has deepened the isolation and exploitation of immigrant women. It is ironic that women and their families immigrate from the 'Third World' to the 'First World' in search of better working conditions and higher standards of living. However, with the restructuring of the garment industry due to the changing locus of control and global competition, although they might have enjoyed a temporary improvement in their standard of living, their hard-earned security has once again become precarious. In other words, 'Third World' immigrant women are undergoing a process of being recolonized in the 'First World'.

Union and State Responses to Work Restructuring[8]

In order to ameliorate the massive displacement of workers in the industry, the two major unions in this sector (garment and textile, which is now merged to form UNITE) came together in the summer of 1991 to form a sector-wide labour adjustment committee, tapping into funding provided by the federal and provincial governments. I will first give some background of labour (or industrial, depending on the level of government in question) adjustment programs. Then I will discuss some of the problems I identified while working with these committees in my various roles.

The concept of industrial adjustment originated in the federal government over thirty years ago. In 1963 the Industrial Adjustment Service (IAS) was established as an integral part of Canada Employment and Immigration Commission's (CEIC) programs and services.[9] It was originally called Manpower Consultative Service. According to an internal IAS document, the major principle of IAS is to 'ensure job enrichment, job redesign, and quality of work life, contributing to improved productivity and the general economy'. It is part of the federal government's effort to solve 'human resource adjustment problems resulting from technological and market changes'. As can be seen from these statements, the federal government still regards one of its major roles as facilitating labour market processes in the changing economy. The aim here is to improve productivity; workers' employability is secondary to this overall concern. Federal and provincial jurisdictions in labour adjustment are elaborated in the following paragraphs.

There are two types of IAS committees: developmental (upsizing) and adjustment (downsizing). Developmental committees are set up when companies go through technological change or expansion. Adjustment committees are set up when companies are either downsizing or closed down completely. The primary objective is to 'help workers adjust to the reality of job loss and displacement'. When IAS was first established, the ratio between developmental and adjustment committees was approximately 60:40. This ratio in the early 1990 has reversed (40:60), reflecting the economic recession in Canada.

Two types of adjustment committees were operating in the garment sector in Toronto during 1991–4: plant-based committees and a sectoral (or sector-wide) committee. Plant-based committees were set up for specific workplaces when downsizing or closure occurred. The sectoral committee was initiated by the unions (as mentioned earlier) and set up to coordinate smaller plant closures and develop measures for the long-term outlook of the industry. This is because factories in the garment trade were usually fairly small. In the event of a closure, plants with more than fifty workers had to register with the Ontario Ministry of Labour and follow procedures stipulated by the Employment Standards Act (such as giving notice and severance pay). In this situation, an initiative could be made, either by the employer, employee, or union representative, to access IAS to set up a plant-based committee. This requirement did not apply to factories with less than fifty workers, which could shut down overnight. Workers from these plants were left with no recourse. When we put this scenario together with the description of the organization of the garment industry mentioned earlier, we see that women workers were disproportionately affected in plant closures. Thus, restructuring and job displacement are gendered processes. Given the lack of formal procedures to handle the smaller closures, it was the unions' intention to try to use IAS, together with provincial funding, to help ameliorate the serious and massive displacement of members within this sector.[10]

The Ontario government's involvement in adjustment services was much more recent. It dates back to the early 1980s when an Employment Adjustment Branch was created within the Ontario Ministry of Labour. This was a period of economic recession in Ontario. At that time, the province assisted IAS committees to provide adjustment programs such as counselling services for workers. When the New Democratic Party took office in 1990, the Ontario government entered into a partnership with IAS to provide adjustment services on an equal cost-sharing basis. A large amount of money was allocated to five provincial ministries to carry out adjustment services, and the Employment Adjustment Branch was expanded to form the Office of Labour Adjustment. This infusion of money into adjustment services corresponded with a drastic downturn in the Ontario economy.[11]

Funding of adjustment committees was split among the federal government (30 per cent), the provincial government (30 per cent), and the company (40 per cent). In the case of bankruptcy, which happens to the majority of businesses in the garment sector, the two levels of government covered 100 per cent of committee expenses. There was a division of labour between the federal and provincial governments with regard to adjustment. Whereas the federal government was concerned with the overall outlook and well-being of an industry (hence industrial adjustment), the provincial government's emphasis was on displaced workers (worker or labour adjustment). This division reflects the respective jurisdiction of the two levels of government: the federal government is responsible for the overall economy; the provincial government deals with the *actual* lived realities of unemployed workers.[12]

I will illustrate the limitations of adjustment committees by describing briefly their operation based on the sectoral committee I chaired. Membership in an adjustment committee usually consisted of employer and worker representatives, federal and provincial government consultants (or advisers), and resource people such as personnel from relevant government and community services. The committees were chaired by an impartial person with knowledge and experience in the sector and adjustment activities. In the case of the sectoral committee I chaired, no employer was involved because it was set up to handle workers from plants that were already closed. In this case, membership consisted of representatives from the two unions and two community groups working with 'immigrants', the government consultants, and resource people (from the local college and Canada Employment centres). This committee met monthly to review the situation in the garment industry, evaluate committee goals, and set directions for its future work.

In addition, an Action Centre was set up to handle the day-to-day activities arising out of the adjustment process, such as tracking the workers and providing them with information pertinent to jobs displacement (e.g., how to obtain unemployment insurance, programs and services for unemployed workers, etc.). The centre associated with the sectoral committee was staffed by a coordinator and two displaced workers. The idea was to train unemployed workers to help each other and to help themselves. The paid staff were responsible for service provision for their 'clients',[13] namely displaced workers from garment and textile plants who did not belong to plant-based adjustment committees. The scope of the problem in the garment sector is reflected in the fact that the Action Centre saw an average of over 580 clients a month.[14] This is in addition to the displaced workers who belonged to plant-based committees and did not include non-unionized workers. The staff also liaised with other organizations with similar mandates, including other adjustment committees, government and educational programs (such as Canada Employment Centres and colleges), and community-based organizations providing adjustment services.

Industrial/worker adjustment programs had no formal evaluation procedures. In a closure situation, the effectiveness of the committee was measured by types and levels of activities (e.g., workshops, counselling sessions, contacts with workers) and the number of workers 'adjusted' through the committee (i.e., workers who no longer needed help from the Action Centre). The target was to reduce the number of workers needing assistance and increase the number placed in jobs or in training and other programs. For example, the Action Centre kept statistics on whether clients needed help. In the 'require no help' category, figures were broken down further to indicate the number of people who were employed, in training or other assistance programs (e.g., on welfare, worker compensation), retired, and so forth. An examination of the statistics between December 1993 and July 1994 reveals that during this period, there was an increasing proportion of workers (from about 60 per cent to 90 per cent) requiring no help.[15] Workers were thus seen to have 'adjusted' successfully. In fact, this kind of record keeping masked the transformation of garment workers' livelihood from working in a factory to working at home, since women who worked at home would not be needing help from the Action Centre.[16]

Immigrant Women and Labour Adjustment

The statistics of the Action Centre, however, do not tell us about the kinds of jobs workers got, their working conditions, or whether they actually stayed in training programs. In this section, I place labour adjustment in the larger context of immigrant women in the labour force. Examples of the operation of the sectoral committee are used to show how labour adjustment programs, instead of alleviating the displacement experienced by immigrant women, served to hold them in what I have characterized elsewhere as a captive labour pool (Ng and Das Gupta 1981).

Two points need to be made clear: first, the *effects* of labour adjustment programs on different segments of the labour force vary. In the auto industry, for example, organized labour was able to collaborate with the auto industry to access labour adjustment funds to set up fairly comprehensive retraining program for their workers, who are mainly men.[17] The auto industry is the backbone of the Ontario economy, and the auto workers union is the largest and most powerful union in Canada. The auto industry is also male-dominated, and auto workers are seen as highly skilled workers. I will return to this point in the discussion. Second, by analysing the operation of the sectoral committee, I do not wish to place blame on individuals, such as committee members and Action Centre staff. My aim is to highlight the structural relations at work that produce differential and differentiating effects on groups of people. In this case, I show that the programs did not benefit immigrant women as much as those working with them had hoped.

The key characteristic of immigrant women workers, especially if they do not speak English, is that they are a captive labour force (Ng and Das Gupta 1981). They are both essential to and disposable in a capitalist economy. (When they become redundant, as many are in the garment sector, they become a reserve army of labour, a flexible labour pool upon which new or other industrial developments can draw.) They are available to the low-skilled and low-paid sectors, they have little or no opportunity for job advancement, and they are pushed out or pushed to the margin when industrial decline occurs. Viewed in this framework, labour adjustment efforts perpetuate the captivity of this labour pool while giving the appearance that workers are cared for by state programs, thereby sustaining the myth of free labour and worker mobility under capitalism.[18] Three examples illustrate my argument.

First, one of the key stipulations of IAS committees was that they could not receive other funding, nor could they use IAS money to purchase training for unemployed workers. The mandate of the Action Centre was to provide counselling and assessment services (which could be purchased with IAS funding), to refer workers to other agencies in the service delivery network (such as community-based agencies and local community colleges), and to place them in jobs (which were dwindling in the garment sector).

When the sectoral Action Centre staff attempted to refer many non-English-speaking workers to other community and government services, however, frequently staff members were told that these workers were not eligible for the programs. For example, many programs (ultimately state funded) required English language proficiency. Participants were selected on the basis of their perceived ability to succeed in the program. Non-English-speaking workers with low educational and skill levels were seen as less likely to succeed in the programs. These eligibility criteria, coupled with the shrinking social safety net characteristic of this period of economic contraction and restructuring, meant that workers at the bottom rung of the labour hierarchy were most disadvantaged.

Second, I want to point out the incongruity between and among government programs that resulted in some workers falling through the cracks, as it were. The story here mirrors the stories of other groups, such as single mothers and elderly persons, in this collection, raising serious questions about the common-sense notions of caring and benevolence. An incident from the sectoral Action Centre illustrates my point. Since many of the Action Centre's 'clients' lacked English proficiency and therefore could not get into existing training programs in the first year of its operation, the coordinator negotiated with the English as a second language (ESL) network in the city to launch a year-long ESL course for a group of twenty-six workers, using Section 26 of the UI (unemployment insurance—now employment insurance) provision. This provision enabled workers to take language and training programs while on UI. On the eve of the course, the federal government announced that funding provided under Section 26 had run out, and that all programs were to be suspended. While this particular group of workers were permitted to take this course after much lobbying and protest, the Action Centre was unable thereafter to make use of this provision for other workers. This example points out the misfit of many state and community programs in the adjustment process.

The final example concerns the notion of action plan. One notion of a successful adjustment process was the development of an individual action plan. That is, with the help of the Action Centre staff, an individual develops a set of goals for retraining, skills upgrading, and future employment, and a time frame and strategies for achieving these goals.[19] In fact, action plans were by and large irrelevant to workers in the lower echelon of the garment sector. Most workers in this captive labour pool had little formal education and training. Employers deploying this labour pool made use of skills that workers (mostly women) acquired in domestic settings (sewing being one such skill). Since these workers' wages were an essential part of the household economy, unless they received equivalent subsidies for language and training programs, workers were unlikely to take advantage of these programs because their immediate financial need overrode other considerations. As I and authors in other chapters have pointed out, women's caring responsibilities in the family are determinants in the 'choices' they make around paid work. Their caring responsibilities are the reason why many immigrant women saw homeworking as a viable alternative, when in fact homeworking serves to keep them captive in dead-end labour pools. Indeed, globalization is made possible because of the availability of docile and flexible labour pools of (mainly) women and children, and because it can depend on women's caring responsibilities for the reproduction of other workers. I will elaborate on this in the next section.

In this discussion we see that the problems arising out of the structure of the labour market and the organization of the service delivery system are treated as individuals' attributes. Workers' failure to secure employment is seen as a deficit in either their language, their skills, or their (inferior) ability. What remains invisible is how the capitalist labour market is organized hierarchically in a globalized economy. While industrial adjustment may benefit employers who are contemplating reorganization, or a select group of workers in the high-skilled sector(s) such as those in the auto industry mentioned earlier, it was another means through which many immigrant women are held captive.

In sum, state processes, together with the restructuring of the garment industry, all contribute to locking immigrant women in particular locations in society. This is what I mean when I suggest that 'Third World' women are being recolonized in the 'First World'.

Discussion

Gender, Race, Class, and Capitalist Relations

What I described earlier is the convergence of gender, race, and class relations in (re)shaping the experience of 'immigrant women' in Canada. In this section I will explain my conceptualization of gender, race, and class in order to see them as relations that intertwine in multiple and complicated ways in shaping people's everyday life. The purpose here is to provide an analysis that would enable us to describe people's experiences in an integrated way rather than fragmenting them according to the analyst's theoretical categories (see Ng 1993).

Frequently the concepts of gender, race, and class are used as competing categories for determining social status. I want to move away from treating race, gender, and class as *categories* designating different and separate domains of social life to discovering how they are *relations* that organize our productive and reproductive activities, which are located in time and space. That is, gender, race, and class are not merely theoretical categories; they are concrete social relations that are discoverable in the everyday world of experience.

I use the term 'gender' in the same way that feminists developed the term in the 1970s to distinguish it from sex differences. Gender is not a term used to designate biological differences between men and women. Rather, it refers to the *process(es)* whereby sex differences are made real or objectified as differences between men and women, and where these differences are valorized in differential ways. Namely, men are seen as superior and there-fore more valued; correspondingly, women are seen as inferior and there-fore less valued. Thus, gender refers to the *relation* between men and women. Treating the skills that women acquire in domestic settings as 'natural' is an aspect of gender relation. In the process of differentiating men from women, these skills, which are social in origin, are seen to grow out of the natural differences between men and women, and less value is attributed to women's skills in relation to those acquired by men in terms of the production process. Put in another way, more value is attributed to skills deployed in commodity production, and less value is attributed to skills acquired in and used for reproductive purposes.

For instance, sewing is regarded as a woman's skill; sewers are paid less than cutters in garment production. This process of valorization and differ-entiation (a) produces social difference as gender difference; (b) devalues the skills women acquired (for instance, the notion that women don't have to be trained for garment work because it is their 'natural' skill); and (c) produces and reinforces women's inferiority socially and economically. This is *sexism*. In industrial restructuring, women are the ones to become home-workers. Men in the garment industry retain the higher-skilled and better-paying jobs. This is precisely how sexism operates systemically in society.

Marie Campbell's description of nurses' work provides another poignant example of how sexism operates in a hospital setting.

Similarly, people's physical and phenotypical differences are made into absolute differences in the construction of 'races'. This construction was deployed by Europeans in colonization and imperialist expansion (Miles 1989, 1993). *Racism* (that is, the ideology of the superiority of one 'race' over another) was used to justify the subordination of groups seen as inferior. Thus, racism encompasses both the ideology *and* the practice of inferiorizing groups of people on the basis of their perceived racial differences. The historical process of racialization is expressed in contemporary reality by, among other phenomena, a labour market that is segregated by race and ethnicity. The garment industry with its gender, ethnic, and racial hierarchy is an example of this process of inferiorization.

Finally, my understanding of the term 'class' is consistent with how Marx uses the concept in *The German Ideology* (Marx and Engels 1970) and *Capital* (Marx 1954). That is, class is not used to indicate people's status in terms of occupation, salary, education, etc., which is how stratification analysts operationalize the term. It is used to refer to a *process* whereby people's lives are transformed in terms of the relation and means of production (Braverman 1974). Although this transformation hinges on economic relations in capitalist society, it is not *simply* an economic relation. It is fundamentally a transformation of people's way of life or *mode of livelihood*. Thus, in the case of the restructuring of the garment industry in Toronto, we see how garment workers' livelihood is transformed from wage workers to homeworkers. Belinda Leach's chapter provides another example of the transformation of full-time to part-time employment for women workers in rural areas.

In this discussion I want to preserve an understanding of capitalism, not only as an economic system but as a *mode of production and reproduction*. That is, capitalism is a way in which people produce and reproduce their livelihood under specific material conditions that goes beyond the economy. It is a dynamic process whereby people's livelihood is being transformed and reorganized according to the requirement of capital accumulation. Gender, race, and class are essential ingredients in this continuous process of transformation. In the sketch I provided of the garment workers earlier, it is clear that we cannot isolate gender, race, or class as the primary determinant of their experience. Rather, they are concrete relations that are interwoven; they work in complicated ways to give particular shapes and contours to people's everyday life.

Whereas industrial development was largely confined to national boundaries by the national bourgeoisie until the 1970s, and the so-called 'developed' countries augmented capital accumulation in the 'Third World' by resource extraction (thereby underdeveloping them), globalization signifies the stage in capitalism whereby capital has developed the capacity to move beyond national boundaries.[20] This has led to the restructuring of practically all industrial sectors worldwide and the concomitant reorganization of everyday life in both 'developed' and 'developing' parts of the world. The description I gave of the reorganization of the garment industry in Toronto is part and parcel of globalization, which affects groups of people differently on the basis of gender, race, and class, as I have pointed out. The result of globalization at the micro level, as demonstrated by the garment trade, is the renewed impoverishment of immigrant groups who were able to secure better livelihood before the restructuring process. Thus, we see that globalization has created 'Third World' enclaves within the geographic boundaries of the 'First World'.

I am not suggesting that garment workers were not exploited before. I am saying that globalization, with the resultant restructuring of the garment industry in Canada, has led to an increase in the exploitation of immigrant women. In this way women from 'Third World' countries are being recolonized, this time in the developed part of the world to which they fled to escape from the effects of underdevelopment. There is a further difference between garment workers as members of an industrialized workforce and their status as homeworkers. As homeworkers, 'immigrant women' are without the benefit of union and labour standard protection. They become self-regulating—the ultimate form of colonization.

The State in a Globalized World

Finally, I want to comment on the role of the state in this period of restructuring.[21] The role of the state in Western capitalist social formations has been a subject of heated debates, especially in neo-Marxism.[22] Here, I bypass the traditional debates as to whether the state is instrumentalist or relatively autonomous in capitalist societies.[23] The strategy is to see what the experiences of immigrant women in the garment sector examined earlier tell us about how the state works in this period of globalization and restructuring. My analysis builds on an understanding of the state that I developed earlier (Ng 1996; Ng et al. 1990). It is rooted in the works of Marx and Engels:

> The social structure and the state are continually evolving out of the life process of definite individuals, but of individuals, not as they appear in their own or other people's imagination, but as they really are, i.e., as they operate, produce materially and hence as they work under definite material limits, presuppositions and conditions, independent of their will (Marx and Engels 1970:47–8).

At the same time, the state is not a monolith but 'an embodiment of struggles between classes . . . which (a) legitimizes certain courses of action, thereby rendering other (alternate) forms of action illegitimate; and (b) organizes how people relate to one another' (Ng 1988:89).

What we see in this period is that as capital transcends national boundaries, it is facilitated by the state through the development of policies, programs, and strategies in relation to the requirement of capitalist accumulation *both* within the nation and internationally. Although these policies and programs appear to be neutral, by examining various sites in which women find themselves, in the home as well as in the workplace, this collection shows that in fact the effects of state policies and programs are highly gendered and racialized. Within the nation, the realignment of the labour market with new requirements of capital (e.g., a flexible labour force) is a major concern. Viewed in this light, the federal industrial adjustment program was a means to facilitate this realignment through its dual upsizing and downsizing function. It is understandable that in the more recent period, the destabilizing effects of globalization would make labour rather than industrial adjustment an emphasis. The provincial government is understandably more concerned with economic downturn and worker displacement because the effects of a destabilized workforce are lived in local sites. This accounts for the different philosophies of the federal and provincial programs I examined.

Meanwhile, labour adjustment programs are not intended to take care of workers on a long-term basis. Rather, their purpose is to facilitate the redeployment of labour that is flexible, pliant, and able to respond to the changing demands of industries as they strive for profit augmentation. The experience of garment workers in the labour adjustment process illustrates the seeming contradiction of the state: it both cares for workers and keeps them captive as a flexible labour pool. The analysis conducted here shows how the state is part and parcel of the reorganization of class relations.

What we see during globalization is the changing role of the state in relation to its citizenry. Whereas in the postwar period, its role in social and welfare provisions was expanded, it has now contracted. In addition to my study, studies on daycare, social assistance, and elder care in this volume point to the contraction of the welfare state, as well as the state's efforts to reorganize the labour force. What all these studies reveal is that the outcome, if not the intent, of the changes currently occurring within the state are deeply and increasingly gendered and racialized. These processes indicate how class relations are being reconfigured in late capitalism. The changes documented in this book mirror changes in the economy: gains made by disadvantaged groups such as the working class, women, minorities, the elderly, etc., are being eroded.

Internationally, nation-states, together with transnational corporations, are working collaboratively to facilitate capital mobility and augmentation. The establishment of free trade zones and deindustrialization within 'developed' countries (such as garment production) are thus simultaneous and compatible, rather than contradictory, processes. The kinds of negotiations that occur among heads of states, such as the Asia-Pacific Economic Cooperation

Conference in Vancouver in 1997 and the Multilateral Agreement on Investment negotiations in Paris in 1998, not to mention the North American Free Trade Agreement, are instances of how nation-states work cooperatively to maximize and smooth transnational movements of capital.[24] As I and others have demonstrated, these efforts have differential effects on the livelihood of groups of people on the basis of their gender, race, and class.

What we are witnessing right now is the consolidation of a *regime of ruling*[25] that enables the coordination of capitalist production and movement internationally. As we have seen from this analysis, these kinds of processes that are occurring in Canada and elsewhere in the world have negative impacts on the lives of ordinary working people regardless of where they are located geographically. Thus, in the age of globalization, we need to rethink categories we take for granted in describing the world. The most obvious of these in the context of this chapter are divisions between development and underdevelopment, between the 'First World' and the 'Third World', between private and public. With this re-examination comes the need to understand how globalization actually operates in local sites as an everyday phenomenon. The studies in this volume start to document this process. After all, it is in the lived actuality of our world that we develop ways of resisting and transforming the detrimental effects of globalization.

Notes

1   The development of this analysis would not have been possible without the nurturing and insights of the network members to whom I owe so much. Renita Yuk-lin Wong, Nandita Sharma, and Teresa Macias helped with background research at various points. I am also indebted to Kathryn Church, Eric Shragge, and Jean Marc Fontan for sharing with me their own research, which furthered my own.

2   The two major unions for this sector were the International Ladies Garment Workers' Union (ILGWU) and the Amalgamated Clothing and Textile Workers' Union (ACTWU), which were merged to form a new union, UNITE (Union of Needletrades, Industrial and Textile Employees), in 1995. The adjustment committee is called the Apparel Textile Action Committee. For details, see Roxana Ng, *Apparel Textile and Action Committee Final Report, March 9, 1993–July 8, 1994.*

3   This project was funded by the Technological Adjustment Program, administered by the Ontario Federation of Labour (OFL) and funded by the New Democratic Party government. Its purpose was to provide research dollars to enable unions experiencing rapid technological changes in their sectors to investigate and strategize around these changes. In setting up this program the OFL appointed academics as resource people for unions that were funded to conduct research. I was the academic resource person to ILGWU from 1990 to 1995.

4 I am deliberately using 'garment workers' and 'immigrant women' interchangeably in this chapter to highlight the overlap between these two groups of people. Elsewhere I have argued that 'immigrant women' is a socially constructed category that may or may not correspond to someone's legal status (Ng 1993:281). Although not all garment workers are women or immigrants, the majority of those with whom I have worked were women and immigrants from the 'Third World', and thus occupy a unique place in the Canadian labour market.

5 It is not easy to name the divisions we have created to describe the current state of the world as terminologies change over time. I am using terms such as 'First World' and 'Third World' in quotation marks to indicate their constructed character. I am also using terms such as 'developed' and 'developing' to indicate the 'First World' and 'Third World' division. At the end of this chapter I will re-examine this binary logic in light of my analysis.

6 Since there are few studies on the garment industry in Toronto, data from this section are based largely on the research done by Jan Borowy for the International Ladies Garment Workers' Union (now UNITE) between 1991 and 1994, with myself as the academic resource person and my experience as the chair of the sectoral labour adjustment committee (mentioned in the next section) from 1991 to 1994. I am indebted to Jan Borowy and Alex Dagg, the ILGWU regional manger, for sharing this information with me.

7 I owe this insight to members of the network.

8 Data for this section are based on my experience as chair of the adjustment committee mentioned in the chapter introduction, on reports of the adjustment committees, and on the research I conducted for ILGWU (Ng 1994).

9 CEIC was eliminated and amalgamated as part of the mega ministry of Human Resources Development Canada in 1993.

10 Although there was no strict guideline about the minimum number of workers for plant-based committees, government consultants generally used fifty people as an overall guideline for setting up plant-based committees. In cases where the plant had less than fifty workers, sometimes a committee was set up for two plants if they closed around the same time.

11 In 1993 the OLA was renamed the Adjustment Advisory Program and became part of the function of the Ontario Training and Adjustment Board (OTAB). OTAB was eliminated in 1995 when Conservative (Harris) government came into power.

12 Space does not permit a full exploration of the interplay of geography, space, and the state in the restructuring process. For a more thorough discussion, see Jenson et al. (1993).

13 It is interesting to note that in setting up the labour adjustment action centre, unionized workers (the centre's staff) adopted the terminology of the service delivery system by referring to former unionized members as clients.

14 Statistics provided by the Apparel Textile Action committee (ATAC) staff, December 1993 to July 1994, in the ATAC Final Report, 9 March 1993–8 July 1994, Appendix 4, ATAC Client Status, 1 December 1993–8 July 1994.

15 Apparel Textile Action Committee, Final Report, 9 March 1993–8 July 1994, Appendix 4, ATAC Client Status, 1 December 1993–8 July 1994.

16 Since the Action Centre did not ask for the sex of their clients, it is impossible to know the gender breakdown from the statistics. I don't mean to suggest that this kind of record keeping was developed to conceal the changing livelihood of garment workers. I am saying that statistics do not tell the full story of people's lived reality.

17 This is based on my personal observation and communication with people in the labour adjustment field during my tenure as the chair of ATAC.

18 I thank members of the network, especially Lyn Ferguson, for this observation.

19 See Ng (1994).

20 I want to make two comments in this regard. First, according to this view, Canada's relation to the US is that of a 'Third World'-'First World' one as Canadian analysts in the 1970s concluded. Second, my characterization here is simplistic. The point I want to make is that globalization marks a change in how capitalism works.

21 I am using the term 'the state' here as a shorthand to refer to the multiple and complex apparatuses and departments that constitute the activities of ruling in modern society.

22 For two concise and comprehensive reviews, see Jessop (1990) and Barrow (1993).

23 I want to thank Keith Denny (Denny 1998) for sharing his summary article with me, and Renita Y.L. Wong for doing the bibliographic search on the state.

24 Indeed, UNITE, the garment workers' union in Toronto, would claim that NAFTA is partially responsible for the decimation of the garment trade in Toronto as retailers and manufacturers moved south in search of cheaper labour.

25 The term 'regime of ruling' is borrowed from George Smith's analysis of the regulation of homosexuals and AIDS treatment (Smith 1995) and inspired by Patty Simpson's adaptation of this term in her work on development, which she calls 'the development regime' (Simpson 1998). I am using the term to refer to the complex conglomerate of relations and apparatuses developed among and across nation-states to coordinate capital mobility and regulate production and labour to facilitate capital augmentation—a key development in this period of globalization.

References

Barrow, C.W. 1993. *Critical Theories of the State: Marxist, Neo-Marxist, Post-Marxist*. Madison: University of Wisconsin Press.

Borowy, J., and T. Johnson. 1995. 'Unions Confront Work Reorganization and the Rise of Precarious Employment: Home-Based Work in the Garment Industry and the Public Service'. In *Re-shaping Work: Union Responses to Technological Change*, edited by C. Schenk and J. Anderson, 29–47. Toronto: Ontario Federation of Labour.

Borowy, J., et al. 1993. 'Are These Clothes Clean? The Campaign for Fair Wages and Working Conditions for Homeworkers'. *And Still We Rise: Feminist Political Mobilizing in Contemporary Canada*, edited by L. Carty, 299–330. Toronto: Women's Press.

Braverman, H. 1974. *Labour and Monopoly Capital: The Degradation of Work in the Twentieth Century*. New York and London: Monthly Review Press.

Denny, K. 1998. 'Looking at the State We're In: Plura, Marxist and State-Centred Theories of the State'. Unpublished ms, Ontario Institute for Studies in Education, University of Toronto.

Jenson, J., et al., eds. 1993. *Production, Space, Identity: Political Economy Faces the 21st Century*. Toronto: Canadian Scholars' Press Inc.

Jessop, B. 1990. *State Theory: Putting Capitalist States in Their Place*. Cambridge: Polity Press.

Johnson, L.C., and R. Johnson. 1982. *The Seam Allowance: Industrial Home Sewing in Canada*. Toronto: Women's Press.

Leach, B. 1993. 'Flexible Work, Precarious Future: Some Lessons from the Canadian Clothing Industry'. *Canadian Review of Sociology and Anthropology* 30, no. 1:64–82.

Marx, K. 1954. *Capital*. Moscow: Progress Publishers.

_____, and F. Engels. 1970. *The German Ideology*. New York: International Publishers.

Miles, R. 1989. *Racism*. London: Routledge.

_____. 1993. *Racism after Race Relations*. London: Routledge.

Ng, R. 1988. *The Politics of Community Services: Immigrant Women, Class and State*. Toronto: Garamond Press.

_____. 1993. 'Racism, Sexism, and Immigrant Women'. *Changing Patterns: Women in Canada*, edited by S. Burt, L. Code, and L. Dorney, 279–308. Toronto: McClelland & Stewart.

_____. 1994. 'Worker Adjustment in the Garment Sector: Comparing Plant-Based and Sector-Based Committees'. Supplemental report in *Facing Factory Closures in the Garment District*. Toronto: International Ladies Garment Workers Union, Ontario District Council.

_____. 1996. *The Politics of Community Services: Immigrant Women, Class and State,* 2nd edn. Halifax: Fernwood Press.

_____, and T. Das Gupta. 1981. 'Nation Builders? The Captive Labour Force of Non-English Speaking Immigrant Women'. *Canadian Women's Studies* 3, no. 1:83–9.

_____, et al., eds. 1990. *Community Organization and the Canadian State*. Toronto: Garamond Press.

Simpson, P. 1998. 'An Inquiry into the Textually Mediated Practices of Women Development Workers Affiliated with the Canadian Executive Service Organization'. *Sociology & Equity Studies Ontario Institute for Studies in Education.* Toronto: University of Toronto.

Smith, G. 1995. 'Accessing Treatments: Managing the AIDS Epidemic on Ontario'. *Knowledge, Experience, and Ruling Relations*, edited by M. Campbell and A. Manicom, 18–34 . Toronto: University of Toronto Press.

Author Index

Subject Index

abused women, 30–51: abuse continues after separation, 36–7, 44–6; cuts cause more women to stay, 45, 46, 47; emphasis on market, 31, 34–8, Falkiner case, 32, 33, 40–1, 42–3, 44; idealization of family, 31, 36, 38–43; Lalonde case, 45–6; 'man in the house' rule, 38–9, 44, 99; statistics, 33–4

children, history of protection, 164–84: abuse, 164–5, 166, 180–1; foster care, 169, 172; mother blamed for problems, 166, 171–3; professionalization of care, 166, 167, 170–80; residential care at Earlscourt, 166–80; risk assessment, 164–5, 166, 180–1, 181n1

community centres, volunteering in, 142–63: context, 143–6; four aspects, 149–50; 'hoax' associated with cuts, 142–3, 152–4; 'scary dance' with unequal partners, 143, 154; shadow work, 18, 150, 156; three-sphere model, 147–8

daycare, mothers as volunteers in centres, 118–41: child care essential for workfare, 123; 'consumer' mothers and 'client' mothers, 133–5; recent changes in welfare state, 122–5, 137; volunteers in welfare state, 105–6, 108, 119–22; Winnipeg case-study, 125–35

elderly women, 52–72: being managed, 54, 55–6, 58, 60–1, 66; care deficit ('thinning of needs'), 58–9; care providers for, 56–7, 62–4; disabled people and, 57–8, 65–6; making demands, 54, 57–8, 59–60, 67–8; managing, 54, 56–7, 58, 59, 61–4, 66–7

garment workers, homemaking and family, 226–45: changes in Toronto, 227–9; class, gender, and race, 227, 230, 237–9, 240–1; family care, 230; government adjustment services, 231–40; recolonization of immigrant women, 231, 236, 239; weaknesses of adjustment programs, 234–6

nurses, 186–208: gender relations, 198–99, 200–1, 202–3; intelligent action fills task-based holes, 194–201, 204; management approach reorganizes caregivers, 188–91; managerial concepts or everyday work, 192–4, 201–4

rural job changes, 209–25: gender relations, 220–1, 222, 223; layoffs affect income and life quality, 215, 216; loss of jobs affects women more, 216–19, 222–3; restructuring in the rural context, 210–14, 222

single mothers, changing media image, 73–92: appearance in the news less frequent, 78–9; change from 'helpless' to 'bad', 83–6, 88; growth of statistics, 82–3, 88; increased reliance on 'experts', 79–82, 88

welfare mothers, caring in everyday lives, 17, 93–115: care not recognized, 12, 103–6, 110–11, 112, 127–8; caring and need, 100–2;